Anthropology, New Global Order and Other Essays

About the Editor:

Kamal K. Misra is Professor and Head, Department of Anthropology, University of Hyderabad, Hyderabad. He had his academic training at Utkal University, Bhubaneswar; Jawaharlal Nehru University, New Delhi; and the University of Kent at Canterbury, United Kingdom. He is also a recipient of Commonwealth Academic Staff Fellowship and the Fulbright Fellowship. Dr. Misra has taught at Utkal University, the University of Hyderabad and at Austin College, Texas, USA. He specializes in Environmental Anthropology, Anthropological Linguistics and Theory in Anthropology. He has extensively carried out fieldwork in Northeast, Central and South Indian tribal and rural communities. His publications include *Social Structure and Change among the Ho of Orissa* (1987), *Tribal Elite and Social Transformation* (1994), *Text Book of Anthropological Linguistics* (2000), and *Peoples and Environment in India* (2001), co-edited with M.L.K. Murty. He has over 50 research papers published in national and international journals, and book chapters. Dr. Misra is on the Board of Editors of *Indian Anthropologist*, and *Man and Life*.

ANTHROPOLOGY, NEW GLOBAL ORDER AND OTHER ESSAYS

Edited by

Kamal K. Misra

Associate Editors

P.V. Rao, R. Siva Prasad, B.V. Sharma

CONCEPT PUBLISHING COMPANY, NEW DELHI-110059

Cataloging in Publication Data—DK
Courtesy: D.K. Agencies (P) Ltd. <docinfo@dkagencies.com>

National Seminar on Social Anthropology in the Era of Globalization (2002 : Hyderabad, India)
Anthropology, new global order and other essays / edited by Kamal K. Misra ; associate editors, P.V. Rao, R. Siva Prasad, B.V. Sharma.
p. cm.
Papers presented at the National Seminar on Social Anthropology in the Era of Globalization, held at Hyderabad during 7-8 February 2002.
Includes bibliographical references.
Includes index.
ISBN 8180692019

1. Ethnology—Effect of globalization on—Congresses. 2. Tribes—India—Congresses. I. Misra, K. K. (Kamal Kant),1954- II. Rao, P. V. III. Siva Prasad, R. IV. Sharma, B. V.

DDC 301 21

ISBN-81-8069-201-9

First Published 2005

Published and Printed by
Ashok Kumar Mittal
Concept Publishing Company
A/15-16, Commercial Block, Mohan Garden
New Delhi-110059 (INDIA)

Phones : 25351460, 25351794
Fax : 091-11-25357103
Email : publishing@conceptpub.com

Preface

'Globalization' has become a buzz word today, as all of us presently live in a globalized world, which in common parlance refers to quick trans-national flow of men, material and information at a supersonic speed. The traditionally protected spatial and cultural boundaries of the nations are opened up for migrants and multi-national corporations creating a global ambiance and an aura of multi-culturalism. This has led Inda and Rosaldo (2002) to define globalization most simply "... as the intensification of global interconnectedness". Along with intensification, globalization also implies a "fundamental reordering of time and space". With the speed at which things move and due to faster accessibility, a situation of "time-space compression" has emerged as one of the end products of globalization. When the process of globalization is deepening everyday with greater shrinking of space and shortening of time, the dichotomy between 'global' and 'local' is becoming more and more subtle and gradually indistinguishable. Given anthropology's conventional commitment to the study of small and bounded local communities, globalization has far reaching implications for its theory and methods. With this background and keeping in mind the challenges anthropology currently faces and shall be facing in the near future, I had convened a National Seminar on Social Anthropology in the Era of Globalization at the University of Hyderabad on 7-8 February 2002 to review the stands taken by the anthropologists on this matter and to elicit their views on the appropriateness of anthropological theory and method in handling the issues emerging due to time-space compression and global-local interface. All but one chapters included in this volume were presented and discussed in the Seminar, which were later revised for the present volume.

As the process of globalization is vast and varied so are the chapters in this volume, the scopes of which extend from the structure of globalization to its many empirical manifestations. Areas of ecology and environment, local governance, health and hygiene, education and literature, and their interconnectedness with the swift process of globalization have been discussed in various chapters of this volume. Despite situational and experiential differences, the common finding of the chapters in the volume relates to the fact that no matter one likes or not, globalization in its varied representations is an inescapable feature of the modern socio-political order. Its impact on the poor and marginalized must be understood with reference to the politico-historical background and the socio-economic contexts in which these societies are situated. Hence, the future tools of anthropological research must be re-oriented to probe into the nature and directions of change in such societies, which are caught between primordial loyalties and the processes of homogenization. Since such challenges are not new to anthropology, it should devise methods of application such that the beneficial impacts of globalization should benefit the most vulnerable sections of the population.

This volume would not have seen the light of the day, but for the support and encouragement of many individuals and institutions. I owe special thanks to my colleagues, research scholars, alumni and students of the Department of Anthropology, University of Hyderabad for making the Seminar a success, and subsequently helping me in editing this volume. I am thankful to all the authors of the chapters for their patience to bear with the long gestation period for the publication of this volume. The University of Hyderabad deserves my thanks for providing funds and infrastructure for organizing the Seminar in 2002. I have a special debt to the Fulbright Foundation, USA for awarding me a Scholar-in-Residence Fellowship during 2003-2004, and to Austin College, Texas, USA for hosting me during the period of Fellowship. Most of the final works was completed while I was teaching at Austin College, Texas. I am especially thankful to Dr. Janet Lowry of the Department of Sociology at Austin College for all her help, advice and encouragement. I owe special thanks to Dr. Oscar Page, the President and Dr. Mike Imhoff, the Vice-President of Austin College for their academic and moral support. I am also thankful to Dr. Karen Nelson, Dr. Jackie Moore, Dr. Ivette Vargas, Dr. Tom Baker and other colleagues in Sherman, USA for their constant support and encouragement. My special thanks are due to Mr. Tom Lowry for many logistical support and friendly gesture. I am, however, solely responsible for any mistake or omission. Last but not the least, I owe a special debt to M/s Concept Publishing Co., New Delhi, in particular to Mr. S.P. Sinha, for taking keen interest in publishing this volume for the wider audience.

August 15, 2004

Kamal K. Misra
Hyderabad Central University

Contents

List of Tables

List of Contributors

Dr. N. Subba Reddy is Honorary Fellow at the Centre for Economic and Social Studies (CESS), Begumpet, Hyderabad, India since 1991. Before joining the CESS, he had taught Anthropology at the Universities of Lucknow, Guwahati, Andhra and Madras. He was also a Senior Visiting Fellow at the CESS between 1986 and 1991. He was retired as the Professor and Head of the Department of Anthropology at Madras University, Chennai. Prof. Reddy has extensively worked among the tribes of Andhra Pradesh and Tamil Nadu in India, and has published more than 40 papers in international and national journals of repute, besides contributing chapters to various anthologies.

Dr. Ajit K. Danda was the Director of Anthropological Survey of India, Professor and Head of the Department of Sociology and Social Anthropology at North Bengal University, and Research Professor and Research Coordinator of the Asiatic Society. He is the President of Indian Anthropological Society, Member-Secretary of the Indian Confederation and Academy of Anthropologists, Editor of the *Journal of Indian Anthropological Society*, and Fellow of the National Academy of Sciences, India. He has 26 books and 174 research papers to his credit in English, Bengali and Hindi.

Dr. Leif Manger is currently Professor of Social Anthropology at the University of Bergen, Norway. His main research interests have been household adaptations in oasis environments, mountain environments and savannah plains; trade and communal labour; and socio-cultural processes of Arabization and Islamization. His major publications include *From the Mountains to the Plains: The Integration of the Lafofa Nuba in Sudanese Society* (1994), *Survival on Meagre Resources: Pastoral Adaptation of the Hadendowa in the Red Sea Hills* (co-edited 1996), and *Muslim Diversity: Local Islam in Global Contexts* (edited 1999). His currently working on a monograph on Yemenese diaspora in the Indian Ocean region.

Dr. Simon Charsely is Senior Lecturer in the Department of Sociology, Anthropology and Applied Social Sciences at the University of Glasgow, United Kingdom. His principal publications are: *The Princes of Nyakyusa* (1969), *Culture and Sericulture* (1982), *Rites of Marrying: The Wedding Industry in Scotland* (1991), *Wedding Cakes and Cultural History* (1992), *Challenging Untouchability: Dalit Initiative and Experience from Karnataka* (with G.K. Karanth, 1998), *Reshme Krishi Samskruti*

Matthu Abhivrudhi (in Kannada, trans. by U.D. Bongale, 2001), and numerous articles in professional journals.

Dr. Premananda Panda is Senior Faculty in the Department of Anthropology, Sambalpur University, Burla, India, and a member of the National Literacy Mission in New Delhi. Dr. Panda is in the Editorial Board of many professional journals, *viz. Journal of Oriental Anthropology* (Allahabad), *Prasar: Contemporary Journal of Adult and Population Education* (Jaipur), etc. His monograph on the Binjhal is under publication. Dr. Panda is a regular contributor to national and international journals of Anthropology.

Prof. P.K. Biswas is a faculty at the Indian Institute of Forest Management, Bhopal, India, which is an autonomous institute of the Ministry of Environment and Forests, Government of India. He has extensively worked in the areas of participatory development, joint/community forest management, decentralized governance, and rural and tribal development, and has contributed numerous articles to professional journals and anthologies.

Dr. V.N.V.K. Sastry is Director, Tribal Culture, Research and Training Institute (TCR & TI), located in Hyderabad, India. His principal publications include, *Between Gond Rebellions* and numerous research articles on Applied Anthropology. Dr. Sastry had earlier worked as Project Officer of Integrated Tribal Development Agency, General Manager of Scheduled Tribes Cooperative Finance and Development Corporation, Joint Secretary of Scheduled Tribes Residential Educational Institution Society, and Joint Director of Planning in the Department of Tribal Welfare, Government of Andhra Pradesh, India.

Binoy Sharma was Post-Graduate student in Forest Management at the Indian Institute of Forest Management, Bhopal, Madhya Pradesh, during 2000-02.

Amol Bholerao was Post-Graduate student in Forest Management at the Indian Institute of Forest Management, Bhopal, Madhya Pradesh, during 2000-02.

Dr. Amitabh Pandey is Lecturer in the faculty of Social Anthropology at the Indian Institute of Forest Management, Bhopal, India. His areas of research interest include common property resources management and cultural conflict resolution.

Dr. Debasis Debnath is Assistant Professor in the faculty of Social Anthropology at the Indian Institute of Forest Management, Bhopal, India. His areas of research interest include tribal studies, joint forest management, and ecological anthropology.

Dr. V. Subramanyam is Associate Professor in the Department of Anthropology, Andhra University, Waltair, India. Dr. Subramanyam has undertaken extensive research among the tribes of Andhra Pradesh, particularly in the Eastern Ghats region. He has published one monograph, many papers in journals of repute, besides contributing chapters to many anthologies. Dr. Subramanyam has completed 7 research projects and currently working on a major research project, funded by the University Grants Commission of India.

Dr. Sudhir Jacob George is on the faculty of the Department of Political Science at the University of Hyderabad, Hyderabad, India, and is currently the Head of the Department. Besides International Relations and South Asia, he specializes on the tribal problems of North East India. His principal publications include *Chakma Refugees in Tripura* (co-author, 1991), *Intra and Inter-State Conflicts in South Asia* (edited, 2001) and several articles in national and international journals.

Dr. N. Sudhakar Rao is currently Professor in the Department of Sociology at the Assam Central University, Silchar, and also the Registrar-in-Charge of the University. He possesses vast research experiences and has undertaken many research projects in different states of India. His principal publications include two books titled, *Organized Power and Unorganized Resistance* (1998) and *Ethnography of a Nomadic Tribe* (2002). He is the co-author of *Yanadi Response to Change: An Attempt in Action Anthropology* (1995). He has published many articles in referred national journals and anthologies.

Aravinda Meera Guntupalli is a doctoral scholar and research assistant in the Department of Economics at the University of Tüebingen, Germany. Her research interest is focused on anthropometrics and health determinants of regional productivity development in India. She has published a few papers on reproductive behaviour among the tribal communities of India.

Vilas Kovai has been working as a Social Scientist (Grade 1) with the International Centre for Advancement of Rural Eye-Care, a Department of L.V. Prasad Eye Institute, Hyderabad, India. His research interests include interventional research, concept development, qualitative research, and programme planning and management relevant to rural eye-care.

Sannapaneni Krishnaiah is a Scientist associated with L.V. Prasad Eye Institute, Hyderabad, India.

Bindiganavale Ramaswamy Shamanna is a Consultant associated with L.V. Prasad Eye Institute, Hyderabad, India.

Ravi Thomas is a Director of L.V. Prasad Eye Institute, Hyderabad, India.

Gullapalli Nageswar Rao is a Director of L.V. Prasad Eye Institute, Hyderabad, India.

Dr. N.K. Das is Superintending Anthropologist (Cultural), Anthropological Survey of India, Ministry of Tourism and Culture, Government of India. His principal publications include *Ethnic Identity, Ethnicity and Social Stratification in North East India* (1989), *Kinship, Politics and Law in Naga Society* (1993), and has edited many other titles, including *Religion, Culture and Philosophy: Critical Studies in Syncretism and Inter-faith Harmony* (2003). He has over 100 research articles published in various journals of repute.

Dr. B.V. Sharma is Senior Lecturer in the Department of Anthropology, University of Hyderabad, Hyderabad, India. His research interests are primarily in the areas of educational and medical anthropology. His study report on *Community Contribution to Tuberculosis Care: Asian Experience* has been published by WHO in 2002. His another report on *Unqualified Health Provider in Rural India* is under publication. He has many articles published in various journals.

Dr. P.H. Mahammad is currently working as a Project Associate for Andhra Pradesh Rural Poverty Reduction Project at the Centre for Economic and Social Studies, Hyderabad, India. Besides rural cooperatives, his research interests include sensitizing and capacity building towards elimination of child labour. He has published articles on child rearing and socialization, and handloom weavers of Andhra Pradesh in professional journals.

Dr. Kamal K. Misra is Professor of Anthropology and the Department Head at the University of Hyderabad, Hyderabad, India. His broad research interests spread over the areas of Environmental Anthropology, Anthropological Linguistics, and Anthropological Theory. His principal publications include *Social Structure and Change among the Ho of Orissa* (1987), *Tribal Elite and Social Transformation* (1984), and *Textbook of Anthropological Linguistics* (2000). He is the co-editor of *Peoples and Environment in India* (2001). Besides these books, he has published over 50 papers in many journals of repute and in different anthologies. He is currently working on a monograph on indigenous environmental knowledge and development.

1

Anthropology and the New Global Order

An Introductory Remark

KAMAL K. MISRA

The Preamble

Understanding the issue of changing global social order with the help of the oft quoted concept of globalization, to my mind, is veritably timely, when all of us live in a world in which uninhibited transnational flow of money and materials, images, information and people have generated intense debates on the impact of commodities and capital on cultural and biological diversity. While the process invariably stirs the minds of the common people, anthropologists are still more concerned, as globalization in the form of Western hegemonic influence, attempts to intrude into the distinct ethnic and cultural identities of many non-Western societies. Anthropologists debate among themselves about the nature and direction of the globalization process, its historical beginning, the Western agenda of its consolidation, and its influence—good or bad—on economic and cultural lives of millions of people in the developing countries. They also debate about the efficacy of the theories and methods earlier developed within the domain of anthropology in understanding the non-Western societies, which are currently undergoing the process of globalization (Eriksen, 2003).

Before embarking upon the debatable questions listed above, let us understand how the process of globalization is looked at from different angles. In common parlance, globalization is all about an aggressive spread of market economics and communication technologies, often under the control of the Western Multi-national Corporations (MNCs), threatening the very existence and sustainability of local cultures and values in the non-Western societies. Even some scholars believe that it is an expression of the advancement of 'modernity' over 'tradition', which is characterized by the loss of cultural identities due to the imminent process of cultural homogenization in these societies (de Rivero, 2001). But anthropology has persistently resisted such simplistic formulations. On the contrary, it seeks to document and analyze the subtle and innovative ways in which many intrinsic as well as extrinsic forces help these societies to create and re-create their identities and attach meanings to them within the broader politico-economic environments that encompass them. Anthropological theories address to the competing paradigms in understanding cultures and the representation of cultural identities keeping in mind the relevance of different prisms and categories, such as ethnicity, gender, class, nation, etc., in which cultures as socially recognized systems of meaning are produced and represented. Therefore, identities and their varied manifestations under different temporal and spatial contexts have engaged the attention of anthropologists and other anthropologically informed scholars.

In India, the new policy of structural adjustment in the form of globalization, liberalization and privatization, which began in early 1990s, has been posing severe challenge to many tribal and rural communities in terms of establishing their identities in this fast changing world of Western hegemonic cultural homogenization, as revealed by many empirical studies. For instance, commercial agriculture requiring heavy investments is driving small and marginal farmers in remote inaccessible areas of India into distress. The operation of transnational corporations has forced the rural artisans to give up their traditional crafts, unable to face the stiff competition from outside. There are instances that many traditional occupational groups like the weavers have to give up weaving in favour of either farm or industrial labour. The tribal communities, already threatened by deprivation and exploitation, are now burdened with the threat of aggressively expanding market forces and to encroachment into their economic and cultural milieus. Traditional subsistence cultures in India and other developing countries are increasingly giving way to an atomized and consumerist culture, characteristics of the West, in the emerging scenario. Therefore, at the present juncture, it is imperative to assess—(1) What role anthropology could play in this increasingly globalized world in understanding the interface between the global and the local? (2) How should anthropology respond to the new challenge of understanding a society under a different disposition by using its conventional paradigms and methodologies, when markets increasingly interact with political forms, social institutions and cultural values? (3) What are the demands of the global and transnational phenomena on anthropological field inquiry? and (4) How useful could be the anthropological findings in understanding the nature of identity formation in local cultures under the stress of emerging global transformations? The chapters that follow in this volume, directly or indirectly, address to some of these basic questions. The volume also includes chapters that articulate some of the contentious issues relating to the indigenous and marginalized populations and the issues pertaining to their environment, health, education, entrepreneurship in the context of an emerging new global social order.

History of Globalization Studies in Anthropology

Although the study of globalization has constituted an integral part of the Anthropology syllabi in many Universities now, it was rather a latecomer to this field of study. The process of local-global nexus was given a backseat due to the common assumption that ideally small-scale preliterate societies are 'bounded' entities and relatively free from most of the external global forces, which can be studied and understood in their own right. This evidently confronted with the global reality and interaction between the local and the global. The strong fieldwork traditions in studying different tribal societies by the British anthropologists reinforced such an assumption. The relation of these societies was believed to be at the most with the neighbouring clans and communities either for marriage or for barter. Subsequently, in the French structuralist tradition, there was no room for distinction between local and global. Our reading of Hegel, Marx and Lévi-Strauss leads us to their conceptualization of the logic of wholes and parts. For them, "... the world never begins with parts that somehow come together into larger wholes. Rather the wholes, or structures, are already immanent in their parts, and the parts can have no autonomous existence" (Ekholm-Friedman and Friedman, *in press*). Even the Structural Marxism, which was popular in the 1970s tried to eliminate a more static approach and more orthodox materialist models, and insisted on the concept of 'social reproduction' as the framework of analysis against the assumed nature of society as a closed entity. It went out to understanding social form, "....as constituted by socially organized processes of production, distribution and consumption, the basic framework by which a population reproduces itself over time" (*ibid.*). Apparently this implies population as a self-reproducing whole without necessarily articulating itself with a larger world.

In more recent times, within the domain of Anthropology, a new approach has emerged claiming the field of globalization as a "cultural" field. This approach assumes globalization as a new phenomenon in human history and hence, deserves new concepts and methodologies. Keeping this in mind many empirical studies have been conducted in situating today's global interaction as a matter of tension between cultural homogenization and cultural heterogenization. New concepts like Americanization and commoditization are invented and used. As a part of this approach, Appadurai's seminal work refers to the new global cultural economy as a "complex, overlapping, disjunctive order", which is difficult to be understood in terms of either the centre-periphery models or push-pull effects or surplus-deficit models. On the contrary,

Appadurai suggests that men, materials, money, technology and information flow in a rather chaotic set of disjunct circuits between the economy, culture, and politics around today's globalized world that bring us together. He proposes the relationship among the five dimensions of global cultural flow in terms of ethnoscapes, mediascapes, technoscapes, financescapes, and ideoscapes for exploring such disjunctures (Appadurai, 1996). Wallerstein's world-system theory with the primacy of endless capital accumulation via commodification of everything characterizes the modern world as "....larger than any juridically defined political unit", whose linkages with its parts is primarily economic (Wallerstein, 1998). Among other innovative thinkers, Ronald Robertson conceptualized globalization as the processes of both "compression of the world and the intensification of consciousness of the world as a whole" (1992). He suggests, it involves crystallization of four main components of 'global-human circumstance', such as societies, system of societies, individuals and humankind. His main contention is that globalization as a process both connects and stimulates awareness of connection and dissolves the autonomy of actors and practices in contemporary world order. In this process of relativization, all units engaged in globalization are constrained to assume a position and define an identity relative to the emerging global whole (1992: 29). Although some of the powerful writings underscoring various linkages between local and global have been published in the 1990s, much before that Clifford Geertz's *Agricultural Involution*, Andre Gunder Frank's *Capitalism and Underdevelopment*, and Eric Wolf's *Peasant Rebellions in the Twentieth Century*, etc. have already indicated that more often than not the local cultures could be best understood in terms of their articulation with the social, economic and political forces of the larger social world.

One of the most outstanding recent contributions is by Ekholm-Friedman and Friedman (*op. cit.*) distinguishing between 'global' and 'globalization'. For them, while global is a purely structural concept, globalization is empirical and behavioural, manifested through contact, movements, diaspora formation, global communication, and the like. For them,

"Global systemic anthropology is about the history of the human species, the forms of its social life and culture, understood in terms of the structures of social reproduction, that have guided its trajectories. This framework encompasses the study of cultural forms of symbolic structures and ritual practices of everyday strategies of life. It does not aim to replace them, but to contextualize them" (*op. cit.*).

Whether globalization is a new phenomenon or as old as the human civilization, whether it is unilinear and singular or multiple, whether it is spatial or social or occupational or ideological, whether it relates to compression or extension, it is a new social order that requires new tools to understand. The new genre of anthropology, as never before, has undermined this process of modernity—singular or multiple—and has tried to reflect on its various dimensions.

The chapters in this volume are arranged according to five major thematic sections, keeping in view the theme(s) of the chapter(s). While the first section deals with the issues of anthropology and globalization, other sections that follow include ecology and sustainable development, local self-governance, globalization and health, dalit identity and literature, tribal education, and global market and local primordiality.

Anthropology and the Forces of Globalization

Reddy, in Chapter 2, sets the debate on the core issue of equality *vs.* efficiency of the process of globalization and suggests some meaningful corrections, if the process has to benefit the larger sections of the global population. He agrees with the fact that globalization certainly brings into close interaction different nations, ethnic groups, religious communities and economic classes. The significance of anthropology in this context is that it makes one aware of the vast diversity of cultures existing in the world and insures one against the shock of the strange and bizarre. It also imparts the lesson that one should understand the other from the latter's point of view and should not cast the other in one's own image. It cannot be overemphasized that it is a very important principle to follow when people belonging to different cultures have to interact and deal with each other. His exemplary analysis of an emic approach is supported by the anecdotes of gesture of cordiality in American and French cultures, semantic difficulties in international communication, and his own experience at Andhra University about the holding of hand by fellow classmates and its interpretation of homosexuality by the American students. His contention of looking at globalization from the point of view of local cultures brings to the fore the role of anthropology not only in understanding, but also in setting the right direction to the process for the benefit of the poor and marginalized.

Reddy, from his vast experience of working among the tribal population in India, has noted with discontent how the ideally beneficial process of globalization has ultimately ended up with tribal miseries and tribulations. His examples come from his association with many tribal development projects and their implementation. The callous response of the governments of Madhya Pradesh and Gujarat towards 'proper' rehabilitation of the displaced tribals in Narmada Dam Project, the attempt of the Government of Andhra Pradesh to lease out land in the Scheduled Areas to Multi-national Companies in contravention to the provisions of the Fifth Schedule of the Indian Constitution, and a remarkable decline in the budget allocation for the Tribal Sub-Plan (TSP) over the years in the state of Andhra Pradesh, etc. have made him to painfully conclude that as if tribals have become disposable materials. Nevertheless, Reddy's exuberance of optimism with the new global order is certainly plausible, if it aims at redressing the present imbalances in population densities, per capita resource base and the quality of life. Without a sincere pursuit of that ideal, he believes, all talk of globalization is a mere shibboleth, which would finally facilitate bigger fish eating the smaller fish after a deceptive camaraderie. Ideal globalization would require sacrifices on the part of developed countries. Tariffs and immigration laws should work in favour of the developing countries, which should work with a huge sense of discipline and responsibility. Integrity from all sides is the desideratum to achieve that ideal.

The tone of 'cautious optimism' set by Reddy with respect to the new global order represented by homogenization and liberalization and its impact on the impoverished and marginalized groups in the developing countries has been shared by Danda in Chapter 3. In this chapter, Danda immaculately delineates the hypothesis of 'melting pot' in articulating the ethical issues involved in inflicting transformation through globalization on the local cultures by 'unwarranted' invasive strategies. He aptly questions: is there any wisdom in asking the people to opt for borrowed knowledge, foregoing their traditional self-wisdom that provided them with both confidence and pride for generations together? What does the so-called course of history mean to them and whose history does it actually reflect? If stages of history reflect colonial prejudice, how much could its validity be taken for granted in the post-colonial world? In order to answer these vital questions, which set the current discourses on globalization *vis-à-vis* the marginalized population, Danda takes the cue from the formulations of Ralph Linton. He reminds Linton's differentiation between the solid, well integrated, fairly stable cultural core and relatively fluid, ever changing zone of alternatives surrounding the core. When a new element is introduced into a culture, it undergoes a period of repeated trial with the competing traits behaving as alternatives within the given culture complex. The transformations often come at the end of this process and acceptance by the society. On the contrary, Danda suggests, the 'bombardment' of alternatives from outside, which apparently does not give any scope whatsoever for trial, upsets the internal balance of a culture. The results that follow include loss of human dignity, commoditization of human labour, emergence of a situation of chaos due to the availability of umpteen numbers of alternatives, and extinction of tribal and marginalized groups in extreme circumstances. Danda, therefore, suggests that the course of history cannot be uniformly perceived, as it may have been a boon for a selected few, but certainly devastating for many others, who continue to remain at the receiving end. This reinforces Reddy's convictions articulated in Chapter 2 regarding cultural dislocations among the tribal oustees of many major hydro-electric projects and other government-sponsored developmental interventions. Both Reddy and Danda at least agree on the point that the much-hyped process of globalization lacks the basic compassion for the humanity as a whole. Finally, Danda touches upon the role of anthropology in understanding the process of globalization and invites fellow anthropologists to seize this opportunity to set aside the 'colonial' mind-set in looking at the course of history by deconstruction of a sick system in favour of reconstructing a brave new world.

In Chapter 4, Manger's highly stimulating contribution echoes the call of Danda to look at the course of history in understanding the process of globalization. Manger carries forward Danda's message a little further and attempts to substantiate his argument with the help of his decade long study on Hadrami diaspora in Hyderabad, Singapore, Sudan and Southern Ethiopia. Manger aptly remarks that Hadramis are constantly and continuously undergoing the process of globalization ever since the first wave of migration from the Hadramaut area in South Yemen began around 1750 A.D. But since the same community migrated into different countries in different continents, Manger asks, how their identities emerge and evolve in the diaspora? He prefers to take an anthropological historical line of analysis by saying that the emerging identities of the Hadramis partly depend on contemporary realities of the concrete communities, and partly their own notion of 'historicity', that is the way people use history and historical narratives to create and establish their identity. Therefore, Manger tries to argue that what is understood today as globalization and its relationship with deconstruction or reconstruction of identities among the technologically simpler societies, are not new, but have been the lifeline of the Hadrami diasporic community for the last two thousand years or more. Because of this, he asserts, societies, cultures and nation-states have never been isolated entities; rather the flow of population and ideas from time immemorial has characterized them as open and mutually dependent domains.

In order to explain his way of understanding globalization, Manger attempts a critical assessment of the seminal contributions of Manuel Castell and Anthony Giddens. Manger prefers not to identify globalization as the logical end point of modernity, as the latter is precisely an ambiguous concept. Neither does he intend to dichotomize concepts into traditional and modern, modern and post-modern, and local and global, etc., as it blurs the vision of historicity. He suggests an alternate analytical framework of looking at the 'forces', 'connections' and 'imaginations' of globalization, taking cue from the outstanding contributions of Michael Busawoy *et al.* His forces are the economic, political and cultural forces of globalization; connections are the ones that make the forces sustainable through networking; and imaginations are the people's reactions to the process of globalization, either by justification or normalization or resistance to the process. He justifies this framework as it is historically grounded, theoretically driven and a macro-ethnography, combining comparative ethnography and history. Manger then discusses at greater length the process of globalization of the Hadrami diaspora through the concepts of forces, connections and imaginations reflected through the real historical transformations in two different historical epochs of, what he calls, global imperialism and global post-modern.

Charsley's position on contextual understanding of globalization in Chapter 5 is not different from the views expressed by either Manger or Danda or Reddy in earlier chapters. In fact, Charsley begins his chapter with a note of caution that the trend of 'exaggerating the newness of present' (like the logical endpoint of modernity) in anthropology needs to be probed objectively. He asserts that globalization does not necessarily mean a straightforwardly new phenomenon or complete change in the life style of the people, except perhaps an accelerated pace of change in society. Further, the impact of globalization may be more perceptible among the urban upper classes than among the rural people in general and the lower classes in particular. He cites the example of the impact of cable TV network in rural Andhra Pradesh as one of the facets of the impact of the globalizing process. Against the general impression that growing popularity of cable TV has marginalized many folk performers and the degree of social interaction has decreased considerably. Charsley's findings go much beyond to locate the internal socio-economic and political forces, which often play a rather decisive role in transmitting which channels and what videos the cable operator can make available for the subscribers. This leads Charsley to suggest, "At least the sociology, the economics and the physical layout of a village would have to be studied. The significance of anything new here would only be understood by locating it within contexts themselves involved in on-going process of change". Similarly, he observes the resurrection of popularity of the traditional *puranic* theatrical genres like *yakshaganams,* as the viewers feel 'bored' with the monotony of the cable TV programmes, against the general perception that the introduction of cable TV has swayed away the very existence of many folk performances in rural areas.

Charsley then hints at another danger, the danger of pushing aside 'culture', which has been the fundamental concern of anthropology, by the current agenda of globalization. He refers to the ideas of Malinowski and Geertz in explaining culture, and contends that anthropology should be all about the lives of people, which are primarily based on a variety of understandings, values and priorities. Human beings are creative and frame their own lives by choosing the best from among the opportunities available for them. And how and why they appreciate and choose from the bewildering variety of opportunities should be the central concern of anthropological study. He appeals that agenda of globalization should not undermine the cultural concerns, which are the foundation of anthropology. In Indian rural areas, he believes, cultural differences are still very much in existence, despite the scare created by globalization towards bringing about cultural homogenization. India still lives, Charsley states, with its distinctive south and north, linguistic states, dialectical regions within states, castes, classes, religious groups, which overlap each other and the geographical divisions.

Panda in Chapter 6 looks at the process of globalization as a global extension of differential power relations between different players, which was hitherto observed within limited geographical scales with a restricted scope. He contends that for the developing countries the asymmetrical power relations between the nations are of particular relevance, as globalization is associated not only with cultural, but also conceptual hegemony. He begins with a very sensitive question regarding the process of globalization in countries like India *vis-à-vis* the common citizens. Panda seeks the clarification as to whose interests the state serves through the regime of liberalization and privatization, and what impact these forces exert on the traditional resources and intellectual property rights of the people living close to the nature?

In carrying forward his arguments, Panda enlists land, water and forest as the commons in the era of globalization. He suggests that it is imperative to look at how globalization affects the system of land tenure, water management and management of forest resources, and how property relations are integrated with the customary laws, traditional authority structure, gender, etc. in the present context. Similarly, he ponders over the relationship between social organization, indigenous knowledge system and intellectual property rights in the era of globalization. He contends that in the changing global scenario, it is necessary for the anthropologists to keep a track of international conventions, bio-piracy issues, roles of diverse knowledge systems and the prospects of sustainable resource management. Panda, in fact, advocates for integration between globalization, local institutions in less developed countries and development in the real sense. He observes that although globalization is projected and conceptualized as a levelling mechanism towards homogenization, in reality, even within the local areas, differential access to opportunities and information have created schisms between the groups. Therefore, he calls for investigations into how local institutions, household structures, community practices, social networks, public policies, etc. mediate interactions between global processes and local responses, and thus shape the fortunes of different social groups in different places. Against the usual apprehensions of the scholars, Panda seems to suggest that the rule of the market is difficult to resist and cultural autonomy is bound to be jeopardized leading to the loss of traditional knowledge and skills. But at the same time when there is growing assertion by the rural and tribal populations of their right to life with dignity under the Constitution and International Conventions, Panda suggests, people-centred planned economic development could be the best way out. Otherwise, he sounds a word of caution that there could be ethnic conflicts, and communalism could have different expressions disturbing the internal harmony of the local communities.

Ecology, Indigenous Population and Sustainable Development

In an attempt to link up the indigenous population, their ecology and development in Indian context, Biswas contends in Chapter 7 that even in the present age of liberalization and globalization, there can be no financial asset if there are no ecological assets, and sustainable development is closely intertwined with environmental conservation. Development of the forest dependent communities, he asserts, is only possible when there is a harmonious balance between conservation of forest and livelihood security for these people. Since the question of livelihood is closely associated with the question of right over the resources, Biswas contemplates on the debate of considering whether forest area has to be the property of the state or a private property or under the exclusive ownership right of the indigenous people who have been living there since generations. He outlines the difficulties in the privatization of forests in India, although privatization has been the hallmark of the current process of globalization, because of the fact that primarily in India, privatization of forest simply meant plantation or specialized husbandry. Secondly, the impending political difficulties in having large tracts of forestland by private parties outside the usual land reform parameters. The third and the most important is the issue of leaving forest for the management by the indigenous communities, who lack 'both capital and expertise' required for the scientific management of forest. Therefore, Biswas is inclined to suggest that even if forest is leased out or sold to private agencies, the forest communities must actively participate in the system from practical and ethical considerations. He argues in favour of granting tenurial right of the indigenous communities over the forest to augment the process of livelihood security. This should be complemented with a decentralized decision-making process at the local level in tune with the spirit of the Panchayats (Extension to the Scheduled Areas) Act of 1996, if these communities are to be saved from the endemic situation of impoverishment in most of the tribal pockets of India. He concludes by saying the anthropological/sociological tradition of empirical appreciation of the local situation and indigenous institutions would go a long way in understanding these issues better and looking for a solution, if it is needed.

Sastry in Chapter 8 has carried forward the nexus between tribals, land and forest in India, and has used an experiential narrative among the tribes of East Godavari district in Andhra Pradesh to demonstrate the losses of common property resources in recent times in the tribal areas and eventual sense of deprivation and insecurity by the tribals in their very homeland. Sastry contends that the end-result of tribal frustration has not come about overnight, but by a long process of alienating them from land and forest. He recounts how the tribal cultures have developed definite values and beliefs with subsistence as their epicentre. For example, how all resources, particularly land and forest falling under the village boundary, were common properties, and were often safeguarded by the boundary deities. But the process of acculturation, penetration of modern market forces, increasing intervention by the state by way of imposing legislation in the tribal areas, etc. have eroded the very concept of common property, thereby leaving the tribals in a situation, where the earlier mechanism of assured food for everybody in the community is in a state of complete disarray. The most important turning point in alienating tribals from their land was, for Sastry, various measures by the British Government in India and Provincial Governments in declaring forestland as state-owned property. Subsequent Forest Acts in Independent India led to a deplorable condition of tribal alienation. Even some of the policies of the government went against the interest of the tribal population due to its myopic vision and lack of efficient implementation. In order to substantiate this point, Sastry takes recourse to the contentious issue of Minor Forest Produce (MFP) and the role of the Girijan Cooperative Corporation (GCC) in the State of Andhra Pradesh. With commercialization and marketability of forest produces in mind, he shows, how the GCC has unintentionally induced the tribals to leave the forest without many gum-producing trees today. Further, trees, which were once common properties, are now being owned individually in many communities because of their market values. Grazing lands, which were also common properties, are no more seen in many tribal areas due to over-grazing and rise in livestock population. On the whole, he argues that the concept of common property among the tribals, which ensured their livelihood till recently, has changed irreversibly and has lost its significance in the tribal life of India, for which he urges to re-examine all the protective and promotive policies for the tribal in the changing context.

While Sastry contends irreversibility of common property resources in tribal areas, which is undoubtedly true in many regions of the country, still there is a ray of optimism in the new regime of global concern over commons. Sharma, Bholerao and Pandey in Chapter 9 of this volume have tried to prove this through their organized fieldwork and empirical data from the endemically drought prone villages of Rajasthan. The study is conducted in the tribal dominated Patedi village in Dungarpur district of Rajasthan, which has been inhabited by the Bhil and a few SC households. It is said that the village has a high rate of literacy and being a Gram Dani village, the traditional panchayat has a major role to play in village affairs, leaving the developmental works to the statutory panchayat. The primary hypothesis of the study is that poverty in rural areas is due to the ill management of resources rather than their scarcity. In tribal areas, where the community spirit is at its high most of the times, the authors argue, judicious management of common property resources could alleviate the poor tribals from poverty and destitution.

Sharma, Bholerao and Pandey have observed that after plantation in village common land many benefits flow to the villagers, which include grass, wind blown twigs, dead and dry fuel wood, timber, etc. that are freely collected by the villagers. From the third year onwards, the villagers also got fodder. Availability of fodder helped increase the livestock population in the village with corresponding rise in income. These of course are besides the wages given to those who worked for plantation on the common land of the village. Even during the drought year of 1997-2000, there was only temporary or distress migration in the village and not permanent migration in search of jobs outside the village. The authors conclude that the tribals are also capable of managing village common property resources for their advantage with a little support from either the government or the NGOs, which help in supplementing their income and ensuring better standard of living.

Village common property resources could be many and varied. The tribal villages in the proximity of forests have an additional advantage of having Non-timber Forest Produce (NTFP) as one of the common properties, which Sastry has already highlighted in Chapter 8. While Sastry's observations are general and experiential, Pandey and Debnath in Chapter 10 have attempted a field-based study on the bearing of NTFP on tribal economy as well as the cultural practices in 3 tribal dominated districts of Madhya Pradesh. In addition, the study probes into differential dependence of tribal communities on NTFP due to their differential economic organizations in the districts of Mandla in the east, Betul in the south, and Khargone in the west parts of Madhya Pradesh. The representative tribal communities in these 3 districts include the Baiga, the Korku and the Bhil, which are at different levels of subsistence. While the Baiga primarily depends on shifting cultivation, the Korku is a community of agriculturists, but supplement their income with the procurement and marketing of NTFP. The third category, the Bhil, is least dependent on NTFP, as its members go out in search of wage labour once the *Kharif* harvest is over. The authors have observed that the relative dependence of the Baiga, Korku and Bhil on NTFP is 46 per cent, 13 per cent and 5 per cent due to their differential economic pursuits. The use of NTFPs in food and fodder, in ethno-medical practices, in fairs and festivals and for markets also vary among these tribal communities because their requirements of materials and accessibility to resources are different. The study emphasizes on the fact that management of these common resources like NTFPs in tribal areas needs to be done keeping in mind the variations in the use of resources and their importance in the total subsistence pattern of the local communities. No blanket policy could be useful, which does not take cognizance of differential uses of resources by different communities. Hence, the local communities and their knowledge about the resources have to be given due importance in policy making on NTFPs.

The later half of the 20th Century in India was marked by the interventions of many international agencies to inject the spirit of community participation in the development process, particularly in the rural and tribal areas. The international conventions of indigenous people were critical of the government apathy in many countries by further marginalizing them. During this time, the World Bank had played the role of a powerful catalyst in Indian villages creating an ambience of development through capacity building and decision-making at the grassroots level. Around that time, the adoption of National Forest Policy, 1988 by the Government of India may be considered as a watershed in the history of forest-tribal relationship. The Joint Forest Management (JFM) programme came into being in early 1990s in many states. Chapter 11 by Subramanyam is an empirical study of JFM in the Visakha agency of Andhra Pradesh, which had adopted it since 1994. Subramanyam has sought to analyze the role of anthropology in understanding the forest-tribal nexus in the context of centuries of suppression of the tribal communities under the imperialist Forest Acts and Policies.

In one of the study villages Subramanyam finds active participation of the tribals in JFM programme. It has helped them in improving their economic condition as well as for the regeneration of degraded forestland. Surprisingly, they have stopped clearing new *podu* plots in the reserved forests, which they were doing earlier quite frequently, despite the act being considered as illegal by the Forest Department. A large number of tribal residents have shown interest in horticulture and plantations having commercial value around their settlements. In fact, the villagers expressed their eagerness to be supplied with the saplings of silver oak, eucalyptus, jofra, neredu, kagu or ganuga, usiri, jack, mango, etc. by the Forest Department. They have a feeling that afforestation is helpful in receiving higher rainfall and reducing soil erosion. This reflects a changing tribal awareness of forest protection and regeneration, although they have been accused of damaging the vast forest wealth over generations. The villages where JFM is not in operation, the people participate in the afforestation programme undertaken by the ITDA, although they feel that it is not as effective as JFM, as the latter is funded by the World Bank. This, of course, implies better incentives to the local tribals and greater participation in the afforestation initiatives. Under the changing circumstances where the tribal is a willing participant of forest conservation and regeneration, Subramanyam concludes that the psychology and culture of the tribal people should be properly understood by the planners and policy makers in the Government to implement these programmes effectively. If the tribal people are made to understand the evil effects of deforestation and importance of conservation, they could come forward voluntarily to take up afforestation programmes. Subramanyam has echoed the experiences of West Bengal in the successful implementation of JFM and the participation of tribal people in forest regeneration efforts, although the programme did not show a promising result in many other states in India.

Local Self-Government and Tribal Administration

In an increasingly globalized world today, the indigenous or the tribal populations do not only have their share of natural resource management, but also in local self-government. Mahatma Gandhi's vision of *gram swaraj* or the village self-government echoes the tribal spirit of managing their own affairs without violating the federal structure of polity of modern India. In his discourse in Chapter 12, George succinctly delineates the debate between the members of the Constituent Assembly who were ideologically committed to Nehruvian liberalism and the assimilationists with regard to the issue of tribal autonomy within Independent India. Because of their number, the Nehruvian liberals won the debate culminating in the inclusion of the Sixth Schedule into the Indian Constitution that paved the way for formation of Autonomous District Councils (ADCs) in Assam. It may not be inappropriate to state that ADCs are smaller democracies within the larger Indian democracy. The Constitution literally made all possible provisions for these 'mini' democracies to be politically, economically and socio-culturally autonomous by retaining and preserving tribal customs and worldviews. The Sixth Schedule of the Constitution has granted legislative, judicial, administrative and economic powers to the ADCs, without of course being detrimental to the interests of the country and the state as a whole, so that these institutions could independently decide their own developmental priorities without any external intervention.

From his case study from Meghalaya, George explores various dimensions of functioning of the ADCs and their predicaments in the present context. It is evident from the analysis that the ADCs have not been able to successfully mobilize resources, either from the State Government or from the taxpayers within the jurisdiction of the ADCs, which could have contributed to the economic development of the district. The ADCs also do not have any control over the state budget and they find it difficult to mobilize the MLAs of the district to argue in favour of them in the Assembly. In the social arena,

ADCs could have made profound impacts on the tribals but for the poor implementation of the constitutional provisions. Although primary education was under the control of the ADCs until 1990s, the State Government had to withdraw it due to the failure of these institutions to manage the school system properly. The power of the ADCs to administer justice has been still elusive, as the Governor has never authorized the local courts to try any major case. In their efforts to codify the customary laws, various interest groups have tried to twist these laws to the annoyance of the public. Perpetuation of kingship or chieftaincy among many of the tribal groups in north-east India has jeopardized smooth implementation of the constitutional provisions granted to the ADCs in directing its efforts in the welfare of the tribal communities. As a third tier of India's federal political system, it has, however, created immense political consciousness and participation, and has provided more political opportunities at the local level than are usually seen in other tribal areas not covered under the Sixth Schedule of the Constitution.

Globalization, Anthropology and Tribal Health

Besides the issues relating to tribal administration and tribal development policies, matters connected with health and hygiene in the tribal and rural areas of India has drawn the attention of the anthropologists in recent times. Despite the popular slogan, "Health for all by 2000 A.D." by many national and international agencies, health remains an area of vital concern for all in most of the developing countries of the world, including India. Since health is not an isolated physiological phenomenon, but is a function of socio-biological and cultural practices, genetic attributes and environmental conditions, there is a need to look at health from a holistic perspective.

The New Economic Policy of the Government of India has been criticized for its policies of cutting or reducing subsidies and decreasing expenditure on public health and education. Undisputedly this has largely affected the poorer sections of the Indian society. When the policy of liberalization and penetration of global market forces into the remotest parts of the country has widened the gap between the rich and poor, introduction of 'health fees' in many government-managed hospitals has certainly hit the deprived and marginalized sections of the society. Poverty, unemployment, malnutrition among children and general deterioration of health conditions are attributed to the new economic policies and the general trend of globalization.

In Chapter 13, Rao aptly expresses concern that the existing practice of studying health culture by the anthropologists in the era of globalization poses new challenges. He calls for better conceptual frameworks, methods, tools of data collection and analysis in the study of health and has proposed a holistic anthropological paradigm its scientific understanding. Rao's conceptual framework places health at the intersection of social structure, cultural values and environment. The concept of good health is primarily, Rao maintains, rooted in the cultural values of the people. This is developed by the human-divine relationships or the worldview, which guides an individual to adopt a particular strategy in dealing with the ill health. Similarly, many social factors, such as the family, gender, concept of person, social inequality, social position, decision-making, religious taboos, etc., also determine the concept of ill health and sick behaviour. In the same vein the environmental factors like the altitude, temperature, biosphere, etc. have tremendous impact on human biology, and therefore, on human health. To sum up, Rao argues that no one factor discussed above is less important in the understanding of human health, as it is not just a bio-medical exercise, but must include a much wider holistic perspective.

Rao further suggests that for a micro-level understanding of health, one should place individual at the centre, whose perceptions and experiences matter in maintaining good health. These perceptions and experiences largely come from the process of socialization in a family, the society at large that regulates the normative behaviour of an individual and a family, and the state, which has its goals, ideologies and philosophy that provide education, legal system and health care. All these impinge upon the individual and the society and mould perceptions regarding health and sickness. Rao, therefore, proposes that at the micro-level, individual experiences and perceptions of health stand at the cross-section of family, society and the state, and hence, all these should be studied from a holistic perspective.

In order to show the relationship between body and health, Rao suggests that healthy body is not only an embodiment of physical state, but also connected with the human psyche. Since body is intimately linked with food habits, nature from where food is derived and psyche, the micro-level analysis should take into account these essential components to understand individual perception of a healthy body. Similarly, for the restoration of health, at the micro-level, he suggests that analysis should be made of various options available for the sick individual and the persons attending on the sick person, and how choice for restoration is made. On the whole, Rao underlines the need of the macro-level analysis of health and health behaviour holistically by analyzing the mutual bearing of social structure, culture and environment, while at the micro-level, analysis should include individual, body and restoration of health. Our anthropological understanding, he suggests, could go a long way, if health is understood from all these dimensions, when health care for the poor and marginalized is being relegated to the periphery under the regimes of new economic policy and globalization.

From the general understanding of health system, if we focus our attention on specific epidemics like HIV/AIDS, socio-economic inequality as a by-product of a globalized economy and large-scale migration of labour force from rural to urban regions have their role to play. In Chapter 14, Meera rightly remarks that the incidence of HIV/AIDS in India has spread from high-risk population to bridge population, and finally to the general population. She emphatically states that the poor and marginalized, particularly women, are most vulnerable, the social and economic dependence being the root factor.

While tracing the history of anthropological research on HIV/AIDS, Meera notes that the focus of much important research on HIV and AIDS over the course of the past decade has moved from behaviour, in and of itself, to the cultural settings within which behaviour takes place, and to the cultural symbols, meanings, and rules that organize it. Further, the anthropologists recognize that while individual cultures are more or less internally coherent systems, they are also part of nations, which are, in turn, connected with other nations of the world. Thus local cultures are not completely autonomous, independent systems; they are influenced by international circumstances and events. So anthropologists must take cognizance of globalization and the global context into account in the research on HIV/AIDS. Meera lucidly explains and emphatically argues that there exists an intimate relationship between political, economic and behavioural dimensions of sexuality that results in the vulnerability of poor and destitute. She cites the examples of prostitutes in Mumbai who are immigrants to the city from many parts of the country; the *hijras* engaged in 'institutionalized prostitution' and the regular blood and organ donors, who are the victims of HIV/AIDS. Finally, Meera suggests that the theoretical models and methodological skills traditionally associated with the discipline of anthropology are becoming more and more recognized as essential tools in dealing with HIV/AIDS as a disease that afflicts collectivities as well as individuals, a disease of societies, cultures and nations. She opines that it would be one of the many challenges before the anthropologists in the 21st Century. It would indeed be the responsibility of the anthropologists to demonstrate the social and cultural dimensions of health care and prevention of diseases in an economically liberalized world, where epidemics like trades spread beyond imaginations.

Although globalization agenda is normally understood in terms of economic liberalization and privatization, in many ways it includes providing good quality of life to the people in the third world. Health is an integral part of such an agenda. There have been many global initiatives to make available universal immunization, proper nutrition for mothers and children, quality eye care, etc. to the people of the developing countries, particularly the marginalized and poor among them. In Chapter 15, Kovai *et al.* present an assessment of such a global initiative, "Vision-2020: The Right to Sight", to reverse the trend of avoidable blindness and visual impairment by 2020. The study is undertaken in the state of Andhra Pradesh, and among the most vulnerable rural population in the state. The study aims at understanding treatment-seeking behaviour for visual impairment, mostly caused by curable refractive errors and cataract. Very interestingly the study indicates that among the sample population, visual impairment includes cataract (47.7%), refractive error (41.2%) and other causes (10.9%). Surprisingly, about 97 per cent of the patients did never feel the necessity of an eye test, as they never felt decrease in vision in the last 5 years. More than half of the patients did not visit an eye hospital for personal reasons, 37 per cent for economic constraints and 21 per cent for social reasons. There is, however, a significant correlation between age and health-seeking priority. This is, of course, with the approach of blindness, and not before that. The study indicates that literacy has a significant role to play in treatment-seeking behaviour of the rural population in India. In order to achieve the global objectives of Vision-2020, the study suggests that elimination of illiteracy, increased awareness and removal of economic constraints for eye care should be taken into consideration. Indirectly though, the study indicates that identification of the vulnerable population should be with the help of anthropological methods, leaving the rest to the ophthalmologists and others.

Dalit Identity and the Genre of Dalit Literature

The Chapter 16 by Das portrays the anger and resentment of the dalit population in India and their expression in the dalit literature. Quoting Khare, Das agrees that anthropology should not merely seek truth but also social justice. He contends that anthropological discourses in the past did overlook the issue of independent dalit identity and ethos, while binding them in the hierarchical framework of Indian castes. Das delineates the emergence of dalit literature in south and north-west India and explains with excerpts how anger, sorrow amidst optimism are vividly expressed in dalit poetry and autobiographies. One wonders why the news of caste-based oppression and exploitation of the dalits still find their place in Indian newspapers, when there is a parallel slogan of a global village. Will our politicians allow us to dream of a global village at all, devoid of inequalities and exploitation?

Das has drawn our attention to the genre of dalit literature, which goes hand in hand with political revolts and is marked by revolt and negativism, since it is closely associated with the hopes for freedom of a group of people who, as untouchables, are victims of social, economic and cultural inequality. Generations of suppression are burst out in dalit poetry, when the poet says: "*Earlier men could have been the wretched slaves of the soil. I refused to make compromise ...*". Das has analyzed the dalit poetry, which he names as *vidrohi kavita* (revolt poetry), in Maharashtra, Gujarat and Andhra Pradesh, trying to find a common tone of resentment against traditional caste society and the low rank assigned to the dalits there by the higher caste groups. But Das expresses immense self-confidence and awareness among the dalits in the present times as a category of oppressed for centuries. As a reaction to this, dalit literature is rich with the expression of fearless, aggressiveness and a great optimism of a just society.

Globalization, Anthropology and Tribal Education

It is an established fact that while the process of globalization strives to bring nations and communities into its fold, as it stands, the indigenous people or the tribes are not yet benefited much from this process. One of the reasons of this deprivation is the lack of education, about which anthropologists often show their concern. In Chapter 17, Sharma draws our attention to the less rigourous attempts by the anthropologists in studying problems in formal education and calls for a sound methodological approach to underline the significance of ethnography in understanding tribal formal education. Conventionally, he opines, anthropologists are obsessed with the informal education and process of socialization among the tribal communities, paying less attention to the formal school education. He aptly remarks that anthropological studies generally lack the qualitative rigour and fail to understand in depth the culture-school incongruence phenomenon. The need, therefore, is a special emphasis on cultural differences in value orientations and learning styles in schools and community and identify the schools with specific school cultures that would help optimize the use of cultural resources a specific tribal community possessed. His argument is to look at the phenomena of child experience at home, at peer groups and the influence of school environment over a period of time collectively contribute to the success of schooling, and the negative role of any one of these factors often leads to the failure in schooling.

Global Markets, Primordial Sentiments and Enterprise

Although globalization is largely understood as an overarching policy of trade liberalization and privatization, the role of culture as a primordial factor is not given the attention it deserves. Culture expressed through various primordial loyalties is present in all cultures though, its manifestation is more in many traditional cultures including that of India. In Chapter 18, Mahammad examines how certain cultural factors, such as kinship, caste and other primordial ties help the communities to continuously strive for sustaining in any profession notwithstanding severe hardships and crises they have to face. On the contrary, to the communities without such cultural networks literally fall prey to many external market and other forces in an increasingly globalized world, eventually facing a situation of complete bankruptcy. As a case study, Mahammad has chosen the traditional weaving communities in the state of Andhra Pradesh to show how many primordial ties boost the spirit of entrepreneurship and how they operate as shock absorbers at the time of crisis.

In sociological and anthropological literature of development, primordial bonds are often characterized as stumbling blocks in the process of development. But in the present condition of a vulnerable market force, Mahammad argues, these primordial sentiments bail the entrepreneurs out from difficult economic crises. He argues that the innovativeness and adaptability by sections of particular occupational groups to market changes show the prevalence of more enterprising qualities among that particular endogamous group, unlike earlier characterization of these groups as averse to transformations. In fact, it is in the backdrop of the penetration of globalization process into the Indian economy (which made the economy more market oriented) that the paper dwells upon the dimensions of entrepreneurship and development among the traditional weaving castes/ communities.

Conclusion

Globalization, economic liberalization and privatization are the inescapable features of the modern world, no matter how these are perceived by different nations, communities and groups. States seem to be helpless in preventing globalization, as "The wave of debates about multiculturalism that has spread through the United States and Europe is surely testimony to the incapacity of states to prevent their minority populations from linking themselves to wider constituencies of religious or ethnic affiliation" (Appadurai, 1996: 22). Appadurai aptly observes that the 'diasporic public spheres' are the crucibles of a post-national political order, which are geared by enormous expansion of mass media, movement of refugees, activists, students and labourers (*ibid.* 22-23). Against this state of incapacitation, many scholars have been very pessimistic regarding the impact of globalization on the poor and marginalized. It is observed, "The history of majority of the countries of Latin America, Africa and Asia, since their independence, has merely recorded a gradual process of dysfunction and global marginalization" (de Rivero, 2001: 2). Many scholars have gone to the extent of invoking the principle of Social Darwinism by stating that little did Darwin suspect that his theory of natural selection would apply to the modern global market and technological revolution. This pessimism is however negated by many scholars citing that under the globalization regime, inequality was at its lowest level by the end of 2000 in last 50 years, poverty has declined at a faster rate between 1985 and 2000, and even many poorer countries have grown faster economically than the richer countries (Bhalla, 2002: 1). Despite all these arguments and counter-arguments, the empirical studies included in this volume express a common concern that cultural studies under globalization must not forget the politico-historical background and socio-economic contexts of the cultures and communities that form the microcosm of an anthropological enquiry. It is strongly expressed by many in this volume and elsewhere that human societies are not immutable entities and human beings have always the flexibility of choosing one out of many possible opportunities left before them, which ultimately decide the nature and direction of their society and culture. Anthropological tools and methodologies need to be redesigned to probe into these enquiries, when cultures are caught between primordial identities and the processes of homogenization.

REFERENCES

Amin, Samir (1997), *Capitalism in the Age of Globalization: The Management of Contemporary Society*, London: Zed Books.

Appadurai, Arjun (1996), *Modernity at Large*, Minneapolis: University of Minnesota Press.

Austin-Broos, Diane (2003), Globalization and the Genesis of Values, *Australian Journal of Anthropology*, 14 (1).

Barnet, Richard and John Cavanagh (1994), *Global Dreams: Imperial Corporations and the New World Order*, New York: Simon & Schuster.

Bauman, Zygmunt (1988), *Globalization: The Human Consequences*, Cambridge: Polity Press.

Bhalla, Surjit S. (2002), *Imagine there is no Country: Poverty, Inequality, and Growth in the Era of Globalization*, Washington D.C.: Institute for International Economics.

Braman, Sandra and Annabelle-Sreberny-Mohammadi (1996), *Globalization, Communication and Transnational Civil Society*, New Jersey: Hampton Press.

Brecher, Jeremy and Tim Costello (1994), *Global Village or Global Pillage: Economic Reconstruction from the Bottom Up*, Boston: South End Press.

Chossudovsky, Michel (1997), *The Globalization of Poverty: Impacts of IMF and World Bank Reforms*, London: Zed Books.

Clarke, Susan E. (1998), *The Work of Cities*, Minneapolis: University of Minnesota Press.

De Rivero, Oswaldo (2001), *The Myth of Development* (Translated by Claudia Encinas and Janet Herrick Encinas), London: Zed Books.

Ekholm-Friedman, K. and J. Friedman (in press), *Essays in Global Anthropology*, AltaMira Press.

Eriksen, Thomas Hylland (ed) (2003), *The Globalization: Studies in Anthropology*, London: Pluto Press.

Friedman, T.L. (1999), *The Lexus and the Olive Tree*, New York: Farrar, Strauss, Giroux.

Gupta, Satya Deva (1997), *The Political Economy of Globalization*, Boston: Zed Books.

Haynes, Jeff (1999), *Religion, Globalization, and Political Culture in the Third World*, New York: St. Martin's Press.

Hoogvelt, Ankie M.M. (1997), *Globalization and Post-colonial World: The New Political Economy of Development*, Baltimore: John Hopkins University Press.

Holton, R.J. (1998), *Globalization and the Nation-State*, New York: Macmillan Press.

Inda, Jonathan Xavier and Renato Rosaldo (eds) (2002), *The Anthropology of Globalization*, Malden: Blackwell.

James, Harold (2001), *The End of Globalization: Lessons from the Great Depression*, Cambridge, MA: Harvard University Press.

Kiely, Ray and Phil Marfleet (1998), *Globalization and the Third World*, New York: Routledge.

King, Anthony D. (ed) (1997), *Culture, Globalization and the World System*, Minneapolis: University of Minnesota Press.

Lewellen, Ted C. (2002), *The Anthropology of Globalization: Cultural Anthropology Enters the 21st Century*, Westport, Conn: Bergin & Garvey.

Lewis, Mark (1996), *The Growth of Nations: Culture, Competitiveness, and the Problem of Globalization*, England: Bristol Academic Press.

Maitra, Priyatosh (1996), *The Globalization of Capitalism in Third World Countries*, Westport: Praeger.

Mittelman, James H. (1996), *Globalization: Critical Reflections*, Boulder: Lynne Rienner Publishers.

Mlinar, Zdravko (1992), *Globalization and Territorial Identities*, Vermont: Avebury.

Robertson, Roland (1992), *Social Theory and Global Culture*, London: Sage.
Sassen, Saskia (1998), *Globalization and Its Discontents*, New York: New Press.
Schaeffer, Robert K. (1997), *Understanding Globalization*, New York: Rowman & Littlefield.
Stiglitz, Joseph E. (2002), *Globalization and Its Discontents*, New York: W.W. Norton.
Thomas, Caroline and Peter Wilkin (1997), *Globalization and the South*, New York: St. Martin's Press.
Tomlinson, John (1999), *Globalization and Culture*, Chicago: The University of Chicago Press.
Wallerstein, I. (1998), *Utopistics Or, Historical Choices of the Twenty-First Century*, New York: The New Press.
Waters, Malcolm (1995), *Globalization*, New York: Routledge.

2

Anthropo-Sociological Perspectives on Globalization

N. SUBBA REDDY

Introduction

The word globalization epitomizes what is conveyed in the saying that the world has become small. It means that diverse peoples from distant places are brought into close interaction. If this interaction is for 'common good', then globalization is a welcome phenomenon. But if it favours some against others, it should be unwelcome to the latter and also to impartial observers.

There is a dialogical discussion on the subject between Thomas Friedman, the author of *The Lexus and the Olive Tree* and Robert Kaplan, the author of *Warrior Politics*, published in the *Journal of Foreign Policy*. Friedman who is a protagonist of globalization says: "Globalization is the integration of everything else. Globalization enables each of us, wherever we live, to reach around the world farther, faster, deeper and cheaper than ever before, and at the same time allows the world to reach into each of us farther, faster, deeper and cheaper than ever before". From the other side, Kaplan who is more concerned with the common good says that under globalization people come together "so that the highest morality is the morality of order, with everyone giving up a share of his independence for the sake of greater order". He is skeptical of the results of globalization at least in the short run. He says: "Globalization is not necessarily good news.... And the news could get scarier because more interconnections will lead to complexity before they lead to stability" (Friedman and Kaplan 2002: 64-65).

Taken in its ideal form, globalization squares with the main thrust of anthropology. But in its actual form it seems to be at odds. I will first briefly deal with the positive side and try to show how anthropology can be of help in the process of globalization for the common good, and then come to the latter to show where the findings of anthropology and other social sciences are unable to back the results of the current processes of globalization. The relevance of anthropology in the context of diverse people coming into close interaction is that it prepares one to meet and engage with people of varied cultures. It also imparts the lesson that one should understand others from the latter's point of view and should not see them in one's own image. It cannot be overemphasized that it is a very important principle to follow when one has to deal with people of widely different social and cultural backgrounds.

Understanding Across Cultures

Different ethnic groups in the world have distinct ways of thinking, acting and responding, and have different worldviews. These differences are noticeable not only between primitive tribes but even between modern nations of the developed world. Bateson (1962: 188) narrates an interesting conversation between an American father and daughter. The daughter asks her father why the Frenchmen go on waving their arms during a conversation. The father asks the daughter why she goes on smiling during a conversation. Finally, both of them agree that these gestures express cordiality and that their absence would indicate that the parties are cool or cut-up. And the French express their cordiality in their own way.

In an essay on semantic difficulties in international communication, Edward Glenn (1962: 52) narrates how words with same denotation have different connotations in different countries. The French word for taxpayer is contributable. But the French, given to the Cartesian way of thinking, sense a connotation in it different from the English who are conditioned by their pragmatism and empiricism. When these words occur in a discussion, the idea that comes to the mind of the French is whether everyone contributes equally to a cause, whereas the idea that comes to the mind of the English is whether one gets the maximum benefit at the least cost. Glenn (1962: 52) also refers to the serious differences that arose at a conference between American and Russian delegates when the former moved an innocuous resolution in favour of expanding economy. The Russian delegate strongly objected to it because the Russian equivalent for the word 'expanding' takes a reflexive form and has the connotation of self-expanding which, in the Marxist-Hegelian way of thought, conveys the idea that what expands, necessarily contracts and collapses.

A distinct characteristic of Arabic culture has been noted by Glenn (1962: 49). For the Arabs a simple, unstressed 'no' does not mean a final negative reply. It is only a signal for further negotiation. Only when it is repeated a few times in an emphatic form, it means a final negative reply. Similarly a simple 'yes' does not mean the final acceptance of a deal or a proposal. Huntington (1996: 227) observes that the American soft attitude is being mistaken by Japan and China and finds the following explanation for it: "Because of the American penchant to identify 'good' relations with friendly relations, the U.S. is at a considerable disadvantage in competing with the Asian societies who identify good relations with the ones that produce victories for them (advantageous). To the Asians, the American concessions are not to be reciprocated; they are to be exploited".

Some problems arise because of the discrepancy of assumptions and expectations between the parties concerned. At an annual meeting of the Fulbright fellows in America at which I was present, some scholars from Western Europe complained of the cold and cut-and-dry attitude of their research guides in America. They said that when they arrived in America and reported themselves to the professors at the host institution, the latter straightaway showed them the laboratory where they had to work and asked them to report their progress after a month. There were no more words exchanged and no query showing personal warmth. They said that it took them a few months to adjust themselves to the new human climate.

The reverse was the case with a few students from Wisconsin University who came to study Telugu at Andhra University. They were happy that whomever they met gave his time freely which was a pleasant contrast to the situation back in America. But they faced one problem because of the differences in the meaning of a particular practice in the two cultures. Whenever the American students walked from the hostel to the university department, the Indian students accompanying them held their hands to express their cordiality and affection. The American students felt embarrassed because it would suggest homosexuality in their society. When an American student brought this to my notice, I advised him to hold a book in each hand when he walks and thus avoid holding of hands without offending anyone.

Cultural History and Intellectual Property Rights

In anthropological studies, diffusion of ideas and artifacts from one culture to another forms an important part. Culture history tells us that any useful idea or invention disseminates, willy-nilly, from place to place and from people to people, and is sometimes re-shaped and adapted to suit the local culture and local genius. Wheat and coffee were first grown in the Middle East. Cotton and tea were first cultivated in India and silk in China. While India invented the steel-making process, China invented printing with clay moulds. Gunpowder originated in China. The world owed to India the conception of Zero and the calculation of stars' ascension and eclipses. Potatoes, tomatoes and tobacco were the gifts of Red Indians of America. While some of these products were readily borrowed, some were not, though more useful. Tobacco seems to have been readily accepted by the cowboys but not tomatoes. George

Washington Carver, a Black American agricultural scientist had to eat tomatoes on public platforms to demonstrate that they were not poisonous but nutritious, in order to persuade the white farmers to cultivate them.

Did any one pay any royalty to the original growers of those crops or the inventors of those techniques? Against such a background, it is very difficult for a student of culture history to understand or appreciate the very idea of intellectual property rights, which is one of the main planks of globalization. If any one has the attitude that he cannot pursue any serious research without the expectation of royalty, he is not worth the name of a scientist and deserves nothing but contempt. A notification or acknowledgement of a discovery should be a reward by itself. What a strange situation it is, when farmers have to go to M.N.Cs for seed and grow the crops without any scope for raising the seed themselves.

Culture of Consumption and Environmental Crises

The most striking feature of globalization as we witness it today is the culture of consumption. The world seems to be caught in its swirl and is being carried away by its forceful current. There have been two extreme views about it, one pessimistic and the other optimistic. Some thinkers starting with Malthus, Ricardo and Mill have warned us against the non-sustainable level of resource utilization long ago. The loudest warning in the recent decades was sounded by Meadows and his team in their book, *Limits to Growth* (1972). While some of their predictions went wrong, there is still one which needs to be heeded. They warn that industrial civilization may collapse by 2100, unless there are curbs on the growth of population and industrial production. Even if it is ignored as too alarmist, there are other voices to be heard about the environmental catastrophe which may ensue if the present rate of resource utilization continues.

Bodley, in his book, *Anthropology and Contemporary Human Problems* (1976: 31) refers to the oil spills, off-shore drilling and dumping in the oceans and says that this may lead to the elimination of marine phytoplankton which produces 70 per cent of the atmospheric oxygen. Asimov (1971) notes that there has been an abnormal increase in the human sector of global biomass (including domesticated plants and animals) and a corresponding decrease in the earth's natural biomass. He cautions that we may reach a stage when every gram of material on earth is transferred to the human sector and every natural competitor is eliminated. According to his estimate this stage may be reached by 2436 A.D.

There is a smug claim that progress is measured by the quantum of energy consumed per capita. But is it not a lop-sided development if 35 per cent of energy output is utilized by one country *i.e.*, the U.S.A., as noted by Bodley? To the same order belongs the fact that 60 per cent of the world's copper output is being consumed by three countries, *i.e.* U.S., Russia and Japan. There are other facts which sound paradoxical. While the energy from fossil fuels is being used to substitute the human labour, and home appliances have multiplied, the hours of work put in by housewives in America seem to have increased but not decreased. Bodley (1976: 66) reveals that while the housewives in America put in 52 hours of work in a week on the average in 1920, they have put in 55 hours of work in 1970. It only shows that wants are multiplying faster than human ingenuity and the man is caught in a vicious circle.

As against these pessimists, there are, of course, many optimists. Even in the days of Malthus, there was Godwin who believed in the possibility of infinite increase in the means of subsistence through changes in technology and in social relations. In the recent decades, Barnett and Moarse (1963) are known for their firm belief in perpetual growth through discoveries of new sources of energy. But this is a bit of crystal gazing and there is as much chance of the prophecy being fulfilled as being falsified. Wisdom may lie in being cautious and not in being over optimistic.

Bodley (1976: 59-61) cites the difference between high and low energy cultures presented by the environmentalist, Earl Cook, in the *Scientific American*. In primitive cultures the consumption of energy per capita per day has been 4000 to 12000 kilocalories. Before the fuel revolution, the energy consumption in most of the (non-primitive) societies was 26000 kilocalories per capita per day. After the fuel revolution, it rose to 70000 kilocalories. In America it went on rising to reach 230000 kilocalories by 1970. A warning that emerges from these facts is that the waste heat generated by this vast amount of energy consumption may destroy industrial civilization unless the energy consumption is curtailed.

Anthropology offers certain perspectives in this regard. In simple societies, all matter is considered finite and non-expandable and people adjust themselves to nature. This is in contrast to the modern man's assumptions about the infinity of resources and mastery over nature. The cultures at the lower level of evolutionary progress have been far more efficient in energy output and input ratios than the advanced cultures. The impact of primitive cultures on the environment has been always moderate enough for nature to cope with and replenish. Odum (1971: 211) points to the fact that subsistence economies maintained a stable self-regulating ecosystem, but the picture began to change after the fossil fuels came to be used in the food systems. He ridicules the so-called efficiency of factory farms. According to him, factory farms utilize only 0.25 per cent of solar radiation into useful energy, whereas tropical forests utilize 3.5 per cent of it. The larger yields on factory farms are made possible only through fossil fuels replacing the loop of the natural system, which, in effect, means conversion of oil into food (the oil used in tractors, weeders, harvesters, sprayers, etc., besides chemical manures and pesticides).

Rappaport (1971) compares potato cultivation in U.S. with sweet potato cultivation in New Guinea. In terms of food value, the production in the U.S. is 10 million calories per acre, whereas it is 5 million calories per acre in New Guinea. But there are no inputs in New Guinea except human labour while the inputs in America amount to a staggering figure, and they are such that they cause environmental degradation in the long-run. So the lesson that one should learn from these facts is that there should be curbs on the consumption pattern and on the utilization of energy and other resources.

But who can stop the march of the juggernaut of consumerism? The Chairman of the American Federal Reserve in his testimony before the House of Representatives Financial Services Committee on July 15, 2003, refers to one feature of current American economy as most gratifying. That is the number of people taking loans for buying houses has increased. If borrower is the benefactor of economy, then consumer is the king.

Other Actualities of Globalization

When we consider the phenomenon of globalization as it is unfolding today, there is much in it which makes a student of anthropology or of any social science uneasy. The defining features of globalization are free market, non-regulation, abolition of subsidies, free competition in trade which implies abolition or lowering of tariffs, consumerism and privatization. Some of the precepts and prescriptions apply only to the poorer nations and not to the richer countries. For instance, America expends enormous amounts on subsidies to enable the farmers to export the grain to other countries on competitive terms. In some situations in certain years, even burning of grain stocks to boost the prices is an accepted practice. The major industries of America like the automobile and airways corporations could not have survived but for the government pouring in enormous public funds to enable them to stand on their feet. It should be clear to anyone that in such a situation the poorer nations with modest resources are unable to compete in the international market. Steward Wallis, Director of International Division, Oxfam, in a recent press interview says that if the poorer nations are allowed to raise the level of their international trade by 1 per cent, the resulting benefit would lift 12.8 million people out of poverty. In his view, the trade laws are rigged in favour of the rich nations and the current trade practices generate extremes of poverty and prosperity (*Times of India*, July 25, 2003).

Equality *vs.* Efficiency

What is the fountainhead of the culture of consumption? One view is that it stems from inequalities between men which sets in motion the process of commoners trying to catch up with the Joneses, and the latter striving to remain a few steps ahead of the former. A logical deduction that emerges from it is that if the inequalities are reduced, the culture of consumption may lose its momentum, but if the inequalities persist, the culture of consumption will aggravate, and the outcome may be even greater inequalities. So the present pattern of globalization may never bridge the gap between the rich and the poor. There is another view, which may be termed as the top-down view which holds that when there is overall economic growth, the benefits will trickle down to the lower strata who would ultimately stand to gain from the net growth in economy. According to this view any redistributive interventions may retard the very growth process, which would spell a decline for every section of the society.

The differential impact of global economy on different strata and the related question of equality *vs.* efficiency received wide attention from economists and other social scientists. Pranab Bardhan covered this subject comprehensively in an extension lecture delivered in South Africa under the title, "Social Justice and Global Economy" (2001: 461-480). The argument that openness enhances growth and reduces poverty is characterized by him as a doubtful proposition. He cites the findings of Harrison and Hensen in support of this view (*ibid.* 468). The wage inequalities, according to him would not decrease but would increase, and the conditions of workers in the non-trading sector may actually deteriorate in the context of globalization (*ibid.* 469). With the rise in food prices resulting from trade liberalization, the plight of the poor worsens (*ibid.* 470). The differential mobility of employers and employees depresses the bargaining power of the labour (*ibid.* 470). The experience of Latin America and Africa reveals that the benefits of global economy have not tickled down to the poor (*ibid.* 473). On the other hand, some redistributive projects actually enhance productive efficiency rather than reduce it (*ibid.* 473). In his opinion, globalization may help disseminate technology, but the benefit often does not extend beyond a particular firm or particular partnership even within the same industry. One may also recall in this context the well-known thesis of Andre Gunder Frank (1971) that underdevelopment is often a product of the interaction between developed countries and the less fortunate nations of the world.

Galbraith (2002: 11-25) in a seminal paper with a telling title, "A Perfect Crime", examines the impact of globalization on the inequalities in the world. He finds the data complied by the World Bank experts Deininger and Squire inadequate for his purpose. He then turns to the data on manufacturing pay compiled for the period between 1963 and 1966 by the U.N.I.D.O. which was analyzed by the Texas University Inequalities Project. The main findings of this project, according to Galbraith, are as follows: After a brief decline in inequalities during the 1970s, "there is a turn around in 1981-82 just as Reagan took office in the U.S. At the same time there was a shift in the global climate of real interest rates .... The result was to precipitate a global debt crisis.... Poorer nations were forced first to cut down imports, capital spending, and then were pressured to abandon long-standing trade and welfare policies. The years since 1980s have thus seen an empirical test: an extraordinary increase in inequalities has not been followed by any increase in the global rate of economic expansion".

He refers to the prosperity experienced by the U.S. and U.K. during the period immediately following the 1980s when they harped on the magic of the market, and the I.M.F. began haranguing the poor countries to observe "austerity and then financial deregulation and privatization, sale of state assets at 'fire-sale prices' to foreign investors". Galbraith concludes: "The problem is a process of integration carried out since at least 1980 under circumstances of unsustainable finance, in which wealth flowed upwards from poorer countries to the rich and mainly to the upper financial strata of the rich countries .... It has been, it would appear, a perfect crime. And while statistical forensics can play a small role in pointing that out, no mechanism to reverse this policy exists, still less anything that repairs the damage. The developed countries have abandoned the pretense of attempting to foster development in the world at large, preferring to substitute the rhetoric of ungoverned markets for the hard work of stabilizing regulation. The progress is grim: a descent into despair, disease, ecological disaster and wars of separation and survival in many of the poorer countries".

Impact on Weaker Sections in India

In our own country a number of developmental projects funded by international financial institutions like World Bank have been undertaken in the present era of economic reforms. It may be in order to have a look at their impact on the weaker sections and scan the attitudes of the executives imbued with the ideology of globalization. Let me cite a few cases of this nature. Take the river valley projects. It is well known that tribals constitute the largest component of persons displaced by such projects either in the world in general or India in particular. High-sounding promises are made about their relocation and resettlement, but, more often than not, they end in breach and not in fulfilment. In the early stages of the Narmada dam construction, I happened to attend an international symposium on the problems of project-affected people. An officer of the Madhya Pradesh government was also a participant. He made the statement that the project was conferring the benefit of civilization on the displaced tribals as they were now seen living in towns like Bhopal, earning wages and wearing nylon shirts and pants. That was his idea of humanitarian resettlement. It is now clear that the Madhya Pradesh government is no longer in a position to provide land-for-land resettlement for the tribal oustees. In Gujarat where this assurance still exists on paper, its implementation is flawed.

After a lot of controversy, the World Bank itself constituted a committee under the chairmanship of Bradford Morse to conduct an independent review of the progress of resettlement. Here is a sample of what the independent reviewer observed about the conditions of the resettled tribal oustees in Gujarat.

> "In Krishnapura the people have been living in five lines of tin sheds for the last three years. We heard a

> litany of difficulties. In the monsoon waterlogging was extreme....They had a school in the old village, but they did not have any school here. They had many problems with their lands, both in its allotment and in its quality. Some family heads were still not given any plots while many major sons were still not recognized. They were promised that they would get housing plots, a school, a temple, a dispensary and a meeting hall. They were told that the work on the buildings and services would start as soon as they relocated ..... yet, after three years, there was no sign of work beginning. About jobs and employment possibilities there were very few. Their families were broken up. They had lost their animals .....The case of Amroli was even more disturbing. They came from one of the largest submergence villages. But only 19 families moved here (the rest were disinclined to come here after seeing the conditions here). They complained about water facility ... The well (water) was saline. Of the 19 families who were given land, 7 have land that was not cultivable .... The lands in the old village were of better quality .... The lands they were shown were not lands they were given" (Morse 1992, 111-112).

There is one extremely disturbing revelation in the report of the independent review about a collusion between World Bank and the State Governments to whittle down the safeguards embodied in the 1982 policy directive formulated by the World Bank itself. This policy requires that wherever tribal people are displaced there should be special efforts to see that their way of life is not disturbed. But the World Bank sought to distort the very definition of tribe so as to help reduce the number of oustees requiring special attention in resettlement. They interpreted the wearing of a factory made shirt or the presence of the images of Hindu gods in their house (even the image of Ganesha printed on a paper used as a wrapper to indicate the brand of a saree) as an indication that the person or family was detribalized. The result was that out of 19 tribal villages in one sector, 9 were taken out of the category and were labelled as forest-based villages. In the next step, as the forest around was denuded, they were re-classified as plains villages (*ibid.* 63-64). The independent review summed up the matter in the following words:

> "From the point of view of the people themselves, the intent of Indian Constitution, basic anthropological findings and the criteria embedded in the World Bank policy directive ...., a substantial proportion of those likely to be affected by agreement represents a failure to comply with the 1982 operational manual statement" (Morse 1992: 77-78).

In Andhra Pradesh, I was associated with the preparation of a resettlement report in connection with a proposed irrigation project. While the government records themselves show that there is vacant government land in the command area, which could be reserved, and set apart for the displaced tribals, the officers concerned contend that those lands are no longer available.

We may also examine recent policy trends in Andhra Pradesh. There was an attempt in 1988 to whittle down the provisions of a protective legislation (Land Transfer Regulation of 1970) which sought to prevent alienation of tribal lands and to restore to the tribals, the lands illegally occupied by non-tribals. In the middle of the year 2000, a move was set afoot for leasing out tribal lands to a multi-national corporation based in Dubai for mining bauxite ore and for setting up an aluminium plant. The proposal was pursued in a face of a judgment of the Supreme Court spelling out that as long as there is the Fifth Schedule of the Constitution, the lands in the Scheduled Areas could not be leased out to non-tribals. These moves were stayed for the time being. But there is no knowing when the Damocles' sword will drop.

When we look at the Andhra Pradesh tribal sub-plans of the recent years, the picture becomes even more dismal. The allocation to the TSP in the year 1991-92 constituted 5.2 per cent of the total State plan outlay. But by the year 1999-2000, the funds allotted for TSP came down to constitute only 2.8 per cent of the total State plan outlay. If we take the gross figures, the budget estimates for the TSP was Rs. 152 crores in the year 1999-2000, but it is only Rs. 93 crores in the year 2000-01. And there was no separate demand for TSP in the budget of 2001-02. It means that the tribals have become disposable material.

The Government of Andhra Pradesh prides itself as the forerunner in the adoption of information technology and as the protagonist of economic reforms. If governments that swear by globalization, liberalization and privatization, culture of consumption, etc., also exhibit simultaneously an utter disregard for the interests of the weaker sections, the conclusion is forced on us that they all constitute an integrated package. The leaders of governments in our country seem to be labouring under the impression that in advanced capitalist countries, the state is interested only in maximizing production through liberalization and is not bothered about the welfare of the weaker sections. This seems to make them take the stance that as loyalists to the ideology of economic reforms they should shed the load of their welfare concerns. This is an absurdity, and they should disabuse their minds of it and see what is happening in developed democracies. At this moment, when there is a set back in American economy and the government is seriously considering tax relief in order to galvanize investments, there is also a big debate on how to see that the expected depletion in tax collection does not affect the proposed expansion of welfare measures. Edward Kennedy, chairman of the Senate Committee on Health, Education, Labour and Pensions, released a note at the National Press Club on 16th January 2002, pleading for a bi-partisan support for measures such as provision of education for all pre-school children, expansion of health care for senior citizens, raise in minimum wage and special concessions for employees who have infants to care.

Recently I read an article from which I like to quote the following few lines: "The great question is whether the age of interdependence is going to be good or bad for humanity. It depends on whether all of us can develop a level of consciousness high enough to understand our obligations and responsibilities to each other. We cannot make it if we are led by theories which cater to short-sighted selfishness .... We cannot have a global trading system without a global economic policy, a global health policy, a global education policy, a global environment policy and a global security policy .... In effect we have to create more opportunities for those who are left behind by progress" (*Times of India*, 5 January 2002). The writer of the article is not any known Marxist. But he is a widely known citizen of the world, William Clinton. But Clinton should ask himself whether such a view informs the processes of globalization as we see it today. If it does not, he should address his message more forcefully to the leaders of the richer nations and international agencies.

REFERENCES

Asimov, I. (1992), *The End*, Pent House Publishers.

Barnett, H.G. and Moarse, C. (1963), *Scarcity and Growth: The Economics of Natural Resource Availability*, Johns Hopkins University Press.

Bateson, G. (1962), "Why do Frenchmen?", In S.I. Hayakawa (ed.) *The Use and Misuse of Language*, Greenwich: Fawcett Publications.

Bardhan, P. (2001), "Social Justice and Global Economy", *Economic and Political Weekly*, XXXVI (5 & 6), pp. 467-480.

Frank, A.G. (1971), *Capitalism and Underdevelopment in Latin America*, Penguins.

Friedman, T. and R. Kaplan (2002), "States of Discord", *Foreign Affairs*, March/April, 2002.

Galbraith, J.K. (2002), "A Perfect Crime: Inequality in the Age of Globalization", *Deadalus Writer*, 2002.

Glenn, E.S. (1962), "Semantic Difficulties in International Communication", In S.I. Hayakawa (ed.), *The Use and Misuse of Language*, Greenwich: Fawcett Publications.

Huntington, S.P. (1996), *The Clash of Civilization and the Remaking of World Order*, New Delhi: Penguin.

Meadows, H. *et al.* (1972), *The Limits to Growth*, New York: Universal Books.

Moarse, B. (1992), *The Independent Review—Sardar Sarovar*, Resource Futures International, Ottawa.

Odum, H.T. (1971), *Environment, Power and Society*, New York: John Wiley and Sons.

Rappaport, R. (1971), "The Flow of Energy in an Agricultural Society", *Scientific American*, 224 (3), pp. 117-132.

3

Globalization and the Course of History
Some Reflections

AJIT K. DANDA

I

About one hundred years ago from today, when Israel Zangwill's play *The Melting Pot* (1909) gained popularity in the United Kingdom, many commentators considered it to have very successfully reflected the pre-occupation of mind of the major global powers: the sub-national entities must not insist on their independent identity and instead redefine their socio-cultural goals in terms of the dominant section of the society. The newly founded nation-states in Europe, who were rather over eager to forge socio-political solidarity, if necessary, at the cost of discrete cultural entities and were all out to appreciate nationhood in unitary terms, discovered a *valid* document in it, as per dictum of which they could reinforce their national identity.

After the defeat of the Confederation Forces at Gettysburg in 1863 and all that had followed in the United States of America for several decades thereafter, the tormented psyche of the American nationhood was actually in search of a paradigm through application of which the integrative forces of their socio-political entity could be strengthened. A paradigm could ultimately be found in *The Melting Pot* and a myth was carefully crafted around it in order to project the same as the dominating spirit. So much popular was the theme of the play in the United States of America that the scholars over there, particularly the social scientists adoringly placed the text among important social science documents. Special meanings were attributed to the theme when considered in the context of management of states.

After World War II, capitalizing on the spirit of socialism when many new Third World Nation-states were born with fragmented identity delineations, they too found the theme of *The Melting Pot* quite handy for restoration as well as regeneration of their respective national identities. Looking through over half a century in retrospect, it is observed that seldom did the identities really melt. In certain cases at least they could gain so much strength that they were able to effect fragmentation of the existing nation-states. The bulk of the people, specifically the impoverished lot, adopted a resigned attitude towards these developments. There are still some who even without being vocal about it, by their very behaviour of indifference could reject *The Melting Pot* paradigm altogether. An illustration from my personal field notes will highlight the point.

The forest dwelling Pandos of Chattisgarh, though primarily live on gathering and hunting, know few practices of agriculture and the art of growing food grains. In fact they do clear up patches of forestlands and by dint of their untiring labour, turn them into arable plots, invariably to be usurped by the neighbouring peasant communities. The Pandos do not resist it, neither do they give up the practice of clearing up new patches of forests for application of their skill in food-growing no sooner they get usurped. Such a drama is also being enacted by millions of other marginalized populations from all over the world, without necessarily receiving any media publicity or due recognition.

The model put forward by the hypothesis of *The Melting Pot*, if I am permitted to refer to it so, is no doubt very important, particularly in view of interest of the dominant section of the concerned society. But how does it accommodate the requirements of the impoverished lot?

There are other disturbing questions too, several among whom are very pertinent. How much ethical it is to ask a Pando to share a multi-ethnic ambience, when he apprehends exploitation over there and does not feel himself to be a very confident partner? Is there any wisdom in asking a people to opt for borrowed knowledge, foregoing their traditional self-wisdom that provided them with both confidence and pride for generations together? What does the so-called course of history mean to them and whose history does it actually reflect? If stages of history reflect colonial prejudice, how much could its validity be taken for granted for the post-colonial world?

Through this brief discourse it will not be possible for me to address all or many of the questions adequately. Still they are being referred to here with the explicit objective of drawing attention to the fact that a close probe on some or any of them may suggest that the matter of choice of alternatives before the humanity may not be altogether closed.

The overwhelming inclination of the major colonial powers towards *The Melting Pot* hypothesis and the academic acclaim received by the same suggest as if the die is cast for the global socio-cultural transformation. Although globalization as a concept was not in currency during the early decades of the twentieth century, but did the strategy stand to mean the same to one and all?

Webster's *Third New International Dictionary* (1967) defines globalization as the act of globalizing or condition of being globalized. Could not the behaviour of the United Kingdom, the United States of America, and most of the continental nation-states, demonstrated under the pressure of immediate socio-cultural exigencies, be construed as an attempt towards internationalizing thus diffusing their respective domestic problems? Outwardly, it appears somewhat naïve though, may be a fact that the mechanism of colonial construction with its elaborate trappings were at work to provide a blueprint for the rest of the world. But what has been the nature of consequences?

II

When the British colonizers landed at the Andaman Islands in order to explore the possibility of establishing, what could be called a civilizational outpost there, they found the South Andaman Island already occupied by the Negrito Tribes, in case of several of whom they could either identify or just assign names. Aka, Bea, Kora, Jarawa are some such gatherer-hunter tribes, who all of a sudden discovered with awe that their familiar caring world was disappearing from their horizon very fast. The 'Little Communities', if I am permitted to use Robert Redfield's (1956) cliché here, reacted to this trauma in a number of ways. Some accepted the developments as *faits accomplis* and readied themselves to silently suffer. Some others instantly took up arms (of course nothing more than bows and arrows) and engaged themselves into a relentless war until most of them got killed. Today ten such tribes taken together are survived by only about 30 souls, that too with sufficient transfusion of non-Negrito blood among them. They, nevertheless, bear a new designation, The Great Andamanese. Incidentally, the apparent glorification of the name of the people is not as much due to any achievement of ethnic excellence of the people as it is for their sojourn to the very physical space, which assumed this designation in relation to the dimension of Little Andaman, an isolated island located down south. This explanation is somewhat beside the point. There was, nevertheless, at least one section of the Negrito populations, who considered their adaptation to the rhythm of their tropical green habitat too precious a possession to let it easily forego. Therefore, by volition, they moved out of the area of day-to-day confrontation with the so-called civilization and took cover under the deep green belt along the north-west coast of South Andaman Island and made the southern edge of the Middle Andaman, across the Creek their shelter. They are the so-called Jarawa, a valiant people who decided to resist the onslaught of civilization and fought a battle of accretion for nearly one hundred years. Notwithstanding the fact that the vanguards of civilization did not even know what is the name of this people, they were not let to live the way the people liked.

Permit me to add here in parenthesis that the people were referred to as Jarawa by their distant neighbours (since their livelihood does not allow gathering bands to live in close proximity), meaning 'the other people' (not one of us). This was certainly not their name. Nevertheless, representatives of the civilization often assert the prerogative to call a people by any name they like, thus there are Bison Horn Maria, North Sentinelese, Nicobarese, Lahauli, Kinnara; a privilege denied to the people themselves. The 'authorities' must have the final say; such is the degree of arrogance. If the people have a knowledge the authorities in civilization reserve the right to brand it by a decree as 'non-sense knowledge' or 'no-knowledge', at total disregard to what kind of attachment the concerned people might have had with that specific instruction.

Whether the Jarawa decision to opt for a desolate green cover is backed up by any wisdom, the vanguards of civilization are under no compulsion to understand or respect. Because, as Redfield (1956) asks us to believe that the course of history has on the whole run in such a way as to reduce the distinctiveness of the 'Little Community'. And so much over-powering have been the forces of history that the Jarawa can be left with no open option in this respect; they must submit to the dominating global trend. Thus, the destiny is a foregone conclusion. Perhaps the only question still remains open is who has programmed the course of history and for whom? Redfield further tells us that 'the course of history, as we all know, has been such as to increase the numbers, decrease the isolation and greatly increase the mutual interdependence' (1956:113). Apparently this is a very pious wish and a welcome strategy for development for the humanity as such, but is this at all a fact? What has become the fate of the Negritos of Andaman Islands because of their exposure to the forces of civilization or the developments of history? Greater was the degree of exposure; smaller has become the size of the surviving populations. Greater was the degree of cross-cultural interaction; higher has become the rate of cultural disintegration. In order to examine the issue in the light of further substantive information, let me make another small digression here.

III

In connection with a project on "Tribal Economies and Their Transformation" with specific reference to India, sponsored by the Indian Council of Social Science Research, I had the privilege of examining information on livelihood of all the tribes in India (six hundred and forty-two of them to be precise), including the Scheduled Tribes (four hundred and twenty-seven of them). In order to facilitate analysis of the data when I tried to classify the information, a number of problems and problem related issues emerged. Some of them, which are considered relevant for the limited purpose of this paper, are listed below:

(*a*) All tribes subscribe to a number of economies simultaneously.
(*b*) Their economies more often than not overlap in time as well as space.
(*c*) The maximum number of economies in which a particular tribe involves itself is seven.
(*d*) The minimum such number is three.
(*e*) There are cases, few though (only two to be precise), where it is difficult to determine whether the economic involvement of the tribe in question should be categorized as primary or secondary economy.
(*f*) The total range of economies is as large as ten.
(*g*) From a scrutiny of this list of economies, it is not possible to make out whether there is anything, which qualifies to be called the exclusive tribal economy.
(*h*) The economies in question, on the basis of their respective supporting technology and consequent proliferation of socio-economic and political networks, can be placed in a sequence of progress.
(*i*) The overall sequence of progress is such that there is hardly any other economy, which falls beyond this overall scheme of sequence.

The problems and issues together suggest that despite a fairly impressive record of differentiation of tribal economy in

India, they being devoid of exclusive clusters apparently reflect segmentation. Keeping the other details of data aside, if we pay attention to the sequence of progressive differentiation, because of the interplay of time and space, we observe a unique pattern of continuities and breakthroughs between them to emerge. At certain stages of the sequence, the nature of transformation is so spectacular that their associated consequences can be considered revolutionary or near revolutionary for the humanity.

Once I have given this theoretical framework, no matter how much skeletal it may appear to be, let me put some flesh and blood into it by referring to certain concrete information. The ten economies, on the basis of their nature of progressive differentiation can be organized into the following ordinal sequence highlighting the nature of continuities and breakthroughs:

I.	Gathering	Total dependence on nature for food
II.	Hunting	Total dependence on nature for food
III.	Fishing	Total dependence on nature for food
IV.	Animal Husbandry	Partial freedom from quest for food
V.	Shifting Cultivation	Generation of surplus food enabling humanity to release labour for secondary, tertiary or such other activities leading to development of civilization.
VI.	Terrace Cultivation	
VII.	Settled Agriculture	
VIII.	Crafts and Industries	Civilizational out-fits reinforced
IX.	Arts and Professions	Civilizational out-fits reinforced
X.	Wage Labour	Human labour becoming a marketable commodity robs people of human dignity

The sequence of developments could be assumed as if the course of history, as referred to by Redfield (1956). When there cannot be much disagreement on the sequences of developments, so far as the course of history is concerned, Redfield was nearly silent. Perhaps the socio-cultural antecedents in which Redfield grew up provided him with a mindset, which instead of paying attention to total human consequences found itself relatively more rewarding to be occupied with highlighting integrative and harmonic character of cultures. Thus the fact that the less privileged section of the humanity could have a different kind of appreciation for the same course of history failed to receive his due attention. What transpires thus, as if the stage is set and the course is already defined. The underprivileged need not exercise their mind and/ or try to put up the embarrassing details of their particularist knowledge, which apparently are of no practical significance. Such a strategy speaks of a blockade of mind, if not a sort of prejudice.

I would not even by implication suggest here that Redfield had ever consciously associated himself with such a game plan. Due to his very placement amongst the privileged few, he perhaps had to share a mind-set that taught him to ignore many precise details of indigenous viewpoints and look at the less fortunate ones with compassion. This appears as a typical colonial reflection of the mind, where one is used to view things from higher pedestals.

Redfield, nevertheless, was discrete to observe: "Man makes himself, ...in two senses and the two senses imply a contrast between folk society and at least, modern civilization. Man is self-made through the slow and unpremeditated growth of culture and civilization. Man later attempts to take control of this process and to direct it where it wills (1953:113)."

In other words, during the early and very long period of history, human beings did not look at themselves as makers of either of the future world or of themselves. Intentional making over of society and culture is the conception of civilized man. Thus it is the vanity and consequent urge of the civilized mind to take over control that reflect the pre-occupation of the mindset; perhaps the colonial pre-occupation of the so-called modern man.

There were, of course, other attempts to apprehend the transformation scenario. In the Indian context, reference may be made to the paired concept of Sanskritization-Westernization of M.N. Srinivas (1956) and the double-paired concepts of tribe-caste and tribe-peasant continuum by Surajit C. Sinha (1965). Besides, Sinha also spoke on State Formation and Rajput Myth in Tribal Central India (1962). Despite the fact that they were fairly successful in explaining the broader process of change and development of the society and culture in India, they appear to have borne the reflections of mind of the colonial regime, suggesting a sort of subjectivity to the concepts. What is important to note down in the contexts of Srinivas and Sinha is that political decolonization does not necessarily ensure automatic decolonization of mind of the once colonized subjects. Though sufficiently pre-dated, Linton's (1936) approach makes rather a refreshing exception in this respect.

IV

Ralph Linton (1936) through his discourse on 'Participation in Culture', by way of elaborating the nature and character of such participation had drawn our attention to two very important sets of processes which being in partly manifest but mostly latent state appear to have been in ceaseless operation in every society or culture. What he actually intended to put across was the outcome of his endeavour to explain what have been the exact mechanisms of internal initiative towards metamorphosis that a culture or society become subjected to over time, which in turn results into qualitative transformation. As he envisaged, even in the ideal primordial society, the content of total knowledge is so vast that it is not possible for a single individual to be able to apprehend the whole of it. Nevertheless, the pattern of specialization in activities and the consequent arrangement of differentiation make it possible for the individual members of a society to function effectively as complete whole with respective endowment of only partial knowledge at their command. Such conceptualization merely reflects Durkheim's (1949) notion of organic solidarity. This is outwardly an imperfect arrangement but when the details of the same are examined in the light of totality of the division of labour and consequent distribution of knowledge, it appears not only logical but as if the most desirable alternative that could be available under the given circumstance.

The first among the processes as referred to by Linton is based on the interplay of what he calls universals, specialities, and alternatives of the given culture. He elaborates that when the ideas, habits, and conditioned emotional responses within a society are shared equally by all the constituent members that stand to represent universals. It can safely be speculated in this connection that this can be illustrated by the ideal primordial society, which in reality was perhaps ever illusive.

Elements of culture that are shared by the members of certain socially recognized categories of individuals but which are not shared by the entire population of the concerned society are referred to as specialities. Under this head come the patterns for all those varied but mutually interdependent roles, which have been attributed to various sections of the same society by way of division of labour. As is evident in all cultures, certain things are done by or the exclusive knowledge is possessed by only a designated section of the members, although the overall benefits of the same, at least theoretically trickle down to one and all. Even among the most remotely placed societies known so far, elements of such specialities are quite in evidence.

In every culture or society there are a reasonably fair number of traits that are shared by certain individuals but are not common to all representatives of the society or even to all members or anyone of its socially recognized categories. These have been designated as alternatives by Linton. As argued by him, the cultures of small societies living under primitive technological condition usually include at least a moderate number of alternatives. In a traditional culture, each member of the society accepts the pattern of his own sub-culture to guide one to perfect behaviour and ordinarily one would not imitate the pattern of sub-culture of others, even when he or she is quite at home with them. This suggests that there could be regular transmission of knowledge across sub-cultures but hardly could there be any attempt to transgress their boundaries. In modern society, in contrast, and as is often seen, the sub-cultures tend to merge obliterating the boundary between them. The outcome of such merger becomes evident, when as a consequence of that, the distinctive features of the sub-cultures cease to be specialities and emerge themselves as alternatives.

When a new cultural element is introduced in any society, full acceptance of it is always preceded by a period of trial. During such trial period the competing traits behave as the alternatives within the given culture complex. In fact, it is through repeated trials of alternatives that the second process, as referred to earlier, begins.

As per Linton's formulation, all cultures consist of a solid, well integrated, and fairly stable core formed of mutually adapted universals and specialities and a relatively fluid ever-changing zone of alternatives surrounding the core. For due appreciation of the second process attention to the fluid zone of alternatives seems essential, if not crucial. In other words, for adaptation to the programme of induced changes, role of alternatives appears indispensable. Nevertheless, depending on the degree of exposures to the outside contact, the role of adaptation of alternatives to the culture varies.

Each new trait as soon as it is accepted by any part of the society draws certain traits, which formerly belonged to either universals or specialities, out of the core and pushed them to the fluid zone of alternatives. This in turn reduces the context of the core or universals. Nevertheless, the difference between folk culture and modern civilization, or following Sapir's (1924) dichotomy of genuine and spurious culture is primarily the matter of proportion, which the core of universals and specialities bears to the fluid zone of alternatives. Incidentally, in modern societies the core of culture is getting progressively reduced.

The first process as referred to here, primarily brings about change within the core of the given culture through the internal process of differentiation based on specialization of traits. This being under the influence of shared knowledge has the capability to reduce the core of concerned culture though, do not ordinarily cause any imbalance between the opposed tendencies of centrifugality and centripetality of the cultures. The other process caused by the bombardment of alternatives from outside the system has the potential to create upsets as is reflected through, what in contemporary jargon is called the generation gap. What nevertheless, is evident in both the processes is the increasing stress caused to the core of any culture during progressive erosion of practical knowledge and associated value.

V

From the given description a number of issues emerge out quite prominently:

1. The Negrito tribes of Andaman Islands with the increasing degree of exposures to the outside world (apparent source of alternatives) demonstrate a progressively declining trend in terms of their respective population strength, already leading several of them to extinction.
2. Stages of sequence of livelihoods, as observed through the study of tribes in India, broadly reflect the quest for freedom, which at the post-agricultural phases of developments turned human labour to marketable commodity.
3. After the emergence of civilization, stages of the so-called progress appear directly proportional to the loss of human dignity.
4. The course of history with its apparent trend towards homogenization, in fact, stands to reflect an increasing degree of segmentation as well as virtual stagnation (in terms of social mobility).
5. Availability of alternatives could also grow out of the interaction between universals and specialities (as observed by Linton), leading in turn to harmonic/balanced growth.
6. The course of civilization, understood in terms of progressive degree of differentiation, when devoid of the forces of required integration, leads to a sort of chaos (as has been envisaged by Linton at the phase of increasing alternatives).
7. The alternatives available through induced programmes need careful handling in order to avoid their disruptive tendencies.

8. Despite knowledge of availability of alternatives through induced programmes, there are at least some (like the Pandos of Chattisgarh) who prefer to depend on spontaneous growth.
9. The course of history has been a boon to a selected few but devastating to many.
10. Response to induced programmes under the circumstance cannot be expected to be uniform.

But where do they lead us? The steady processes of degeneration and cultural disintegration, as experienced by the Negrito tribes of Andaman Islands due to their exposure to civilization, has been seriously studied and faithfully recorded by the anthropologists. Apparent indifference towards the forces of so-called progress demonstrated by the Pandos of Chattisgarh did not go un-noticed either. The pattern of progressive differentiation as emerges out of the study of the tribal communities of India has also appropriately reflected the ground realities. The trends of change, however, as substantiated by the models of Sanskritization-Westernization or tribe-caste or tribe-peasant continual also outwardly appear to be valid descriptions. But what do they together really suggest? Can we accept the position that the course of history means one and the same thing to all human populations around the globe? If not what proportion of them refuse to consider the course as really that progressive? The matter perhaps had never been seriously probed. Further, is the course of history that omnipotent or there is scope for its manipulation? If by manipulation of the course it is possible to divert the same towards common good for most of the people from various corners of the globe, is there any justification in meekly submitting to its rather erratic behaviour? Has the process of differentiation emerged out of the course of civilization been compassionate for the humanity as a whole? Somehow such basic questions have scarcely been raised by the social anthropologists. Naturally, the question of dealing with such issues has remained mostly unattended. Despite the fact that social scientists, particularly the social anthropologists, can no longer ignore the matter, not much awareness is yet visible among them in this respect. Reflections from contemporary literature seem to be relatively more down to earth and rich in this respect.

VI

These days often we are confronted with enquiries regarding social relevance of anthropological sciences. The overall reaction of anthropologists in India, whosoever tried to deal with such issues, has rather been defensive. The reasons are obvious; anthropologists during the post-colonial phase have not sufficiently updated their knowledge in keeping with the developments in other disciplines. It is a matter of regret that the syllabus, research methodology, concepts, and theories that we had inherited from our colonial masters have hardly undergone any qualitative change during the past five decades and a half when India experienced a great deal of socio-political changes. Social anthropologists in India have seldom involved themselves in any debate on the need for deconstruction as well as reconstruction (N.K. Bose in 1971 perhaps stood out as a lone exception in this respect). In no post-graduate syllabus in Anthropology do we find any reflections of post-modernist or prognostic approaches. The results of such ostrich-like behaviour have been disastrous to Anthropology and anthropologists. Anthropologists as specialists are scarcely invited to involve themselves in any national planning programme.

The onus for such a state of predicament certainly rests, at least partially, with the fellow professionals. Although rather late, we must learn to contribute substantially to prognostic understanding. For that reason, besides insisting on paradigmatic shift, at least for the time being if we need to borrow ideas from literary sources, we must not hesitate in doing the same. After all knowledge is knowledge no matter from what source does it originate.

Exercises related to the issue of globalization (irrespective of whether the concept is used here in restricted sense), presents us with a unique opportunity to examine whether and how deconstruction can lead to positive action. On the plea of arresting erosion of value, social anthropologists by and large seem to be apathetic towards such exercise. Thus somewhat indirectly though they appear to extend support to the strategy of meek submission to the formulation of course of history. Globalization, although not altogether indifferent to the course of history, as a new innovation in this context has thrown open many new challenges as well as possibilities. I believe social anthropologists will seize this opportunity to spell out where exercise on deconstruction of a sick system can pave the way for reconstruction of a brave new world.

REFERENCES

Bose, N.K. (1971), Bhanga-O-garah (in Bengali), *Desh*. 8th May, 27, pp. 95-98.

Danda, Ajit K. (1992), Indigenous small populations of Andaman and Nicobar Islands, *Andaman and Nicobar Islanders*. Calcutta: Indian Anthropological Society.

Durkheim, Emile (1949), *The Division of Labour in Society*. Glencoe, Illinois: The Free Press.

Linton, Ralph (1936), *The Study of Man*. New York: Appelton-Century-Crofts, Inc.

Redfield, Robert (1953), *The Primitive World and its Transformations*. Ithaca: Cornell University Press.

Redfield, Robert (1956), *The Little Community Peasant Society and Culture*. Chicago: University of Chicago Press.

Sapir, Edward (1924), Language Society and Culture, *American Journal of Sociology*, 29, pp. 401-429.

Sinha, S.C. (1965), Tribe-caste and Tribe-peasant Continuum in Central India, *Man in India*, 45 (1).

Sinha, S.C. (1962), State Formation and Rajput Myth in Tribal Central India, *Man in India*, 42(1).

Srinivas, M.N. (1956), Sanskritization and Westernization, *Society in India*. Madras: Social Science Association.

Webster, A. Merriam (1967), *Webster's Third New International Dictionary*, Vol. 1. Massachusetts: G & C Merriam Co.

Zangwill, Israel (1909), *The Melting Pot*, New York.

4

Understanding Globalization and Need for a Historicized Anthropology

LEIF MANGER

Introduction

My way into globalization is rather indirect. Of course, I had been following the literature in which a post-modern anthropology was emerging, trying to convince us that everything anthropologists had done before was to reify culture and society, and that basically we had never recovered from that greatest of all evils, the Enlightenment. I was never particularly convinced by all this. Not because there were no valid points, but rather because the focus was on a general level that to me did not touch on anthropological *practice*, and therefore did not properly represent what was going on in the discipline. But still I was drawn into the debates. Not in order to understand a post-modern world, but to understand a very old history of migration. The one of Hadrami people from their homes in Hadramaut in South Yemen to areas around the Indian Ocean, including India, and including Hyderabad. Following the Hadramis around in different historical periods, to Africa, to India and to South East Asia, and in more recent times, to Saudi Arabia and the Gulf, I was simply confronted by many of the same issues that concern contemporary globalization.

Conceptual Challenges

The case of the Hadramis takes as its starting point the studies that deal with the area of the Hadramaut in South Yemen and their migration to the Indian Ocean region. Several themes are involved in this. A major one relates to the formation of diaspora communities and the links between the diaspora and the homeland of Hadramaut. A second one is on the major trade systems and the organization of trade across the Indian Ocean, including such themes as transport, credit relationships, solution of the conflicts, etc. Thirdly, the spread of Islam throughout this region, mediated by the migrants, traders and Muslim scholars, helped spread the Shafi'e school of Islam, introducing not only a new faith but also a new platform for organizing communities and their activities. Over time, however, as migration became a continuous adaptation, the links between the homeland of Hadramaut and the diaspora changed. Whereas such links became of basic importance to the development of some Hadrami communities, others developed links to communities not in the homeland but to elsewhere in the diaspora. And processes of assimilation also occurred through which the Hadrami identity disappeared altogether as a recognized identity.

To approach such a history carries with it a number of challenges. A major one has been how to handle comparisons in space and time. The migration has of course brought the Hadrami migrants into very different local conditions, characterized by different ecologies, economies, political systems, economic systems and socio-cultural and civilizational frameworks. However, the spatial extension of migration must be combined with its time dimension, which leads to the second challenge. How to deal with comparative studies in time? Recent studies have shown that the migration patterns, of which the Hadramis were part, go back to the Centuries before Christ, and that the links between societies across the Indian Ocean showed great continuity and were of basic importance to the communities involved. The migration continued through the classical period, into the period of Islamic expansion and later, Western expansion, and finally, through independence, the growth of nation-states until the present day. Obviously, the migration has changed during this long period, including different groups and different destinations, involving people in different activities with different effects on the host communities, but the fact remains that Hadramaut is a type of society in which some sort of migration has been a fact of life for more than two thousand years.

In earlier publications, I have discussed the history of the Hadrami diaspora from about 1750 A.D. until today, which is the period in which the concrete diasporic communities that I studied were established. The four cases were Hyderabad in India, Singapore, Sudan and Southern Ethiopia, and I tried to combine fieldwork in existing diasporic communities with discussions that depended more on historical source material. By such a combination of what can be called both historical anthropology and anthropological history I could show how specific diasporic communities had been established and I could develop descriptions of how they evolved. I could also discuss the various ways Hadrami identities had emerged and evolved in the diaspora, a discussion that partly depended on contemporary realities in concrete communities, but also on people's own notions of "historicity", *i.e.* the various ways people themselves made use of history and historical narratives to create their own identities.

I have also written on the *totality* of the Hadrami migration history, all two-three thousand years of it! Not that I believe that it is possible to deal with such a vast region or such a long history in any empirical detail. Nor do I believe that we have the source material that would allow us to pursue this task. But I do believe that it is possible to put together a general overview, and that this endeavour is worthwhile for two main reasons. The first reason is empirical and relates to the fact that in the course of my work with the Hadrami migration history, I have been struck by the extent, persistence and continuity of links between communities, links that go back to the very early periods of migration. Given this continuity there is a *history of contact* to be written, in which we can see how links between people, between communities, across oceans and continents, do not appear as haphazard occurrences, depending on the genius of a first "discoverer", but must be regarded as a normal part of people's lives, and that what has been going on in so-called "local communities" to an important extent has been shaped by dynamic links to places far away. Such a descriptive history makes us see the Indian Ocean less as a barrier, but more as a bridge. But the issue goes beyond the establishing of historical parameters. I believe the story contains *conceptual challenges*, and that these challenges are of relevance also to contemporary social theorizing. The observation that people and communities in earlier historical periods were not isolated units, but took part in a continuous process of movement, culture contact and interdependences, brings us right into the current debates on contemporary globalization. But now with an important qualification. Such globalizing processes are not new! We see elements of "globalization" way back in time. On the conceptual level, the attempt to understand this long history certainly shows the futility of understanding concepts such as, 'society', 'culture' and the 'nation-state' as isolated, functionally integrated wholes. But it also shows that this discovery was not made by contemporary post-modernists alone, but that it has been part of a rather long history of anthropological theorizing trying to deal with the basic openness and interdependences of human communities, modern and pre-modern alike.

And this is my starting point for my theorizing. I shall look at some contribution that I have found in the globalization literature in order to help me shape my arguments on the Indian Ocean migrations, and, as I said, offer some comments.

Specific Contributions

One contribution that is "hot" these days is Manuel Castells' three volumes entitled, "*The Network Society*" (1996, 1997a, 1997b). These volumes were the theme of a special session in the latest American Anthropological Association meeting in which I participated. Castells is interested in the connections established by the new global technologies of information communication and argues that this type of modern technology creates "space of flows" that replaces the "space of places", and thus changes the ways people are rooted. It creates a polarization between those within the flow of power and those without; the first characterized by "spaceless power", the second "powerless space". Now, this situation brought about by the new information technology also leads to processes that are reacted to by social movements, and that in the process new types of identities emerge. Contemporary identities are to a large extent influenced by what Castells calls "the bipolar opposition of the Net and the Self". Drawing on Alain Touraine, he identifies three types of collective identities coming out of all these processes, they are: (*a*) legitimizing identities, that play along with dominating trends; (*b*) resistance identities, which I think is self-explanatory; and (*c*) project identities, that aim at transforming society.

A second towering contribution is that of Anthony Giddens (*e.g.* 1990). He links his discussion of globalization to modernity, seeing modernity not only as representing technologies, increased speed, time-space compression and the like. He also makes a rather radical statement that the modern world is ontologically different from an earlier, traditional world. The abstraction of time from place, and space from place, lifts life out of the local into the global.

I find much of this fascinating, but I also have several problems with these types of analyses. Let me here focus on two of those problems. The first relates to *history*, the second to *dichotomization*. First, history; obviously there is a sense of history in these contributions, but it is on a high level of generality. There is no focus on *historical transformations*. Such transformations are assumed. Castells argues as if what is *now* is *new*, rather than developing the comparative potential embedded in his analysis, *i.e.* comparison in time, not only space. Then the modern information technologies can be seen in a comparative light of earlier technologies of communication—be they through direct human interaction, letter writing, telephones or e-mails. The same can be done with travel technologies in which the development of new types of ships and new types of sails have been creating important effects in the same way as the steamships revolutionized travels on sea and aeroplanes revolutionized travels in general. Giddens assumes globalization to be the logical endpoint of modernity, he does not engage the actual transformations going on. For what is modernity anyway? When did it start? All institutions defining modernity have different histories; is it a Wallersteinean capitalist system, *i.e.* the long 16th Century? Is it a political modernization, and did it start with the English Civil Wars? With the American Revolutions? Or the French Revolutions? And what type of technologies should be counted? Only those relating to time and space? I rather sympathize with Zygmunt Bauman, who states that as we try to date, the object disappears, exactly because modernity is ambiguous.

And it is at this point we also enter into our second problem, that of dichotomization. Discussions as those hinted at above are at a very high level of abstraction, they are systems oriented geared towards defining "totalities", thus bringing us back into dualisms and dichotomies we should try to avoid, such as modern-premodern, traditional-modern, local-global, etc. What I am saying here is that we might easily end up looking at histories out of context.

An Alternative Way

My suggestion into all this is to focus more on those concrete historical transformations that are relevant to our case of Indian Ocean migrations. There is no way of presenting historical details here, but my points relates to what Michael Busawoy *et al.* (2000) in a recent book called "Global Ethnography" have called for. Their call is summarized in the sub-title of the book, which is "Forces, Connections and Imaginations of a Post-Modern World". My concern is with forces, connections and imaginations, not so much with the post-modern world. The "forces" of globalization being represented by economic, political and cultural forces, the "connections" are represented by how the forces exist through connections in the world, and the "imaginations" are represented by people's reactions towards the globalizing processes, be they justifications, normalization or resistance. Looking at such factors in a long historical perspective I believe would imply a historically grounded, theoretically driven, macro-ethnography, combining comparative history and ethnography.

For this purpose I also want to introduce the concept of *epoch*, not as a history of details, but as a heuristic device in which we can focus on transformations, and what factors are at play in such epochs. The focus is thus on *moments of reconfiguration*, the selection of which is a product of the research question itself. I use three such epochs in my discussions, inspired by Stuart Hall (1991). He coined two such epochs and called them as "Global Imperialism" and "Global Post-modern". The first refers to the time of the British Empire, the second of course to the period of American mass culture. The first is a world of nation states, the second one in which earlier silenced groups come out to react. The change relates to flexible accumulation, politically it is a period in which the nation-state is challenged from above and below, and culturally, essentialisms implied in race and class is replaced by hybridity. I want to add an earlier period also in order to cover my own material, and I call it "Global Empire", *i.e.* not the British Empire, but those earlier empires existing alongside each other before the Western World became hegemonic in the later 18th Century.

Let me continue this contribution by suggesting how such a type of analysis might be developed. Of course, it is not possible to describe this in detail, but in order to give some impressions I shall limit myself to the most recent periods of developments in the Indian Ocean. Hence my focus is on the two epochs of Global Imperialism and Global Post-modern, leaving out the earlier epoch of Global Empire. Within the epochs I seek to look at the three elements hinted at above, *i.e.* describe the forces operating within larger systems, then look at how these forces are manifested in specific places (my examples are from the series of trading towns that have existed in the Indian Ocean throughout the periods), and then also to include people's imaginations and discourses about how the world is at base. In my case these imaginations and discourses are focused on the various Muslim reactions to the globalizing tendencies in the epochs, reactions in which the Hadramis have contributed. The discussion is inspired by contributions both of Castells and Giddens, but what I try to convey is that we have to focus more clearly on the real historical transformations as represented by moments of reconfiguration.

Forces, Connections and Imaginations of Globalization in the Indian Ocean

Global Imperialism

The 18th Century history of the Indian Ocean is one in which we see a basic change in the macro-situation of the region, related to the change in the involvement of European colonial powers from an earlier interest in controlling trade to a focus on controlling territory, thus initiating the period of imperialism (Bayly, 1989). For the British, an important development occurred through their control of Bengal by the East India Company (After the battle of Plassey in 1757, the Company could collect land rents on the authority of the *Nawab of Bengal*, making the Company the chief revenue officer, the *diwan*, a situation that lasted until 1858 when it was disbanded). For Holland their hold over Java (the Dutch East India Company achieved supremacy in 1752, were challenged by the British and regained control in 1816, when the Dutch Government took over and set up a colonial regime called the Netherlands Indies) represented a similar milestone. The glorious past of the Muslim empires was over, and new realities appeared. Not because of Ibn Khaldounian processes of corruption by the leadership, of city life and of wealth, but rather from the development of new regional economies and of new classes. The unifying effects of trade had produced processes of local differentiation. But trade was not the only factor. Population growth in the 16th Century stagnated in the following Centuries and led to uneven developments. Increasing rural differentiation developed. Commercialization led peasants into bondage of larger landowners, who held large estates. Earlier state land was also broken up and commercialized, being less dependent on political office and more as 'freehold property'. Revenue farming made it possible for the rulers to shift the burden of expenditure over to regional leaders, who pushed it downwards to the impoverished peasants. Commercialization, urbanization and the growth of landed classes were the processes that were to bring changes. Such changes were also affected by external links, for instance trade links with the Europeans. The export of raw materials and the import of precious metals played a significant role, leading to the establishment of a financier class. But the export link also increased vulnerability to price fluctuations elsewhere, thus increasing systemic interdependencies. The new regional power-centres that developed within this context weakened the old imperial centres. Egypt under Mohamed Ali is a case in point from within the Ottoman areas. Hyderabad under the Asaf Jahs, Bengal and Awadh from within the Mughal kingdom, and the Qajars in Iran. At the same time 'military tribes' rebelled. Afghan and Turkik tribes from Central Asia (the Rohillas, 'men of the hills') challenged both the Safavids and the Mughals. The Wahhabis in Arabia also belong to this pattern of 18th Century rebellion as did the Maratha Hindu soldiers in India. Tribal societies were also transformed into military dynasties, often creating internal unity by attacking others. But trade links were important also, and many of the areas in which tensions developed were areas in which trade and economic development had led to increased economic tensions. Puritanical movements like the Wahhabis constituted an ideological response to these developments. The leaders of Awadh in India promoted Shi'ism against the Sunnis. One basic consequence of these processes of revolt was the emergence of new political units that were more effectively organized than the loose imperial confederacies they replaced. In fact they might be said to be a first step towards nation-states. The rulers sought to monopolize and protect trade and settle people to tax them. Professional armies were recruited and maintained, often recruited from the minority groups, such as Circassians, Georgians, Afghans, and Arabs, including the Hadramis. New areas of land were developed for agriculture, new sources of labour power were sought, and nomads were settled. Thus control of primary producers was considered important. But so was trade, and battles for control of trade routes were also fought. But as export of primary agricultural products flourished the two things were linked. Raw cotton is a case in point. The quest for revenue was on.

It was the period in which we see the processes so common under colonialism and imperialism, *i.e.* the colonial state began seriously to discipline and control marginal groups, and we start getting the developments towards privatization of land and market oriented economies. Rather than the spread of free trade, it was territorial revenues that the colonialists were after, both the British and the Dutch, and it was in this context that the notion of Britain as a 'Christian Roman Empire' was born (Bayly, *ibid.* 11, see also Cooper and Stoller, 1997). The new political units could threaten Imperial rule and the new rulers became symbols of tyranny, and, as in the case of Tipu Sultan in Mysore, of *Muslim* tyranny. A clearer racial hierarchy was also appearing, as were other types of British prejudices. Urban elites were despised. Nomads and tribes were to be protected. A number of "Consuls" appear representing European powers, playing roles similar to the *maigida, wakil al-tujjar*, or *shabandar* who were already there, but over time during the 19th Century developing into key agents of commercial Westernization. They also represented the new European arrogance, no longer adapting to local Indian Ocean realities but seeking to control and dominate them.

From the end of the 18th Century, European Imperialist interests appeared as a major driving force behind the European interests in the Indian Ocean region, and we see elements well known from other areas influenced by colonialism and imperialism. Privatization of economies, increasing inequalities and a focus on the racial differences between the people living in the trading towns were new characteristics. In the 19th Century the new technologies represented by steamship, the telegraph and telephone, entered the scene, and the building of the Suez Canal helped change sailing routes. With this we see a specific phase of globalization developing in the 19th Century, a globalization that was to continue and to increase in speed into the 20th Century. But in this Century, the overall context changes, from colonial and imperial rule, to nation states and a nationalist ideology, and we see that this change affected the Hadramis in a profound manner. Some Hadramis came out as winners due to their relationships with the power-holders. Others remained at the lower levels of the ladder of economic differentiation, also due to their position in larger systems of power, economy and divisions of labour. But we also see that as Muslims they became part of various Muslim reactions to the extension of European power. The reaction took various forms, from incidents of violent local resistance to the globalized ideological currents of Pan-Islamism in which the role of Islam and of Muslims in the new, modern world were being debated. Such debates continue into the 20th Century, changing with circumstances, but very much defined by the development of the Muslim revival in the 19th Century and the need to define a position in a world.

The western views of Islam coming from the conventional western historiography on Muslims in the 18th Century has portrayed the period as a 'dark age' with a focus on the disintegration of the gunpowder empires and a general defeat to Western powers, portraying Muslim societies as stagnating, as barbaric, and so on. Not surprisingly, the situation is more complex (see *e.g.* Watson, 1983; Al-Hassan and Hill, 1986; Tibbetts, 1981 for counter examples). First of all, the trading towns in which many Muslim traders lived, were commercial centres. Although these centres were traditional, they did not lack dynamism. Such cities offered a choice of commodities, a variety of currency and banking services, and shipping space. And political stability and peace provided by local leaders were important. But such communities were not only trading communities but also the focal points of a series of developments that were to shape the history of the region for the coming centuries. On a general level, the regionalization of the Muslim world in the Indian Ocean brought the development of groups and institutions not related to the state itself. The *ulema* developed independent of the political rulers, and *sufism* developed, and, with al-Ghazali (d.1111), was integrated into the mainstream Islamic thought. *Tariqas* were to play an important role from the 12th Century on. All this was reflected in the Muslim communities in the region. *Qadis* arrived to administer justice and adjudicate disputes among the Muslims; theologians arrived, serving both as intellectual links to the larger world and as agents promoting a degree of standardization in the transregional culture of Islam; Sufis arrived and sought to penetrate the existing cultural boundaries by spreading Islam broadly among native inhabitants. Meanwhile, new converts made pilgrimages to Mecca, where they became acquainted at first hand with Islamic customs and traditions. They became initiated, as it were, into the larger world of Islam. Finally, in many cases, ruling elites recognized political or economic advantages provided within Islam, and as a result they lent official support that enabled the new faith to establish itself securely in their lands. In spite of all intermingling in such towns, the Muslims remained a distinct group, organized religiously around the *mosque*. Members of the groups did not intermarry, but kept close trade relations and dealt with members of other groups. Arabic was important as a language of communication, of religious and literary expression, and of administration, even though Iranian and Turkish were rivals. Membership in the group of Muslims was through faith. And basic symbols to define group-membership were *food habits, articles of clothing and housing*, which all signalled social and religious identities, and helped to keep groups apart. Rules about avoidance of pork for Muslims, beef for Brahminic Indians, milk and dairy products for the Chinese were thus basic markers for members of the various communities. Clothes also helped to differentiate, based on whether people were wearing trousers and robes as dress, whether they were sown or un-sown. The role of public buildings in Islam, expressing the spiritual force of the new religion, also linked the imperial power and architecture.

But the Muslims, although maintaining a boundary

towards other groups, were not an internally coherent group. John Voll (1994) points four styles of Islamic reactions to the developments in the 18th Century. One *pragmatic, adaptationist style* through which Muslims were able to settle in strange territories; a *conservative style,* trying to preserve earlier gains; a *fundamentalist style,* not looking at society but at the Quran for guidance, unwilling to accept compromises, being political activists upsetting social stability; and fourthly, *the personal acceptance of the religion,* focused on local holy men, on the Mahdi or the Shi'a Imam as political representations. We see all these streams represented in the Hadrami adaptations. Their success in building alliances with power-holders in Hyderabad and Singapore illustrate the line of accommodation. The early resurgence of the Mappilas, led by a Hadrami, may tell a story of resistance, perhaps related as much to issues about trade as religion. Other reactions were motivated by religious developments, particularly *sufism.* New theological interpretations that signalled a new fundamentalism were known, for example through the work of Ibn Taymiyyah. Such ideas were also transformed into political action, as represented by al-Wahhabiyy in Arabia. Shah Wali Allah al-Dihlawi (1702-1762) and his establishment of schools rather than a social movement is a local Indian example of a reaction to the disunity of the Muslim society. He reformulated Islam on a broader basis than anyone tradition, thus making Indian Islam more receptive to outside influences than, for instance, the Arabian version of Wahhabism. Southeast Asian Islam was also affected by these trends. Many trading states in the region had introduced Islam, but the religion was by no means dominating. Also, Muslims had adapted to local traditions of Hinduism and Buddhism, making the pantheistic elements of Islam coming to the fore. The Dutch presence in Indonesia gradually made the Muslim leaders depend on them for support, thus accepting many western ways, which again is one backdrop on which to see the growth of fundamentalism. And we see a development of the social organization of the basic unit in sufism, the *tariqah.* Better-organized and more activist *tariqahs* appeared and became vehicles of revival rather than adaptation. The general economic and political situation developed in ways that made these groups able to mobilize outside the religious platform. Increased travelling brought these groups in contact with each other. Indonesian Muslims travelled regularly to Mecca, and it is an interesting fact that some of the leaders behind the Padri movements in Sumatra had been in Mecca during the time of the Wahhabi revolts. It is likely that there was cross-fertilization between different Muslim resistances to developments that made them feel marginalized. Scholars travelled widely, being part of transnational networks, often centred at Mecca and Medina, because of the *hajj*, but other centres like Cairo and Damascus were also important. Religion became the basis for the emergence of new local identities and we find the new types of religious scholars in alliance with new political leaders. The Hadramis were part of these developments and played a role in these networks. They had been travelling to the Gujarat and the Malabar Coasts of India for centuries, and during this period they also established themselves decisively in Southeast Asia. Hadrami families intermarried with the families of Sultans in many of the 18th Century Malay States. They acted as religious leaders, political leaders and traders. In Indonesia, Hadramis played central roles in Acheh, and there were Hadrami imams in mosques at the islands of Bangka and Madura, in Pontianak at Borneo, at Ternate in the Moluccas as well as the more central towns of Java and Sumatra. Their appearance is linked to the central role of South Arabia and Aden during this period, both in trade and as a natural stopping point for pilgrims from east and south.

The 19th Century represents an intensified development of various globalizing forces. One important field is the continuous maritime technological developments. European industrialization and urbanization were forwarded by the introduction of iron, then steel-hulled sailing ships, and eventually steam ships from the early 1800s, developing through the 19th Century, reducing transportation times as well as costs (Hugill, 1993:30). The innovations came first in the commercial sphere, but the military sector followed, on which the *Pax Britannica* developed after 1815. Wood and coal were the first major fuel sources, with a number of coaling stations appearing around the major shipping lines. The opening of the Suez Canal dramatically affected this by reducing the number of stops required, and hence the number of secure coaling stations. Oil fuel freed the ships from many of the problems of coal, the diesel engine further making shipping more efficient in the 20th Century.

Thus there were underlying forces of restructuring the international economy due to the forces of industrial revolution. The search for raw materials, such as raw cotton or timber was only one element, which foreshadowed the shift in the global division of labour due to industrialization. But tools for western influence were also the changes in banking, finance, transportation and communication. Ocean shipping developed to steam and steel. Long distance communication improved. In the 1830s a letter from Europe to India took five to eight months to round the cap on a sailing ship. To receive an answer might take up to two years. By the 1850s the letter from London to Calcutta could go in 30-40 days. By the 1870s submarine cable had been laid and a message from Britain to India could be answered in the same day. And those who wanted to use them had to follow European rules. The postal service was directed by the Universal Postal Union founded in 1874. In the sectors of new technological developments the 'diasporic' ways of doing things disappeared and links between various points in the diaspora were replaced by direct links to the centre. The British shipping with coal stations around the world and telegraphs to increase efficiency, both in terms of sailing orders as well as commercial contacts, were run from England. Exploitation of rivers made this system also reach far inland towards the major grain producing areas of the world. These developments were only to be surpassed when oil and petroleum took over as the main energy sources in the 20th Century, producing diesel engines for ships, cars and tractors, and later aeroplanes, which not only changed trade but also the technological basis of warfare (Hugill, *ibid.*). On the social side, an enormous migration out of Europe also helped change the world order in the 20th Century, first towards German, later American power (O'Rourke and Williamson, 1999). The production in this system revolved around wheat and cotton: wheat to feed the people and cotton to provide raw material for the factories. As population grew the British import of wheat grew, and America, Argentina, Australia and Russia became important wheat producers, but only after Ireland had failed to provide the needed wheat, after the Potato Famine. Cotton could not be grown in Britain and had to be brought from the colonies. Among the colonies, India remained the most important one. Railroads, steam ships and the Suez Canal transformed India into a major source of cheap food and raw materials for Europe. Tea, wheat, oil seeds, cotton, jute came from there. At the same time India was the market for British products. The large surpluses originating from the Indian trade was at the base of British capital accumulation and London's central position in world finance (Arrighi, 1999:263).

The integration of world's economy into a single interdependent whole further developed in the period 1870-1914. Three aspects were central. Further improvement in the means of communication, spreading railways outside Europe and North America, expansion of world shipping, both in tonnage and the shift from sail to steam, which increased speed and regularity. Canal constructions, like the Suez Canal in 1869, the Panama Canal in 1914, helped save distance and time (41 per cent on a trip from Liverpool to Bombay, 60 per cent from New York to San Francisco). Finally, cables laid beneath the oceans linked the continents, followed by the telephone (international lines from 1887), and wireless stations (from 1897). All this paralleled a boom in commerce with a tripling of foreign trade volumes between 1870 to 1914. This is the period of 'finance capital' in the imperial age, an expansion that is related to increasing pressure on the profitability on capital within Britain itself, and which led investors and financial houses ('The Age of the Rotchilds') to channel capital through city to distant places, directly linking up with the imperial project (see *e.g.* Hobson, 1938). However, most of all this was a development between the major countries. Only 11 per cent of the world's trade took place between the primary producers themselves. Investments from the west into these areas helped colonize them rather than develop them. These investments relate to the introduction of the gold standard for European currencies in 1863-74. The flow of capital was paralleled with a flow of labour power leading to the Europization of territories.

But other non-European areas also tried to modernize. Some of the areas were colonies, like the Indian and Indonesian states. Others were quasi-independent, like Egypt. The decline of the old urban artisan communities in the Islamic world were replaced by new forms of indigenous capitalism, partly, but only partly, linked to the industrial revolution in Europe. In the wake of the French Revolution, peasant rebellions flourished. *Rural* sufi groups also followed suit. Millenarian movements signalled this breakdown of the old order and the onset of colonialism. People sought new legitimizations. Universal issues, like Islam *versus* Christianity, replaced local issues. The Sanusiyya in North Africa, the Naqsbandiyya in China, the Salawiyya in the Nile Valley, the Padri in Indonesia (1803-37), all were movements that brought such reformulations. The Mappilas of southwestern India also provided an example of a conflict over the old pepper trade controlled by the Muslim Mappilas, competing with Hindu Nayyar chieftains and also with the Christian Portuguese. Tipu Sultan's success in Mysore helped the Mappilas, but the British defeat of Mysore in 1793 turned the tables and the Nayar retaliated. This case shows how the intensification of religious and ethnic identity through actions of the indigenous state and the violence of popular resistance, the role of indigenous petty capitalism and, ultimately, intervention by colonial power. Here we also see a Hadrami leader in action, Sayyid Fadl. The most important one, however, was the Wahhabiya in Arabia. Challenged were orthodox Muslim leadership and also European colonialists.

The printing press helped 'textualize' issues in new ways. People were more in touch with each other than before within the regions, as between the regions and Europe. Indonesian Muslims had been in Mecca during the Wahhbiyya attacks and brought back the message of purification to the Padri. New groups adapted to the new situations, like the Parsis of Bombay and the Hindu gentry of Calcutta, by founding schools, newspapers and reform societies. In Southeast Asia, the Chinese filled these roles as go-betweens between the colonialist and local groups.

Two Muslims attempts of modernization stand out in the 19th Century, the most outstanding cases being Muhamed Ali (1805-49) in Egypt and the Ottoman *Tanzimat*, started by Mahmoud II in Istanbul, but there were others. And they all looked to the west to find solutions. This, in turn, brought Islamic fundamentalist reactions. In Istanbul, the opposition from the Young Ottomans was liberal in nature, whereas the more Islamic reaction took various forms. One was to emphasize the role of the Sultan as a pan-Islamic ruler (Abdel Hamid II from 1876). The other was to debate with the west, developing a Muslim understanding of modernism. Al Afghani was a key figure here (1839-97). The third theme was a growing absolutism of the Ottoman ruler, as exemplified by Abdel Hamid II, who used Muslim clerics to obtain legitimacy. This ended when the Young Turks revolted and took power in 1908. Nationalism, Arab and Turkish, also appeared, thus making the Ottoman empire a case that shows many of the dilemmas and tensions Muslims found themselves in towards the end of the 19th Century. In Egypt, Muhamed Ali's successors (Abbas 1849-54, Said 1854-63, and Ismail 1863-79) modernized and rebuilt cities and transportation systems. The end result of this policy was that Egypt, rather than developing as a regional Red Sea and Gulf of Aden power, became financially dependent on the West, and with the revolt of Ahmad Urabi, also led to the British political takeover in 1882, bringing in Lord Cromer as the key figure. Also here al-Afghani played an important role formulating critiques, and his follower Mohamed Abduh (1849-1905) even more so. Abduh's aim was to integrate modern western and Islamic ideas and techniques and his public positions (mufti of Egypt from 1899) made him able to propagate them. He inspired both fundamentalism and revivalism.

But in other areas the local states were not strong enough to act as reformers and European colonial powers were the ones spearheading modernization, also leading to Islamic reactions. In India, a series of movements appeared as Islamic reactions. Ahmad Brelwi (1786-1831) is a case in point in Northern India, basing himself on links with the Prophet Muhamed. But after the Mutiny of 1857, the British controlled the areas, and a new development started in which Indian Muslims related to modernism had to accept the British presence. Sayyid Ahmad Khan (1817-98) was a key figure in this, trying to combine western learning with Islamic ones, and establishing schools for such integrated learning. And as with Muhamed Abduh, his thoughts were developed in different directions by later people (Chirag Ali's fundamentalism, or the Deoband position linking back to a traditionalist Islamic identity). The Ahmadiyyas also appeared, eventually to engage in missionary activities outside India. In Kerala, the famous Hadrami *sayyid*, Sayyid Fadl b. Alawi b. Sahl played a central role in a Muslim inspired rebellion, *jihad*, against the British. His family held the title of *tannals* of the Mappilas and in the middle of the 19th Century Sayyid Fadl inspired several attacks by Kerala Muslims on Hindu groups. The attacks were more in the tradition of earlier skirmishes with Hindu groups over the spice trade than real resistance against the British. Nevertheless, Sayid Fadl was expelled by the British in 1852 had left for Istanbul, Mecca and Dhofar (see Dale, 1997; also Bang, 2000). In Southeast Asia the tension between a localized, syncretic faith and a rigorous, cosmopolitan faith existed alongside the conflicts over how to react to Dutch colonialism. Opposition movements were active all through the 19th Century. The early one was the Padri movement in Sumatra. The Java War from 1825 to 1830 was a second incident. A third one appeared in Acheh after the Dutch invasion in 1873. All uprisings had the element of holy wars, led by the *ulema*. And all were affected by Pan-Islamism.

All these movements benefited from the new, modern situation in transport. Their leaders could themselves travel to Mecca on pilgrimage, thereby keeping in touch with the centres of the Islamic world. New communicative technologies also helped the organizations keep open their links to the general intellectual currents in the Muslim world. For instance, Shaykh Muhammad Tahir ibn Jalal al-Din (1867-1957) spread the ideas of Muhamed Abduh's Salafiyyah in the region, and he started a newspaper, al-Imam, in Singapore. He accepted the realities of his times, but continued the efforts to place them in a Muslim intellectual context, leading to organizations that were to characterize the 20th Century Southeast Asian Islam.

Mecca and Madina were also affected, although their religious leadership was conservative, cooperating with the Egyptian and Ottoman rulers against neo-Sufism. Rather it was the Sharif of Macca who kept in touch with the world. The Wahhibis continued to struggle for control after the defeat by the Egyptians in 1818, eventually ending in the 20th Century state of Saudi Arabia. In Oman, the maritime empire declined, and Oman became increasingly dependent on British control. The British take over of Aden in 1839 created a new situation in Southern Arabia, which hindered the development of any particular reactions.

The Muslim reactions to the 20th Century globalization tendencies are not very different from those we saw in earlier historical periods. But many contextual factors are different. One basic factor that changed in this century is the emergence of nation states and of nationalism. Early in the century this process was conceived as a threat to Muslim global unity. The issue of the Caliphate is one example. This was an attempt to restore the Ottoman sultan as a leader of the Muslims, and also a basis for which to call for holy war during First World War. Both attempts failed. The Indian Caliphate Movement was rather strong during the period 1919 to 1925, and they tried to argue for the restoration of the Caliphate. But the Ottoman era was over. In Turkey, the office of Sultan was abolished in 1922 and the Caliphate in 1924.

Rather than a revitalization of the Caliphate, the fight for independence promoted nationalism, and new organizations grew up based on national sentiments expressed in poetry and literature. With independence reform and modernization was embarked upon, under different banners (Arab socialism), signifying a nationalism that was not western. Egypt's Nasser, Algeria's Ben Bella and Indonesia's Sukarno are examples of such leaders. Muslim leaders usually went along with this development, although associations like the Muslim Brotherhood sprang up before First World War reacting to secularism. Muhamad Rashid Rida (1865-1935) was an important voice in this rush towards modernization. His journal, *al-Manar*, became widespread in the Muslim world. Rida argued against secularization and for re-establishment of a Muslim state. Consequently, he ended up a supporter of the Saudi State. The radical stance of the Muslim Brothers was just one further continuation of this line of thinking. Other, more moderate trends were also present in the debates. A series of journals and other publications are typical of this period, in which new ideas appeared, placing Islam *vis-à-vis* the capitalist West, but also communism and socialism leading to new types of ideological and political syntheses.

In India, Muhamed Iqbal and the Muslim League (1906) formulated an Islamic response on behalf of Indian Muslims facing a Hindu majority that eventually led to the formation of Pakistan, engineered by Muhamed Ali Jinnah. In the meantime the Khilafat Movement had put different priorities. More conservative forces among the ulema in Jamiyat al-ulema-i-Hind, wanted more pragmatic policies, whereas al-Mawdudi's Jama'at i-Islami advocated radical ideas setting Islam above nationalism. Tablighi Jama'at were somewhere in between (Metcalf, 1999). In Malaya, the British had preserved the old sultanates, which meant traditionalism. But new thinking emerged with the Young Groups in Singapore (*Kaum Muda*), looking at the Muslim experience in the context of Chinese and Indian majority. Singapore emerged as a centre for publication of religious literature. Students from all over the archipelago, who wanted to further their studies in doctrine or law, went either to Mecca or to the Straits Settlement, where they met and sat at the feet of itinerant scholars from the Hadramaut, and from Patani, Acheh, Palembang, and Java—most of whom had themselves studied in Mecca. The city thus stood at the heart of a communication network, which fed a constant stream of revivified 'orthodox' Muslim thought from the Hejaz into the Malay peninsula and Indonesian archipelago. The efforts to promulgate an Islam of this kind were greatly helped by the publishing facilities, which now sprang up in Singapore. Material from the Arabic and Egyptian press was spread, and although the readership of Arabs, Malay and *Jawi Pernakan* (local born Muslims, offspring of South Indian Muslim and Malay unions) was limited the links between this elite and the mass of people helped spread the ideas also into non-literate quarters (Roff, 1964:83).

Malayan Muslims joined forces with the conservative traditional leadership among the Chinese and Indians, in opposition to the radical Chinese elements influenced by Communism. In Indonesia, Muhammadiyya and Sarekat Islam developed in 1912, the first with Salafiyya overtones of purification, the second being an organization for traders and businessmen, later to develop into an anti-Dutch organisation. The Nahdatul Ulema, formed in 1926, was an organization of conservative ulema. They all represent Muslim organizations springing out of the historical circumstances at the turn of the 20th Century.

Hadramis were active in the diaspora during these periods, but the general trend was that they entered the national movements emphasizing their Muslim identity rather than their identity as Arabs. Many actually left their areas due to anti-Arab, anti-foreign sentiments. Those who stayed behind became nationalized into their new home countries. The middle of this century is thus the starting point of new and weakened relationships between diasporic Hadramis and their homeland. Lack of economic development in Hadramaut due to the rule of conservative sultans was a factor. For a short period the development of Aden as a global city allowed many Hadramis to operate commercially in the homeland in spite of what went on in Hadramaut itself. But this was to end soon. The British left in 1967, and the Quality and Kathiri sultanates quickly became part of the new People's Democratic Republic of Yemen (PDRY). When the new state, PDRY, opted for membership in the Communist block, diaspora-homeland relationships were further weakened.

The Global Post-modern

But the will for political nationalism was soon counteracted by yet another turn in the process of economic globalization. In the second half of the 20th Century a greater geographical mobility of capital, combined with a crisis of the Fordist (Keynesian) mass production led to flexible specialization. An increasing amount of legal constraints on production was being bypassed by the proliferation of personal and familial entrepreneurial economic activities. According to Arrighi, we are again seeing new systemic cycle of accumulation. Some speak of the end of organized capitalism and the emergence of disorganized capitalism, *i.e.* precisely the functional de-concentration and decentralization of corporate powers we have mentioned (Lash and Urry, 1987). David Harvey (1989) calls this a period of flexible accumulation, dating the period of problems leading to it from 1965 to 1973. His analysis is not that capitalism is changing but that they are financial adaptations to solve the crisis capitalism. The main elements of this development can be sketched as follows.

In terms of hegemonic power, the 20th Century is of course characterized by the rise of the USA as a new hegemonic power after the British. Two World Wars and economic recession periods, which helped destroy the gold standard on which the British financial dominance was built, helped bring the USA to its dominant position. The regime of accumulation shifted to one in which multi-national companies dominated the world markets. In Britain, spinning, weaving, finishing and marketing belonged in different companies. The US model was to bring them together in vertically integrated units, whereas the British used 'flexible specialization'. And the Americans, as did the Germans, learnt this lesson during the Great Depression of 1873-96. The context has shifted from colonialism to independent nations, with organizations as the United Nations as fora in which such nation-states supposedly should work out their differences, instead of solving them by war. But the nation-states also became the main vehicle for continuous work towards developing the world economy, although the USA dominated here also. The Bretton-Woods institutions, the International Monetary Fund and the World Bank are as much instruments of American hegemony as they are mediators between independent nation-states. World money was now being part of state building developments. And the development of an American market after the Civil War helped secure a strong national economy, partly through protectionist policies, but it did not develop a global, American, state driven world economy. This is where the multilateral financial institutions became important agents for American interests. It was corporate capital that conquered the world, not finance capital. But once success was assured, foreign markets proved to be limited. The rebuilding of Western Europe (through the Marshall Plan) and Japan, in response to the Soviet power, became answers to this problem. The same did the increasing US military expenditure abroad, after the Korean War until the ending of the Vietnam War in 1973. This all created a long period of sustained growth in the world economy.

The technological developments have continued with oil bringing the Arab countries back into the global picture as oil producers, but also as victims of that position, within the current *Pax Americana*. The use of oil has provided a basis for further developments in transportation, with air traffic as the most significant example. Developments in synthetic products also belong to the picture, as do the lowering of production costs by making access to unused areas more easy and cheaper. The more recent revolution in information technology is also a part of this, with the decentralization of production processes and the development of finance capital as a key resource.

However, the cycle ended and the recession set in the 1970s. Capital surplus was in private hands and the national governments manipulated currency rates to attract it. At the same time, increasingly fluctuating national currencies invited financial speculation. The result might seem like a global financial revolution, but it was not entirely new. Rather, it represented a return to the phase of finance capitalism that has occurred after each period of capitalist expansion before in history. Regardless of its larger scale, scope and technical sophistication, it is a continuation of a *longue durée* tendency since the Italian city-states dominated the world economy. It was a trend towards ever-stronger blocks of governmental and business organization as leading agencies for capital accumulation on a world scale. What the crisis of the early 1970s signified was thus the decline of the US hegemony. It signalled the contradiction of the system. The American capital since the 1950s led to the establishment of the Euro-currency market into which American money kept flowing. This created a financial market beyond the control of any nation-state or any of the Bretton-Woods institutions. It also created European competition with the American multi-national corporations, which again answered by increasing activities. This happened at a time when prices for production inputs (*e.g.* wages) went up. At the same time, in the early 1970s, the price of oil exploded, increasing available capital to be invested in the financial speculations, and also making oil supplies uncertain. It had happened again. The focus on increased purchasing power in the world economy rather than investment in trade and production created a crisis and showed the contradiction between the trans-national expansion of American corporate capital and the national basis of US world power. America's attempt at control, particularly in the Reagan era, is also typical of earlier phases. Excessive pre-occupation with finance and tolerance of debt, deregulation of the economy, 'flexible specialization', and 'informalization', as it happened during Edwardian Britain, Periwig Holland or Genoese Spain (Arrighi, 1999:314). National governments' attempts at control led capital to seek new places, which again increased the possibility of the Second and Third World states to pursue their own strategies. But the American policies changed also that marginalized the position of the South. Easily borrowed money in the 1970s became heavy debt burdens in the 1980s and 90s. But some did succeed, and we saw the appearance of the economic giants in Asia, Japan, Hong Kong, Taiwan, Korea,

Singapore, Malaysia and Indonesia. This happened both through industrialization and also by their position in the on-going financial expansion. The success of the Asian tigers, starting with their position of having favourable labour supply in the Japanese economic wonder of sub-contracting, avoiding some of the rises in production costs the American and European competitors had to face, opened a new perspective on world hegemonic power. The rising centre of the East Asian nations implies that the military centre, the USA, and the financial centre, Asia, no longer coincide. Japan has reduced its input into the American economy and concentrated more on Asia. Hence, the controller of military power does not control surplus capital. These tendencies are not conducive to one single dominant world power emerging. Trans-Pacific trade now supercedes trans-Atlantic trade.

As in earlier periods, there are Muslim commentaries to this state of affairs, and we shall outline a few as they relate to our Hadrami stories. Let me start with a celebrity case.

Usama Bin Laden

Recent decades have shown the emergence of militant Muslim organizations as part of an international network that sees the West in general, and in its contemporary, globalized form in particular, as the enemy. Little information exists on these organizations, but many of them are linked to the name of Usama Bin Laden. As Usama himself is a Hadrami born in the diaspora, namely in Saudi Arabia, he belongs to our story in more than one-way. His family comes from Wadi Du'an, one of the tributaries of the main Wadi Hadramaut, and his father moved to Saudi Arabia in the 1950s, where Usama was born in 1957. As the main international terrorist, the life of Usama Bin Laden is of course surrounded by myths and speculations, and I shall not engage in mythmaking here. But it is possible to isolate certain features of Bin Laden's activities that show how he as a person, and his activities are a "commentary" on the world in which he lives in the same way as the lives and activities of earlier Hadramis and Muslims described in this chapter (Bodansky, 1999).

First of all, the migration of the Bin Laden family signifies the most recent wave of migration of Hadramis to Saudi Arabia and the Gulf. The father developed links with the Royal House in Saudi Arabia and built himself as an economic empire in the construction business. Usama's life has evolved within the context of contemporary globalization and his particular standing must also be interpreted against such a background. The effects of the oil boom of the 1970s brought wealth and facilitated increased travels to the West, for leisure or education, and brought the latest technologies available to the East, and allowed a lifestyle that many interpreted as a threat to Islam. King Feisal's assassination by a "westernized" prince added to this apprehension. Anwar Sadat's flirting with the USA and Israel was the proof of the same. These developments were debated among young people in the Middle East, also in the Saudi universities, where Usama studied. But there were political developments that resulted from these developments. Khomeini's Iranian revolution is one Islamic reaction to what was happening there. The seizure of the Grand Mosque in Mecca in 1979 in order to "save Islam" brought developments to Saudi territory. Another shock came when the Soviet Union invaded Afghanistan. Communists occupying Muslims! And this was actually what made Usama Bin Laden go to Afghanistan, to volunteer in the Afghan *jihad* against the invaders. This was also a period during which he maintained close links with the Royal House in Riyad, but this was to change, which led to his loss of Saudi citizenship and his movement to Sudan that joined the Islamist states after a coup in 1989 that brought Hassan al-Turabi to power. This shift was a result of a move in the Afghan resistance from anti-Soviet sentiment in Afghanistan to an increased emphasis on Islamic resistance both against the West and the westernized Muslim regimes. The American invasion of Iraq in 1990 and the Saudi regime's permission to let American troops operate from Saudi soil were the proofs that things were wrong and that the Saudi rulers compromised their Islamic legitimacy. In Sudan, Usama could operate as a part of Turabi's "universal framework for the Islamic movement", based on originations such as "The Islamic Arab Peoples' Conference" (IAPC) and "Popular International Organisation" (PIO). In Sudan, the "Afghans" who had fought in Afghanistan but were the Muslims from various countries could further develop their organization. The collapse of the Bank of Credit and Commerce International (BCCI) in 1991 not only created an international financial scandal, but also threatened to reveal important financial structures of the militant Islamic groups since many of them used this bank for money laundering and financing clandestine operations. After the fall of the bank, there was a need to rebuild a financial system for Islamic organizations, and Usama Bin Laden was given the job by Turabi.

We shall not speculate to what extent these structures are behind the terrorist attacks on American embassies, naval ships and airlines, nor shall we speculate on possible links with Hadramaut and Yemen; neither the terrorist attack on tourists in December 1998 in Abyan, nor the attack on an American ship outside Aden, carried out by individuals that were said to come from Wadi Duan. And we shall not enter into the debates generated by the events of September 11. But there seems to exist an international network of militant Islamists among whom Bin Laden plays a central role. There is little doubt that the organizations that facilitate the activities of these groups are also mushrooming. The Afghan guerillas played a directly military role in Afghanistan, Pakistan and Kashmir. Islamic NGOs played central roles in Somalia, in the Balkan and in Chechnya. Links to guerilla groups in the Philippines may exist, and as we mentioned, also to new Islamic organizations in Indonesia. It is this reality that is of interest to our discussion here. Not as a case of terrorism, but as a case showing us a continuous Muslim commentary on the world around them, and on the events in that world. As such, they represent a Muslim commentary on the West, but also a radical Islamic commentary on other, more moderate Muslim forces. Times and places are certainly new, but themes and rhetoric show clear continuities.

Southeast Asia, Hadramis and Globalization

The Hadramis who live in Singapore (Manger, 2001) are among those close to the globalizing forces of the contemporary Southeast Asian World. Their lives were shaped by the establishment of Singapore as a global city, a financial centre for world capital and with intentions to develop the economy towards the most technologically advanced sectors. But the case also relates to developments in Southeast Asia in general. We see the Hadramis in Singapore enter the globalization debate in its specific Southeast Asian version. After three decades as an "economic miracle", insular Southeast Asia (Malaysia, Indonesia, Singapore) was hit by a deep recession in 1997. Three years later there are signs of economic recovery, and parts of the region are going through restructuring and transformations in both economic and socio-political fields. This period of Southeast Asian history represents nothing less than a success story in terms of overall economic development, although the adverse effects of increased inequity, labour exploitation, environmental degradation and violations against minority groups have also been significant. The political reactions were profound. Suharto's rule for 32 years finally came to an end in Indonesia in May 1998, and the country carried out its first free election in 44 years in June 1999. In Malaysia we have seen a dramatic political struggle in the political elite culminating with the dismissal and prosecution of the deputy Prime Minister, Anwar Ibrahim. The implications of this move are still unclear, but the situation has highlighted discussions on the role of Islam and political reform in the country. Finally, Singapore was also hit by the economic crisis but to a lesser extent than its neighbours, and the political situation seems less turbulent.

As a historical case, Hadrami entrepreneurs are especially interesting because they did not promote a western-style capitalist development but couched their commercial activities in idioms of Islam, thus generating quite different social effects from those of other entrepreneurial groups. The early importance of Hadramis in the regional economy is connected to their involvement in the establishment of the early trading states in the coastal areas of the Malay world. This involvement developed into commercial interests in shipping between the islands of Indonesia, to and from Singapore and also in the pilgrimage traffic to Jiddah and Mecca. Early involvement in the East Indonesian spice trade was later transformed into Hadrami involvement in money-lending, in labour brokerage by supplying plantation labour, in urban estate developments in Singapore and Batavia (Jakarta), and in the development of newspapers and printing houses. Arabs also entered the important batik sector, in competition with the Chinese, thus also engaging themselves in the manufacturing sector.

Hadramis were central agents in global interchanges that facilitated commercialization and organizational change in local economies; at the same time they affected the "moral economies" in their areas of operation. Families of entrepreneurs have supplied important Islamic scholars and teachers, affecting the region far beyond their purely economic impacts. The Hadramis became prime agents of Islamization in the region. They appear on the scene as teachers, as judges and advisers, not only among commoners, but also close to founders and rulers of various sultanates in the area. In the early 20th Century they were involved in Pan-Islamism, calling upon the Ottoman Empire for protection of their rights, sending youth to Istanbul for education and establishing contacts with the Islamic presses of Istanbul, Cairo and Beirut. These developments helped make Hadramis forerunners in the Islamic reformist movement in Southeast Asia at the turn of the 20th Century, a process that also, interestingly, facilitated development of incipient nationalist movements, especially Sarekat Islam. Through establishment of schools, involvement in printing houses, dissemination of literature both in Arabic and in Malay, and through their involvement as Imams in mosques, thus directly relating to local populations, the Hadramis came to play a significant role in the intellectual developments at the turn of the century.

Similar processes are at work in contemporary Southeast Asia. The Hadrami Arabs engage other Muslim groups, most significantly the large Malay population. Hadrami mosques are still the central fora, where people come for advice and help. The mosques are the sites for negotiation of such varied issues as marriage, relations between in-laws, food regulations, religious conversions and anxieties about secularization of society. But the mosques are also the sites that illustrate the contemporary relationships between Hadramis and various power holders in the region. In the magazine *al-Mahjar* in Singapore (Vol. 6, No.1, April 2001:9) the following story appears from the Masjid Ba'alewi, the Hadrami mosque in Lewis Street:

> "ASEAN Informal Summit, Singapore. Heads of State of the ASEAN Nations and their Foreign Ministers visited Singapore for the Four-Day ASEAN Informal Meeting, which ended on the 26th November 2000. A truly informal kind of summit took place during the ASEAN Informal Summit on Friday 24 November 2000. The congregation at Singapore's Ba'alewi Mosque has the honour of joining a number of ASEAN dignitaries for Friday prayers. Dignitaries present included Dr. Mahathir Mohammad, Prime Minister of Malaysia and Syed Hamid Albar, his foreign minister together with Prince Mohamed Bolkiah of Brunei Darussalam, Dr. Alwi Shahab of Indonesia and Dr. Surin Pitsuwan of Thailand. Syed Hassan bin Muhamad Alattas led the Friday Prayer. In addition to his normal Friday invocations, in his closing do'a, Syed Hassan asked for Allah's blessing for Muslims in the region and their leaders. Datuk Hamid Albar and Dr. Alwi Shahab stayed for lunch at the invitation of Syed Hassan Alatas, the Imam of Ba'alwi Mosque and met local Arabs who regularly attended the Friday prayers and see it as an opportunity to fulfil their silatulrahim."

But other voices are there also. In Indonesia organizations such as *Darul Islam* and *Laskar Islam* appear, with a militant agenda. These organizations represent another effect of the contemporary globalization that of an increasingly globalized militant Islam with links to groups such as those headed by Usama Bin Laden. The effects of such developments remain to be seen, but the organizations can certainly be expected to increase in importance should the political regimes in the region be further destabilized.

REFERENCES

Al Hassan, A.Y. and D.R. Hill (1986), *Islamic Technology. An Illustrated History*, Cambridge: Cambridge University Press.

Al-Mahjar (2001), *Al-Mahjar*, Vol. 6, No. 1.

Arrighi, G. (1999), *The Long Twenthieth Century. Money, Power, and the Origin of Our Times*, London: Verso.

Bayly, C.A. (1989), *Imperial Meridian. The British Empire and the World, 1780-1830*, London: Longman.

Bodansky, Y. (1999), *Bin Laden: The Man who Declared War on America*, Roseville, California: Forum.

Busawoy, M. *et al.* (2000), *Global Ethnography: Forces, Connections and Imaginations of a Post-Modern World*, Berkely: University of California Press.

Castells, M. (1996), *The Rise of the Network Society, Vol. I, The Information Age: Economy, Society and Culture*, Oxford: Blackwell.

Castells, M. (1997a), *The Power of Identity. Vol. II—The Information Age: Economy, Society and Culture*, Oxford: Blackwell.

Castells, M. (1997b), *The End of the Millennium. Vol. III—The Information Age: Economy, Society and Culture*, Oxford: Blackwell.

Cooper, F. and Stoller, A.L. (eds.) (1997), *Tensions of Empire. Colonial Cultures in a Bourgeoise World*, Berkeley: University of California Press.

Eickelman, D. and Piscatori, J. (1990), *Muslim Travellers. Pilgrimage, Migration, and the Religious Imagination*, London: Routledge.

Giddens, A. (1990), *The Consequences of Modernity*, Cambridge: Polity Press.

Hall, S. (1991), "The Global and the Local: Globalisation and Ethnicity", In: A. King (ed) *Culture, Globalisation and World-System*, Binghampton: Department of Art History, State University of New York at Binghampton.

Harvey, D. (1989), *The Conditions of Post-modernity. An Inquiry into the Origin of Cultural Change*, Oxford: Blackwell.

Hasan, M. (1997), *Legacy of a Divided Nation. India's Muslims Since Independence*, London: C. Hurst.

Hobson, J. (1938), *Imperialism. A study*, London: George Allen & Unwin.

Hugill, P.J. (1993), *World Trade since 1431. Geography, Technology and Capitalism*, Baltimore: John Hopkins University Press.

Khalidi, O. (1995), *Indian Muslims Since Independence*, Delhi: Vikas Publications.

Lash, S. and Urry, J. (1987), *The End of Organized Capitalism*, Madison: University of Wisconsin Press.

Manger, L. (ed) (1999), *Muslim Diversity. Local Islam in a Global Context*, London: Curzon Press.

Manger, L. (2001), Hadramis in Singapore: Making Muslim Space in a Global City, *Bulletin of the Royal Institute for Inter-Faith Studies*, 3 (2), pp. 141-176.

Metcalf, B.D. (1999), Nationalism, Modernity, and Muslim Identity in India before 1947, In P. van der Veer and H. Lehmann (eds) *Nation and Religion. Perspectives on Europe and Asia*, Princeton: Princeton University Press.

O'Rourke, K.H. and Williamson, J.G. (1999), *Globalization and History. The Evolution of a Nineteenth-Century Atlantic Economy*, Cambridge, Mass.: MIT Press.

Roff, W. (1964), The Malayo-Muslim World of Singapore at the Close of the Nineteenth Century, *The Journal of Asian Studies*, 24 (1), pp. 75-90.

Tibbetts, G.R. (1981), *Arab Navigation in the Indian Ocean Before the Coming of the Portuguese*, London: Royal Asiatic Society.

van der Veer, P. (1994), *Religious Nationalism. Hindus and Muslims in India.* Berkeley: University of California Press.

Voll, J. (1994), *Islam. Continuity and Change in the Modern World*, Syracuse: Syracuse University Press.

Watson, A. (1983) *Agricultural Innovation in the Early Islamic World. The Diffusion of Crops and Farming Techniques*, pp. 700-1100, Cambridge: Cambridge University Press.

5

Roles and Agendas
Current Predicament of Anthropology

SIMON CHARSLEY

The Background

The task of reviewing the contribution of anthropology to a number of contemporary agendas, which can be summed up as 'globalization' is important. They are ways in which major exogenous forces associated with the expansion of global capitalism impact on the lives of ordinary people and the mini-worlds in which they—and we anthropologists as ordinary people too—have to live. As a general concern it is difficult to imagine anything, which could be more essential or more urgent or more involving.

I want to suggest, however, that there are caveats to be entered. The main one concerns the implications for anthropology as a discipline of taking up the globalization agenda too exclusively, in research and thinking. In addition, there is a simpler one which I would like to address first which concerns our perspective on current change. My arguments here come out of my own experience in anthropology over the past forty years. How could they not do so? To understand them it may be helpful to outline the experience first.

I first met Anthropology in 1960 when Structural Functionalism was still the frame within which the subject was introduced to students in Britain. Evans-Pritchard's African classic of Structural Functional Anthropology, *The Nuer* (1940), was the first text I was asked to study. I hated it, but that grounded my understanding of what anthropology was and even what the word meant. It was a period when the subject was still 'social' in a strong sense: that is to say that 'culture' was not much mentioned. It was something that the Americans focused on: our own rather uninformed prejudices told us that it was a little naïve. Our legacy from the famous Radcliffe-Brown (1952) was 'theoretical' and far superior. I believed it at the time, even if I hated that first of its classics, which I had to study. Radcliffe-Brown had eclipsed Malinowski who was considered a pioneer of fieldwork but weak on the theoretical side. We did not, as far as I remember, study Malinowski's work at first hand.

Interests within anthropology were, however, by then already shifting fast in various directions. In any case, for my post-graduate work I moved from Cambridge to the relatively new centre created by Max Gluckman and his Manchester School. This was very different theoretically. Though Gluckman was himself a fierce critic of Malinowski (see *e.g.* Gluckman, 1963: 207-44), he was in several ways close to the Malinowskian tradition in what he understood himself to be studying and teaching. It was not abstracted social structure and its functions, but real people living and using the social and cultural resources into which they had been born, in terms of which they had been raised and which they subsequently encountered in the course of their lives. His formative work was in the colonial societies of Southern Africa. There colonialism was the framework within which people were living; he, unlike many others at the time, always gave prominence to the issues arising. He had been concerned since the 1940s with the towns newly growing up as well as with rural society. Famously—or for some infamously—he asserted that people could be both 'townsmen' and 'tribesmen'. In the towns they were primarily townspeople, involved in a whole range of urban and industrial institutions and values. They had to be studied as such. In the country they were tribesmen and the contexts of their lives would be quite different, with different possibilities and different constraints, different relationships and forms of association (Gluckman, 1956). They were linked by the lives of people moving between them and maintaining relationships and interests in both. It was a dynamic interaction in which neither side nor both together could nor should be represented as a structure in equilibrium.

This was an anthropology, which had, therefore, already been long concerned with change when I encountered it. It was an anthropology, which nurtured F.G. Bailey and his well-known work on caste and tribe and 'the economic frontier' in Orissa (1957) and T.S. Epstein's influential Mysore study of *Economic Development and Social Change* (1962) on the varying and sometimes paradoxical social effects of large-scale irrigation projects. It brought M.N. Srinivas to Manchester in 1963 as a Visiting Professor and encouraged the development of his pioneering work on Sanskritization as part of a general theory of change in contemporary Indian society (Srinivas, 1966).

Not surprisingly, this kind of anthropology led some of us young Manchester anthropologists into studying development schemes in Africa. They were a major concern in the optimistic era of African independence from the late 1950s. I myself went to Uganda just three years after its Independence in 1962. There I studied change-related topics linked with the migration and resettlement of both refugees and what we would now call economic migrants. I focused on their creation of new communities combining social and cultural resources, which they mainly brought with them from other parts of Eastern Africa with economic opportunities available in their places of settlement. I also studied mechanised farming schemes. These were the cutting edge of development schemes at the time but the results were, as has been only too common with development schemes then and subsequently, depressing.

Later, in the 1970s, I had my first contact with India. This was a study I made of the raw silk industry of Mysore. It was intended as a way of understanding relationships between classes and their dynamics in Indian society. I was trying to avoid caste as a topic: by then it seemed to some of us over-studied and over-emphasised. What resulted, however, was a book on the development of the silk industry from an era of technological innovation in the 1920s to the stirrings of new initiatives at the period of the research in the mid-1970s (Charsley, 1982). Fifteen years later, with many of the issues I had identified in that earlier book still relevant, I was involved again with sericultural development. In tune with the times, that was in connection mainly with a grandiose National Sericulture Project of the World Bank and Swiss Development Co-operation. The component with which we anthropologists were concerned here was 'Beneficiary Assessment'. This was the study of the perspectives and experiences of those intended to benefit from the project, mainly sericulturists and silk reelers, in order to provide a continuous flow of feedback for planning and implementation as the project progressed (Salmen, 1987; Acharya, 1993; Charsley, 2001).

The Newness of the Present

With this background, my first if less central caveat on current pre-occupations with globalization agendas may not be surprising. There is often a tendency to exaggerate the newness of the present. It is attractive to be swept along in the rhetorical flood of those who see the world as rushing into a completely transformed future. But before we do so, let us at least remember that in anthropology so-called 'traditional societies' have seemed to be on the edge of the precipice—or already over it—for even longer than the span of years I have been talking about. Ever since the days of Lewis Henry Morgan in America, arguably the founder of our comparative studies with his systematic work on native North Americans starting in the middle of the nineteenth century (1851 foll.), and very definitely from the time eighty and more years ago when Malinowski made his fundamental studies on a small island on the edge of the Pacific (Malinowski, 1922), it has seemed that the anthropologist was the witness to an old and disappearing order. For Lewis Henry Morgan it was already much nearer to extinction than it was for Malinowski. In the Trobriand Islands of Papua New Guinea he predicted, over-dramatically as it turned out, the imminent disappearance of their old order as its coherence was undermined by colonial interventions. In the American case it was a more direct dispossession and resettlement. Anthropology and 'disappearing worlds' went together long before the conjunction became widely known in the 1970s and 1980s as the title of a long-running and innovative series of anthropological films for British television (Loizos, 1993).

Even when anthropologists have known that what they were studying was not really disappearing, when for instance they have been concerned, as often in India, with the way 'tradition' was persisting to the extent of frustrating 'development', the need to obtain funds has kept this way of presenting anthropology alive. A public reason for anthropological research was needed and it had to be one, which would loosen purse strings. The disappearing and preferably 'exotic' was something to appeal to the lay controllers of resources in Western countries, as perhaps the obstructive nature of tradition was in India. This need to find ways of appealing to people controlling funding who often know little of anthropology is of course a continuing reality of life. Those of us, who seek funds for our own work by making cases to foundations and research councils, and to grants commissions for the support of anthropology as a teaching discipline, must surely be well aware of this particular constraint on the way anthropology has to be represented. Sadly, there is nothing that ensures that ways of representing it which are useful in the short run will be good for the continuation and prosperity of the discipline in the longer run. Representing it as useful for colonial government and receiving support accordingly became a handicap for British anthropology in a number of newly independent countries for a time.

There is no question of course that we have to relate to current agendas of the powerful on whom we depend. Issues arising are important and potentially valuable topics of research for anthropology: there is no doubt of that either. And anthropology has distinctive contributions to make. But, amongst ourselves at least, let us remember that a new word, 'globalization', does not necessarily mean that there is any straightforwardly new phenomenon here or that everything changes. Perhaps the pace of change has accelerated radically, though I am constantly reminded by my current work in villages in Andhra Pradesh[1] that the speed of change and a sense of newness about it is much more apparent to urban upper classes than to rural people in general and the lower classes in particular. For too many of the latter the distresses of their lives are nothing new. They are grounded in much longer histories of changing social and economic relationships and declining access to resources. In anthropology we have been studying these for a very long time already. We have a great store of experience and understanding to call on. Imagining that globalization changes everything tends to devalue this past experience, but the loss is serious if it is allowed to. How significant are those things, which are really new now?

A striking instance, again from current research, concerns the impact we are finding of one of the most obvious and widely known recent 'globalization' change in villages in India. This is the extraordinarily rapid and amazingly widespread of satellite-transmitted cable TV. Its apparently revolutionary impact on everyday life has recently been documented from rural Maharashtra by Johnson (2000). In the three areas we have taken up for study in Andhra Pradesh and there is hardly a village, however small, which does not have its dish and its trails of cables. To start with we were hearing how it had swept away the demand for local live performance, by amateurs and by many kinds of traditional performers. An image was repeatedly presented of an instant privatising of life, with people glued to their TVs to the exclusion of all other more collective activities. It seemed very obviously 'globalization' directly and compellingly at work.

As our research has gone on, however, our sense of what is happening has developed in important ways. I should stress that the topic is not a focus for us but one, which we have come on—almost chanced on—from two angles. One was that when we wanted to show people our recordings of their performances, we thought of the village businesses which, as well as relaying the signals from the satellite broadcasting companies to their cable subscribers, also have the means to put out videos on request. In larger villages there are often more than one of them. This quickly raised the question of who has access to the signals from each particular provider. When, for instance, we wanted to put out material which *Maadiga dappu* players[2] had allowed us to video, we found that although there were TVs in their street none was connected to the particular provider we first approached. This was a local doctor with whom the people concerned had good relationships and to whom they introduced us. Together we had arranged for our video to be played, only to find that scarcely any of the actual performers had been able to see it. Some had connections from another provider whom, for factional reasons as it turned out, we had not approached. I had naively taken the sight of satellite dishes as an obvious indicator of 'global' forces at work, and was now being brought up against some of the local factors determining the variability of 'impact'. At least the sociology, the economics and the physical layout of a village would have to be studied. The significance of anything new here would only be understood by locating it within contexts themselves involved in on-going process of change.

The second way we came across the issue was in surprising claims that began to reach us. An early one was from a bookseller in the local town specialising in the texts of *yakshaganams* who reported a boom in sales in the preceding couple of years. *Yakshaganam* is a mainly *pauranic* theatrical genre particularly popular in Telengana[3]. He also reported his impression that his customers were now buying mainly for performing rather than for private reading. He thought that people had at first been keen on the new cable programmes, and this had contributed to the rather long-term decline in his sales, which was already being experienced. Now, however, people were already bored with the programmes that the cable was bringing in. As is the way with this kind of research, once we had registered this others began talking to us in the same vein. Performers themselves reported a new level of enthusiasm. They thought that it was because the TV material was remote from the experience and language of most people in Telengana[4] and did not have the rewards either for performers or audiences of the *yakshaganams* and other forms long familiar in their villages and lives.

There is a great deal more to this story, and doubtless more than we yet know, but the moral I draw here is that it is easy to exaggerate and over-simplify the 'impact' of external factors when this is what provides the research agenda. The newness of whatever is identified and its significance are the premises on which the research is based. How it relates to whatever else is going on in the society may well, as is illustrated by Johnson's study referred to above, be made to seem peripheral.

So exaggeration of the newness of the present, as focused by this new term 'globalization', is one hazard, which I suggest deserves caution. A sense of the uniqueness of any phenomenon already paralyses the comparative faculty through which understandings may be reached. If, in addition, the contexts, locally as well as on larger scales, into which interventions are being made are not given priority, I think we shall achieve little understanding of what is happening and, even more certainly, why it is not happening in the same way everywhere or for everybody.

The Globalization Agenda and Culture

The main issue for discussion here has already been broached several times. It is the danger of what I see as the fundamental anthropological concern with 'culture' being pushed aside by this current globalization agenda. The discussion now shifts to culture and what is not culture.

As I noted above, my own specimen of an anthropological career was grounded in the structural-functional anthropology of Radcliffe-Brown and in the study of development and change. It was only after my Ph.D. research in Uganda and even my initial study in India that, as a lecturer at Glasgow University, I really discovered Malinowski's work. It was

Radcliffe-Brown and structural-functionalism, which were by then under the cloud from which they have not subsequently emerged. Malinowski, long dead, was again, if metaphorically, basking in the warmth of widespread recognition as the pioneer of an anthropology, which had not posed an opposition between society and culture. He had recognised as interdependent and interacting the aspects of people's lives to which these two labels may apply. Relationships and groups, structures of relationship and grouping, forms in which they could be expressed, the values and meanings attached to them, beliefs and people's idea about 'reality' or realities within which they had to make their lives; all these had to be grist to the mill of a Malinowskian anthropology seeking to understand other people's lives. Malinowski's famous—and famously difficult—aspiration was to see the world as others did, to understand what made life worth living for them, the sources of their pleasures as well as their sorrows (Malinowski, 1922: 517). It was an anthropology, which had revealed as never before the amazing potential of humans for constructing different ways of life for themselves. This, and in particular the many kinds of meaningfulness that are brought into human lives and generated within them, became the focus of anthropology. I think especially of the work of Clifford Geertz on *The Interpretation of Cultures* (1973) as one fertile way in which this Malinowskian tradition has been developed.[5]

Anthropology has to start, I contend, from the perception that lives, which are meaningful and more or less satisfying to those living them, can be based on an always surprising variety of understandings, values, priorities. Human beings are creative and—as I always tell my beginning students—the fundamental thing they have always created is ways of life for themselves. Ways of being, ways of thinking, ways of doing. They are created through the particular histories that people have partly made, largely endured. There is no doubt that economic opportunity is a great solvent of existing values and stimulus to new ideas which begin to allow lives to be shaped in new ways. Economic opportunity is one part of the on-going history through which the culture of particular groups and regions comes to be shaped. But it is far from being the whole story. As we have partly been seeing, though we have not explored it in detail, there are powerful cultural aspects in the how and the why of appreciating and seizing opportunities, hence of outcomes of change in particular places and particular histories. This for me is the central territory of anthropology. Methodologies, which will allow the subtle, interplay of cultural and material advantage and the dynamics of cultural creativity to be revealed, are needed if such issues are not to be lost to understanding.

In principle the globalization research agenda can perhaps be forced to make a space for serious culturally-oriented research. With cable TV I have tried to display a simple instance of how it may be located in 'the local', which can be represented as the inevitable reciprocal of 'the global'. The concept of the local may allow us to re-assert central interests of our subject, which we can raise in the path of the juggernaut too readily perceived as threatening to flatten them. The problem concerns what we shall seek to learn about them if we take our orientation from the agendas of globalization. It is liable to lead in practice to remote and misleading views of the worlds of the people we first study and then represent to others in our writings. They are seen as the objects of development schemes, those exploited by commercialisation, the losers from the privatisation of common property resources, the sufferers from mineral excesses and deficiencies, those whose sexual practices have to be reformed to curb the spread of HIV, those who have to be convinced to respect the new 'human rights' of others or to stand up for themselves against other's infringements of their own rights; and so on. This is an agenda which assumes the dominance of all that is not 'culture', or at least what is not yet the culture of the people concerned: the economic, the environmental, public health concerns, demography, even human rights. The people who are the only and essential agents of response to 'inputs', who may frustrate the most ingenious and best-intentioned schemes, are too often lost to sight. Who are they for themselves and those they associate with? for family, friends, rivals? What are their values, their understandings of their place in their own worlds, their views of the past and the present, what are their pleasures, what makes life worth living, or occasionally does not. These are concerns of the Malinowskian tradition to which I have referred.[6] They are also components of the local human context, which determines outcomes.

The plea now is that you do not allow, here in India particularly, the 'globalization' agenda to devalue cultural concerns. Though they cannot be the whole of anthropology, they must be one of the legs on which it stands, the other being the socio-economic. The latter is prioritised by the globalizing agenda to an even greater extent than the 'common-sense' of the materialistic West has always done. A real effort is needed if anthropology, particularly perhaps in India, is not to surrender to this prevailing trend.

The power of culture is expressed for us in our current research in Andhra Pradesh most sharply and repeatedly by the passion for performing and the dedication to performing arts. This is, to a Westerner, very surprisingly widespread in rural society here and I suspect elsewhere in India too. It is frequently pursued at heavy material cost, in the need for artists themselves to pay much of the cost of performance and in opportunities for other employment foregone. For many of those whose hereditary activity it is there is often a painful moral cost too: preventing themselves being seen as beggars rather than artists is a constant battle. However, in many sections of the society performing is a high point in male lives. It is their access to glamour, and nowhere more so than when, as is usual in Telengana, they can perform female roles from which women themselves are excluded. The idea is common that men can be in various ways better and certainly more glamorous women than biological women themselves. The latter delight in these men-women and their performances. A further aspect, which has to be noticed, is that men's choice to be performers often puts a great burden on their womenfolk. They are rarely themselves performers, being still firmly excluded not only from *yakshaganams* but also from most performing arts. Only too often they must work in the fields to support their families, whilst their performer men folk excuse themselves from such demands. This is an area of life in which local values, understandings, meanings, activities and the ways they shape lives are strikingly visible. It is also an area, which contributes powerfully to the achievements, satisfactions and pleasures, to the richness of lives, which are by material standards poor, often painfully so. Having now, for the first time in a long anthropological career, been myself involved in research into this aspect of people's lives, I am amazed that how it could have previously been so widely ignored in my own and others' anthropological research.[7]

Concern with the astonishing diversity of the cultural creations of humanity is, I would now argue, the one thing, which differentiates anthropology from the wide range of other disciplines with which it shares so many other interests. Without a lively sense of this key dimension, anthropology risks dissolving into one or other of the many familiar non-disciplinary studies dominated by others, into Development Studies, Environmental Studies, Rights Studies and so on. Whilst it is entirely desirable that anthropologists should be contributors to all of these, I do not see how doing so can be the route to anthropology with its own distinctive contributions to make. It is probably not even a way of maintaining it in the competitive academic environment.

Anthropology and the Competitive Environment

Supposing I am right and that it is difficult to maintain any distinctiveness of contribution through such work, does the emphasis on culture provide any realistic alternative? Is anyone other than those anthropologists already imbued with this concern going to appreciate work grounded in cultural awareness? Anthropology has always been relatively small as an academic discipline. Everywhere an academic discipline needs funds, and the sources of funds for anthropology have always been limited. Everywhere there must also be good reasons why new generations will come into a discipline. If these two needs are not met, it will surely stagnate and eventually die. It has, therefore, always been necessary for us to pay attention to the agendas of the powerful: some crumbs may be swept from their tables onto our plates. The different forces of this metaphor in Western and Indian cultures will strike the comparative cultural awareness of the anthropologist. The agendas of young potential recruits to anthropology need attention too. Often of course they largely take their agendas from these same controllers of resources, which both they and we need to tap. Currently it is the apparently unchallenged expansion of liberal capitalism as the answer to the world's problems, as identified by the wealthy Western nations in particular, which grounds this agenda of the resource controllers and those eager to share in that wealth. Anthropology in my opinion has never been and can never be central to this but is constrained to relate to it as best it may.

Are the controllers of the needed resources going to loosen the purse strings for work which goes beyond their immediate agendas into less materially, more culturally focused topics? Are the new generation of students going to appear, ready to enrol in Anthropology courses and perhaps become anthropologists? My recent experience of academic anthropology in India suggests that many here would be pessimistic. There are serious problems of course, but I would like to suggest reasons not to be altogether despondent and, even more tentatively, avenues which might be explored.

I think first of our own experience in Britain. For about the first half of my career in anthropology, culture was under a cloud and crises of identity in anthropology came thick and fast. But in the last 20 years there has been a great welling up of interest amongst the young. Enrolments in Anthropology courses have boomed. In most universities, even belatedly in my own, provision has been expanded. Opportunities for those trained as anthropologists within the academic discipline and beyond it have greatly increased. What has changed here?

A major factor is that Britain has become an increasingly multi-cultural society. It is increasingly linked with other parts of the globe not just through people of British origin settled in them, as in the old days of Empire, but by people from elsewhere who have become part of the British population. They have established their own ethnic identities and distinctions within it but have also often maintained their own home links. Interest in ethnicity and ethnic difference has expanded and contributed to a wider recognition of anthropology and acceptance of its concern with cultural difference as legitimate and potentially important. In India—the example of Andhra Pradesh is at the forefront of my mind of course—interest in cultural difference has always been lively in a society where the cultivation of such differences remains vigorous. Learning about the concerns and the customs of one's fellow citizens and in particular about the distinctiveness of one's own people is no small interest in this society. Cultural awareness and sensitivity are strong and closely linked with identity. Minorities and weaker sections are constantly and for a variety of reasons on government agendas. At present concern with relevant aspects of culture, except perhaps amongst 'tribals', appears in academia mainly within literature and folk culture studies rather than in Anthropology. The possibility of reinforcing interests within Anthropology oriented to valued cultural differences is suggested by the comparison with British experience.

The rise of ethnicity in Britain has been, of course, only one of the relevant things going on over this most recent period of relative prosperity for Anthropology. In that period our exposure through the media, especially television, to glimpses of the lives of different peoples within Britain and across the globe has increased enormously. Mostly these are journalistic views but sometimes they are more or less anthropologically informed. Live contacts through travel abroad and the expanding range of the destinations has played its part too. Tourism as the consumption of a pre-packaged commodity tends to insulate the tourist from engagement with anyone other than the personnel of the industry itself, but the sealing off is rarely complete. The possibilities of escaping it to a greater or lesser extent have expanded too. This has particular relevance for recruitment to Anthropology courses. The so-called 'gap year' between school and university has become a well-known practice amongst the middle classes. Such students do not rush from school to university at the age of 17 or 18 but take a break from education to gain wider experience before going on to the next stage.[8] This may mean jobs within Britain but it often takes the form of lengthy stays abroad. These involve combinations of independent travelling with periods spent living and working, paid or unpaid, elsewhere in the world. Where these are places offering experience of cultures conspicuously different to those familiar in the home society, they provide a basis for interest in Anthropology as a subject for subsequent undergraduate study. This is not to any major extent vocational: Anthropology graduates mostly seek the same kinds of job as other social science and arts students though with a probable bent towards overseas assignments. Those who have done particularly well often wish to go on to research degrees, motivated not by career prospects so much as by the experience offered and sometimes by an intense involvement with the subject. Finding studentships to support these degrees is intensely competitive.

There are clearly important differences between this recruitment situation and current experience in India. I would quickly point, however, to the advantages of having several years of undergraduate experience of anthropological study in engaging and consolidating interests in the subject, sometimes to the point of competing with more obvious career interests. For India it may be difficult to think of increasing teaching at the college level, though I believe that this is currently being attempted in Kerala.

Are there possible parallels for the other sources of recruits identified in Britain? There is an undoubted similarity in the availability of media representations of exotic parts, especially with the expansion of cable TV channels. In both countries this is not what most people watch most of the time, but it is there to support interests and tastes already forming. Experience of other cultures is not in any case such a problem. As the late M.N. Srinivas observed, 'in a culture and society such as India's, "the other" can be encountered literally next door'. 'The other' referred to here were Kurubas, whom he identified as a 'shepherd' caste living and tending cattle in the lane behind his own mainly Brahmin street in Mysore city during his childhood (Srinivas 1996: 204-7). However, few of us can be an M.N. Srinivas, to look on local 'others' with open and friendly fascination. Anxieties, antipathies and tensions on both sides may often make such situations less encouraging for learning than are the voluntary adventures undertaken by young British proto-anthropologists keen to expand their experience. Conspicuously, however, tourism including international tourism is taking off in India, and relatives resident abroad able to lessen the effects of grossly unfair exchange rates are increasingly numerous. A class able to take advantage of travel is growing and it is one for whom educational options are also expanding. Will some of the children of this cosmopolitan class be potential recruits to Anthropology in the future?

Conclusion

This chapter has argued that anthropology has a prime resource in its concern with culture and cultures and a dynamic perspective on these as formed and reformed by the activities of people over time. It always has needed and always will need to respond to the perspectives of the powerful, for anthropologists like everyone else have to eat. But if this means forgetting what is distinctive about anthropology—and here I have pointed to culture rather than to its methods of research since what is to be researched must be prior to the methods for doing so—it is not a viable strategy for keeping it alive and vigorous in the longer run. Cultural difference is not something, which is going away. Though anthropologists have for the best part of the past century or more used the imminent disappearance of their subject matter as a lever to extract resources with which to study it, there is no prospect of everyone in India, for instance, being culturally homogenised. Clones of some imaginary American way of life are not going to replace the rich variety of the present. Even 'local' in relation to 'global' does not altogether catch this. 'Local' here would have to be India, its North and its South, its linguistic states, the regions within states, and all sorts of entities large and small, classes, castes, religious groups, down to villages, which overlap each other and the geographical divisions. They provide key components of the frames within which people make lives for themselves. Will the juggernaut of globalization—to revert to a metaphor already used above—perhaps lose its way in such an immense and richly variegated locality?

To appreciate this as the cultural nature of the society is, to my mind, the strength of anthropology. To forget it is to drain the subject not only of its distinctiveness but of the greatest source of its contribution to the life of its times.

NOTES

1. This is a project on 'Popular Performance and Social Change in Indian Society', based at the Department of Sociology & Anthropology, University of Glasgow, Scotland, and funded by the British Economic & Social Research Council (ESRC) under Grant No. R000239063. In India it is affiliated to the Department of Sociology, University of Hyderabad. Thanks are due to these organisations for their support.
2. *Dappu* is a particular drum, the making and playing of which belongs to the *Maadiga* caste traditionally associated with leatherwork. Its performance is prominent in several spheres of village life.
3. This differs markedly from the more elaborately developed and better-known form from Karnataka so thoroughly analysed by Guru Rao Bapat (1998).
4. This is the region of Andhra Pradesh, which was under Muslim rule until Independence, and in which direct Brahminical influences have been weak. There is a strong sense of differences between the form of Telugu spoken there and the dominant form associated with the more educated and richer coastal region.
5. The concept of culture in anthropology has a long history of controversy. In the course of it, definitions proposed have moved on in theoretically interesting ways (see, *e.g.* Kuper, 1999).
6. I have argued elsewhere (Charsley, 1996) that the negativity of the twentieth-century pan-Indian labelling of people as Untouchables has similarly diverted attention from the positive contributions which the people concerned have always made to the cultural and religious life of the wider community. The agendas of the powerful, however well meaning, almost inevitably place themselves at the centre and have the effect of marginalising others.
7. This is not to say that it has always been ignored. Victor Turner's

later work (1982, 1988) has been influential in America but much less noticed in Britain.

8. In Britain, about 12 years of schooling are followed by 3 or 4 years of undergraduate study in Universities. The Indian pattern of degree colleges and post-graduate universities is not found.

REFERENCES

Acharya, J. (ed.) (1993), *Sericulture and Development*, Delhi: Indian Publishers Distributors.

Bailey, F.G. (1957), *Caste and the Economic Frontier*, Manchester: Manchester University Press.

Charsley, S.R. (1982), *Culture and Sericulture*, London: Academic Press.

Charsley, S.R. (2001), *Reshme Krishi Samskruti Matthu Abhivrudhi* (Kannada trans. U.D. Bongale: 'Culture and the Development of Sericulture'), Bangalore: Pushpaseri Publications.

Epstein, T.S. (1962), *Economic Development and Social Change in South India*, Manchester: Manchester University Press.

Evans-Pritchard, E.E. (1940), *The Nuer*, Oxford: Oxford University Press.

Geertz, C. (1973), *The Interpretations of Cultures*, New York: Basic Books.

Gluckman, M. (1956), Social Anthropology in Central Africa, *Rhodes-Livingstone Journal* XX (Reprinted Manchester: Manchester University Press).

Gluckman, M. (1963), *Order & Rebellion in Tribal Africa*, London: Cohen & West.

Guru Rao Bapat (1998), *Yaksagaana: Performance and Meaning—A Semiotic Study*, Udupi, Karnataka: Regional Resources Centre for Folk Performing Arts [Cover details differ: Gururao V. Bapat. *Semiotics of Yakshagana*].

Johnson, Kirk (2000), *Television & Social Change in Rural India*, New Delhi: Sage.

Kuper, A. (1996), *Anthropology and Anthropologists: The Modern British School*. 3rd ed., London: Routledge.

Kuper, A. (1999), *Culture: The Anthropologist's Account*, Cambridge, Mass: Harvard University Press.

Loizos, P. (1993), *Innovation in Ethnographic Film*, Manchester: Manchester University Press.

Malinowski, B. (1922), *Argonauts of the Western Pacific*, London: Routledge.

Morgan, L.H. (1851), *The League of the Ho-de-no-sau-nee, or Iroquois*, Rochester, N.Y.: Sage.

Radcliffe-Brown, A.R. (1952), *Structure & Function in Primitive Society*, London: Cohen & West.

Salmen, L.F. (1987), *Listen to the People*, Washington: Oxford University Press.

Srinivas, M.N. (1966), *Social Change in Modern India*, Berkeley: University of California Press.

Srinivas, M.N. (1996), Studying one's own culture: Some thoughts, pp. 198-214. *Village, Caste, Gender and Method*, Delhi: Oxford University Press.

Turner, V.W. (1982), *From Ritual to Theatre: The Human Seriousness of Play*, New York: PAJ Publications.

Turner, V. (1988), *The Anthropology of Performance*, New York: PAJ Publications.

6

Globalization and Other Emerging Issues

An Anthropological Analysis

PREMANANDA PANDA

Globalization is a pervasive characteristic of the new millennium and highly topical in terms of the attention now being given to it in the anthropological literature. It is seen as the most current state of a process where technological, economic, commercial, ecological, cultural and military trends, traditionally observable on a geographically limited scale and scope, are extended to the entire globe, leading to the emergence of new players with new and different (power) relationships among them. For the 'developing world', the asymmetrical power dimensions of these relationships are of particular relevance, not only in terms of the cultural, but also the conceptual hegemony associated with globalization.

Although debates on globalization hover around the issues relating to natural resources management, but in reality the themes often include issues of governance, economic systems and hidden values, tourism and global ideology, etc. The central concepts of cultural diversity and marginalisation *vis-à-vis* globalization deserve attention in this global debate. It is more relevant to those developing nations like ours who have gone for liberalisation, allowing international players in economic and cultural areas to have their games on. There are issues of ethnic diversity and cultural uniformity across the national boarders. There has been nested hierarchies that globalization as a concept implies, which ought to be addressed, because under globalization it raises questions as to whose interest does the state serve and what are the related implications on traditional resources and intellectual property rights of people living close to nature and not aware of what the globalization intends to and exerts impact on them? A major challenge is the use of practical cases that offer practical solutions to the global debate on globalization and the commons.

Culture has been a relatively unexplored factor in dealing with common property scholarship. As such, globalization provides a rich palette on which one can examine the relationship between culture and commons' management and use. What role does a deep understanding of culture and globalization play in common property management and use is yet to be known in clear perspective. Concepts of stewardship, inter-generation equity and sustainability, cultural homogenisation, etc. are some of the areas that need immediate attention for the proactive anthropologists to offer prescriptions to safeguard the rural/tribal communities and help them enjoy the rights of full citizenship of free India, and free from any form of bondage either from within and/or from outside forces. "Protected Areas" have been created to cater to the needs of any private party establishing a factory or for any ordnance factory of national defence as a part of security measure, or for the sanctuaries to protect the animals getting extinct and indirectly prevent the forest patches getting exploited and consumed. It is all the same for what reasons that the forest dwellers have been put to difficulties and restrictions imposed upon them on their hitherto known properties of commons. The "Protected Area" (PA) approach has been one of the two "mainstream" strategies for conservation. For urban and industrialised societies, it remains a principal mode of the use of nature, and is held out as a paradigm for the developing world. In India, like in Africa, its impact on land use and state appropriations of nature has been profound. PA advocates have begun to reach out to more people-centred approaches but this initiative has had little impact from social scientists and from an ecological perspective. A few local-level issues have been linked up with globalization and scholars have explored the linkages of protected areas and the development programmes *vis-à-vis* the people. There is, therefore, a need to rethink protected areas in the age of globalization by going beyond wildlife resources.

Land, water and forest are the commons in an era of globalization. Land and water tenure system has long been an important issue for common property scholarship, because common property regimes are always embedded within wider sets of property relations. Globalization has introduced new pressures into national and local contexts. What form does land and water reform and resource tenure take under globalization and what impact does this have on common property resources pose challenges before the socio-cultural anthropologists. Therefore, it is necessary to examine as to how globalization affects the existing forms of tenure and the form of integration between customary laws, traditional authority structure, gender and statutory laws. In what ways do all these encompassing regimes of access and entitlement to resources help to define the character of specific arrangements for the use of common property resources places challenges before the people and power in question? To pay particular attention to promotion of equality in access to resources for all citizens, it is necessary to understand the on-going decentralisation/devolution of resource management and increasing stakeholder involvement in resource management. Further what is the effect of such measures in facilitating the improvement of livelihoods of rural and tribal poor and to what extent are equity issues addressed in the era of globalization also need in-depth examination from peoples' perspective.

Indigenous knowledge systems, integrity of commons and emerging regimes of intellectual property rights in a globalizing world are some of the vital areas of investigation for action anthropologists to study on the locals. The meaning of 'indigenous' remains contested; however, it has implications on issues to do with time-specific, place-specific and personal experiences of particular people within given cultural settings. Case material should highlight social differentiation in common pool resources management, the role of indigenous knowledge systems and their contribution to the future integrity of the commons (*e.g.* the aborigines as a distinct ethnic group).

How do the social organizations, indigenous knowledge systems and intellectual property rights influence the sustainable use and management of the commons resources can be imagined from the recent experiences that the tribal people have. In this changing scenario of global economy it has become necessary to know the international conventions, bio-piracy issues, the role of diverse knowledge systems and prospects for sustainable natural resource management. With regard to the trans-boundary and natural resources management the commons co-operation across boundaries that enhance the management of natural resources for the benefit of all stakeholders (TBNRM) has of late come into the limelight, because of increased competition over natural resources by users at various levels; community, national, regional and international. What form should policy making, legislation, laws and governance between national boundaries under globalization take for effective co-management of CPRs is yet to be defined, and let the anthropologist raise voice before it is too late. The TBNRM perspective calls for the creation of common policies, legislation, laws and governance that are in harmony. We are yet to look beyond our nose in making forest laws as evidenced from the recent amendments, where the forest officials have been more empowered and the people marginalised. Therefore, in the changed global environment the coping mechanism of the people deserves research attention.

New analytic tools for common property resource management have become a popular talk among the business and industrial anthropologists. The past two decades have witnessed technological improvements and the increased use of computer applications (GIS, remote sensing, internet and satellite imaging) designed to support capture, management, manipulation, and analysis of spatially referenced data for solving resource management problems, among others. Have we ever tried to see what role does technology play and what factors inhibit the use and application of these new analytic tools for common property resource management and use? For these issues cost and access to technology, data sharing and standardisation for different users, and ethical considerations is the key.

The SSRC collaborative research network on globalization, local institutions and development has sought to illuminate the mechanisms through which processes of economic globalization are experienced in profoundly different ways in distinctive settings. Despite the putatively homogenizing implications of globalization, growing evidence has suggested that in reality some localities and social groups are better able than others to take advantage of opportunities for enhanced prosperity and well-being, while others have suffered ever-greater degrees of marginalization and impoverishment as a result of those very processes. The community resources management has sought to comprehend those diverse results through a focus on how local institutions, household structures, community practices, social networks, public policies, etc. mediate interactions between global processes and local responses, and thus shape the fortunes of different social groups in different places across points in time. Efforts have concentrated on advancing two working groups: one on industrial upgrading and the other on labour insertion in the processes of globalization. These have been the subjects of international meetings held in various parts of the world, and substantial advances have been achieved both in conceptualizing the key issues to be addressed and in establishing common analytical languages among researchers coming to these questions from diverse perspectives.

The tribes in Asia in general, and India in particular, to a large extent depend on their natural environment for their livelihood. Their economies are closely related to the natural resources. With regard to their own natural resources and style of life, they possess a high degree of skill and knowledge, which they have gained through the long observation and intimate interaction. For centuries, they have been responsible for consuming and conserving the nature and even when they get things from outside they indigenize them such that their subsistence economies contribute to the sustainable practice and the natural resources are not indiscriminately appropriated. Traditionally, their social cohesion for the maintenance of common property resources were very high, and by and large the skill of maintenance was operating through the line of kinship such that the geographical environment for reasons of ethics, politics and spiritual cannot be identified as an independent separable entity.

The non-timber forest produces till this day are given a status of being the produce/collection from the open access resources and therefore, difficult to have any price standardized. As regards Orissa, the state is not in a position till this day to establish the property rights and presumably is the same with other states too with minor variations: The forest produce is subjected to regulated market in an arbitrary way. The reason behind is that these items are evaluated not on the basis of cost of regeneration and restoration, but only because of extraction. The cultural value from the angle of the tribal people is never been bothered. Like traditional anthropologist treating tribal people for their easy research ride, the traders too treat them as well as their resources, easily accessible and priced at their sweet will. With the intrusion of global market, the players from outside will have an almost free ride and the dominant section inhabiting nearby can act as henchmen for the multi-nationals. The frequent intervention of the private parties through state sponsorship has made the status of the community property ambiguous, and neither the tribal nor the state takes care to protect the commons. This is one of the opportunities for the business/corporate houses to exploit the resources of the tribal people. The threat to their resources and the exploitation beyond their tolerance leads to uprising/struggle of the inhabitants against the industrial/business houses.

Most of the people of South Asia still live in villages and follow the traditional pursuits of an agricultural and pastoral economy. The forest collection and the games contribute a share to their subsistence. In the higher altitudes of the Himalayas, the tribesmen live with their flocks of livestock in summer and winter encampments, each remaining unoccupied for some months in a year. The pastoral nomads like the Baluchi tribe in Pakistan generally have only temporary encampments. The Dafla, Apa Tani, Gallong, and other tribes of Arunachal Pradesh establish their villages on the highest parts of the hills, from where the whole valley below is visible. Many tribes site their villages in accordance with the will of God as interpreted by their shamans. Hundreds of villages of the Santhal, Munda, and Ho tribes in middle India are in the forest clearings. The communities like Gadaba of south Orissa live in ancestral village groups. Traditionally each clan of the Bijhal tribe has its mountain and sacred groves. In southern India many tribal villages are located in dense forest, and their economy revolves round forest. In western Rajasthan there are dispersed settlements in desert or semi-desert areas. In the deltaic plains of West Bengal and Bangladesh, countless rivers and streams have caused settlements to be highly concentrated on the strips of dry land. Typical of the area are clusters of houses scattered along the banks of streams and rivulets. Each cluster usually forms a separate residential unit consisting of a number of huts built around a courtyard. Now in most of the tribal areas the non-tribal lower caste people also settled. They, along with the tribal communities, use the commons such as forest, mountain and river valleys. The past settlement pattern befitting to the cultural necessities of the tribal people has been changed.

The response to the global impact on autochthonous has taken a different shape. These get reflected in the events of displacement and resettlement caused due to the big projects launched by the multi-national business houses. The linear settlement is much in evidence in the plain areas of Orissa, Madhya Pradesh, Andhra Pradesh, Kerala, and Tamil Nadu. The abundance of river valleys and the prevalence of the *jajmani* system (in which lower castes perform specialized artisan services for the landowners and cultivators in exchange for a fixed share in the harvest) serve to maintain the traditional linear settlement pattern (Encyclopedia Britannica, 2001). The linear settlement is also found in fishing villages on the sea, or estuaries, or along big rivers. Villages vary from fewer than 50 to more than 1,000 people. The villages of the rich agricultural plain areas are usually larger, while those of the hills and forests are smaller. Some tribal villages are temporary encampments of 5 to 10 huts providing accommodation for up to 30 persons. The tribal villages of the Hill Maler, the Hill Kharia, or the Bondo highlanders in Orissa are slightly bigger, composed of 10 to 30 huts accommodating 30 to 100 persons. Large villages like those of the Waromung in Nagaland having a population of more than 1,000 are exceptional. The villages of the settled cultivators are large and somewhat elaborate in layout. Depending on the extent and fertility of the land, quantum of collection and hunting from forest, the population of an average village varies from 100 to 500 persons. Hindu villages, especially those in the Indo-Gangetic Plain, may have as many as 5,000 inhabitants, divided into a number of hamlets. The natural offshoots of the villages have been created to keep the balance of people and the resources. In caste Hindu villages, the central part of a village is occupied by the dominant castes, while the untouchables live in a far-removed area. Every village has a temple located near the settlement of the higher castes. The houses of the landlords are elaborate; those of the tenants are simple. Most houses are built of mud and tiles, with courtyards and parlours. The village retained its relative transparency so long it behaved as one social unit and share the common culture and some commons even through there were hierarchies maintaining mutual exclusiveness in their transactions. Now things have changed and the world is open to the village through transmitting space media.

The concept of holistic culture and the method of inductive generalisation from direct observation are powerful tools that help business firms to understand environmental relation at home and abroad as well as behavioural interactions within the corporation (Terpstra and David, 1985). The process of globalization was internalised by its first wave, which expanded the European power and colonisation of a major part of world. The second wave began after ex-colonies gained political independence and was characterised by universalisation of production and consumption pattern of northern industrial nations across the world and therefore, as it exists that 2 per cent of people of the world own 98 per cent of world wealth. Shiva (1988) writes that since the universalization is based on 20 per cent of world population predominantly in North consuming 80 per cent of the world's resources, globalization of the production and consumption has led to mal-development and not development in the South. The last quarter of the 20th Century has opened new fields and opportunities for anthropological research and practice in the public and private sector (Baba, 1986). Arensberg (1978) has noted, "We need more insight into the dynamics of large scale business organisation for many reasons. For managing it, for teaching management to mange it, for efficiency, for taming business organisations for human use and social responsibilities and for coming to terms with the powerful force and study growth shown by large scale business organisation in national and international life".

The outsiders to extract the natural resources including timber have used the tribal habitats, such as hill slopes and foothill areas. The trade relations for the sandalwood, bamboo, teak, and a few medicinal plants are fast disappearing, and the state policies of development have been shifting its emphasis from extraction to conservation. In the plain areas, in many cases, long time habitation has given the non-tribals the right over land and resources, while for the tribals inhabiting for many generations are never allowed to have rights over the resources. The *podu* land and the forest managed by the tribal people have never been viewed by the state administration as a feature of management. The lack of formal rights over certain kinds of land, such as the *podu* land by the tribal people deprive them the opportunity to make use of any kind of intervention by the state for developing the management of their natural environment. They have a thorough understanding of the negative effects of *podu* cultivation and have adopted to cultivate specific type of crops. Mixed crops in the *podu* fields, the soil condition of the hill slopes, etc. play an intimate role in people's interaction with nature. Their knowledge of transforming the forest to farm and farm to forest, and adoption of a nature intensive lifestyle never took place in the formal education in agriculture, although we have learnt that mixed cropping has benefited as an added merit to protect plant and soil and conserve moisture and nutritional balance of the soil (Davis, 1995). That the traditional knowledge is important for sustainable development and environmental maintenance has been one of the major events that caught attention in the 1992 Rio Earth Summit and has been documented in agenda 21 of the United Nations and International Biodiversity Convention. As these people have limited skills, their opportunity for alternative means of livelihood is highly restricted in the past. The erosion of community right was caused due to the survey method adopted by government to assess the status of land. Since in Orissa the plane table method has replaced the chain survey method, which does not accurately measure the land that remains above 10 per cent slope, the land is registered as government land by officially de-recognising the community rights. They, therefore, are quickly pushed further to poverty and other forms of exploitation with changes imposed on them and their commons.

One of the greatest facilitators of globalization is the GATT and free trade agreement of 1990, which was designed to move control of food production from small farmers to the hands of a few transnational corporations. Panda notes that GATT policies of trade liberalisation, imposition of intellectual property rights and import of agricultural products are causing displacement of large number of small subsistence farmers, mainly women, belonging to indigenous communities and have destroyed local food economies (1998). GATT intends the term 'trade' to include the intellectual property rights, services, investments, and agriculture. After many negotiations and deliberations by several countries in 1995 the Uruguay Round of Agreements came up. In India, policies of neo-liberalisation have started in the 1980s, which began to be implemented in the 1990s. On 31st December 1999, the Indian Government reached an agreement with the United States laying down a schedule for phasing out most of India's remaining quantitative restrictions on imports, although the deadline given by WTO was April 2003.

A few decades back the quantitative restrictions banned the import of certain items or required certain licences for such import or even place limits on the quantities that could be imported. However, by this agreement, Surjeet reports, 714 out of 1429 items became freely importable from 1st April 2000 and the remaining 715 from 1st April 2001. To help the native producers, the Government of India levied additional customs duties on items like milk powder (60%), wheat (80%), paddy (80%), broken rice (80%), maize (70%), etc., which has already been opposed by the imperial counties. It is also known that India cannot compete with America and European nations because their agriculture is highly subsidized. The rapid export expansion of goods and services reached its height during last decade from 4.7 trillion to 7.5 trillion dollars, that means an increase of 59.5 per cent. The share of export of the developing nations, accounting for around 10 per cent, has shown a decline trend. This implies that between the nations there is a sharp increase of inequality. The sectors like energy, telecommunication, mining, and transport, which hitherto remained Indian monopoly, are being siphoned to world market at a price suitable to outsider business houses. With regard to the tribal people, the exploitation of minerals, like Bauxite and iron ores causing devastation to the forest and the sources of water, and thereby to the forest dwellers, directly hit their livelihood resources and the people had to face bullets for Bauxite.

Since globalization refers to the process of integration of the world into one huge market with no entry and no exit barriers, the commons of the tribals, like forest can never escape from such clutches. Even political and geographical barriers become redundant. Ohmae observed that under this era of globalization two important event cropped up, such as, collapse of Soviet Union, and the second, spectacular rise of the South Asian tiger economies. Under the changed scenario the investment industry, information technology and the individual consumers have made the nation state redundant (Mishra, 2000). The anthropologists are now apprehensive of the tribal identities because the process of globalization might change the ethnic identities and could encourage faster process of assimilation of the distinct features of heterogeneity. The rule of market cannot be resisted and the cultural autonomy will be jeopardised. There could be displacement of knowledge and skill due to the physical displacement. Administrators with anthropological inclination become apprehensive of globalization. Taking the concrete examples from Bastar, Madhya Pradesh, Sharma on the basis of people's version writes that people's assertion is clear, and categorical command over their habitat is the only guarantee of their right to life with dignity reinforced by the Constitution and the international conventions. Therefore, where people have decided that commons are not saleable commodities, any tall promises for such resources cannot be accepted and therefore, in response to the globalization, people centred planned economic development needs to be reoriented. Otherwise, ethnic conflicts are inevitable and communalism will have different expressions in which there will be inherent fights between the cultural systems of tribal and others. To understand the people and their culture either cross-culturally or holistically the need of the hour for anthropologists is to change their mind to look up rather than down. Keeping the impact of globalization in mind, if we really study the tribal communities, who have been uprooted tangibly and intangibly from their habitat, the subjects like business anthropology, industrial anthropology, mining anthropology, anthropology of disaster management and the like must become the areas of interest.

REFERENCES

Agrawal, Anil and Narain, Sunita (1991), Technology Control, Global Warming and Environmental Colonialism: The WRI Report, *Social Action*, 41 (3).

Arensberg, C.M. (1978), *Theoretical Contribution of Industrial and Development Studies in Applied Anthropology in America*, In E.M. Eddy and W. L. Partridge (eds.), pp. 49-78, New York: Columbia University Press.

Baba, Marietta, L. (1986), *Business and Industrial Anthropology: An Overview National Association for Practice of Anthropology*, Bulletin 2, A Unit of American Anthropological Association.

Grey, Andrew (1991), *Between the Spice and the Melting Pot; Biodiversity Conservation and its Impact on Indigenous People*, Copenhagen IWGIA.

Mishra, S.K. (2000), The New Millennium: Challenges and the Total Quality Culture, In P. Panda (ed) *On Managing Excellence in the Dawn of the 21st Century*, ISTD MTI Sambalpur Seminar Proceedings, pp. 63-68.

Misra, K.K. (1987), *Social Structure and Change among the Ho of Orissa*, Delhi, Gian Publishing House.

Panda, Premananda (2000), Is Globalization an Age of Transition? An insight to its Managerial Implications in the dawn of 21st century, Paper Presented in Eastern Regional Seminar on Managing Excellence in the Dawn of 21st century. ISTD Sambalpur, Chapter Orissa.

Panda, S.M. (1998), Indigenous Peoples and Environmental Crisis in the 1990s: Experience from Asia, Paper presented in 14th ICAES, Virginia USA.

Shiva, V. (1988), *Staying Alive: Women, Ecology and Survival in India*, New Delhi: Kali for Women.

Sharma, B.D. (1995), *Globalization: The Tribal Encounter*, New Delhi: Har-Anand Publications.

Terpstra, V. and K. David (1985), *The Cultural Environment of International Business*, 2nd Edition, Cincinnati: South Western Publishing Co.

7

Indigenous People in India
A Case for Reforms of Property Rights and Empowerment

P.K. BISWAS

Introduction

India is a developing country. The majority of its population lives in rural areas. Since independence there has been considerable activities in the field of economic development. The government and various international donor agencies for the upliftment of the poor have spent a vast amount of money. And yet the level of development remains alarmingly low. There is still much poverty, malnutrition, unemployment, and under-employment. This is truer for the rural poor among whom the indigenous people or tribals constitute a significant proportion. These indigenous communities in India largely occupy the forested regions, where for a long period in their history they have lived in isolation from the mainstream of life but in harmony with nature.

The forests support development of indigenous people, which can sustain economic, environmental and social well-being. Development is not merely in terms of economic growth (GNP/GDP), but essentially social development, with emphasis on equitable distribution, freedom of expression and qualitative aspect of life. The contribution of forest is immense in terms of ecological conservation and economic sustenance of the poor in general and indigenous people specifically.

Contributions of Forests for Development of Indigenous People

It is a fact that indigenous people or tribals and forest are intimately related. They have been co-existing with mutual benefit to each other since time immemorial. Tribal life is connected, in one way or the other with forests right from birth to death. Their folklore, rites and rituals revolve around the forest. In times of distress the forest is the last resort for them. Even in areas where forests do not exist, indigenous people continue to periodically visit the distant forests to procure traditional requirements. Apart from this, some financial benefits accrue to them from the collection and sale of non-timber forest products (NTFP). Forests are their economic resource base and occupy a central position in tribal economy. In other words, tribals and forests have a symbiotic relationship.

For several tribal groups living in or near forests, about 30 per cent of their diet is derived from forest resources (*i.e.* wild vegetables, tubers, fruits, nuts, bamboo shoots, small animals, etc.). Medicinal plants are important in the primary health care system. The indigenous people have developed interesting, and often sophisticated knowledge system of ethno-medicine and use of a vast variety of plants for medicinal purposes (NFAP, 1999).

It is a recognised fact that, forests essentially provide three different kinds of benefits: *job and incomes,* often needed to supplement inadequate returns from agriculture; *produce* such as fuelwood, fodder and building materials for the homes; and less directly but just as importantly—a range of *environmental benefits,* without which other activities, such as agriculture, might be impossible (FAO, 1979).

Forest is the second largest land use after agriculture and it is a source of goods and services used by the indigenous people. In remote forest fringe villages about 300 million tribals and other local people depend on forest for their subsistence and livelihood and about 70 per cent of them depend on fuelwood to meet their domestic energy needs (Biswas, 2000). Tribals and other less favourably placed groups—depend on forests and the wastelands, which are suitable for fuel and fodder trees and various kinds of shrubs and grasses (Chowdhry, 1983). Without doubt forests play a significant role in the development and sustenance of indigenous people whose existence depends on a close and ecologically sustainable relationship with the forests they inhabit (Biswas, 1988).

The agricultural sector, which is also important for survival of indigenous communities, depends almost entirely on livestock for the energy needed for various farm operations. The economics of maintaining cattle, sheep, and goats is largely dependent on forests as a source of fodder—be it leaf or fruit fodder.

Wood (timber) is also required for making various types of ploughs and agricultural implements, each with a different life span. The bullock-cart is the main means of transport in the rural sector. According to one estimate, there are about 13 million bullock-carts in India, which accounts for an investment of about Rs. 30,000 million. About 20 million people find direct or indirect employment in the bullock-cart transportation system in India.

The indigenous communities also require small timber for the construction of houses. Timber, bamboo, grass, creepers and barks are useful for this purpose.

Forest offers scope for the development of cottage industries for the tribals. Many trees provide source of raw materials, such as *tassar* and silk production, rearing milch cattle, *pattal* (leaf-plate) making, basket weaving, oil, papermaking and others.

As mentioned before, the potential of NTFP for poverty alleviation among tribals is tremendous. The indigenous communities collect various kinds of forest products throughout the year to sustain their employment and supplement their income. Activities related to NTFP provide employment during lean periods in the agricultural cycle and provide a buffer against risk and household emergencies. These constitute a part of the household activities where old women and children also contribute and in several cases can be the main source of income. Therefore, tribal life is profoundly affected by whatever happens to the forests.

Indigenous People and Management of Forest

Management means the organization and control of an enterprise or undertaking. Forest management from this point of view broadly refers to the organization and control of access to and utilization of trees, woodlots, plantations and natural forest and associated resources including benefits derived from them. It involves professional foresters, institutions like village level organizations, NGOs and the indigenous people.

In the context of forest management, we have to understand the legal status of forest as a resource for the indigenous people. Forest has essentially been the state property. The high profile of the state in the forestry sector, and in particular, its control over reserved forests dates back to the colonial period. The Indian Forest Act of 1865 was the first attempt at establishing monopoly-holding rights by the state and these were formalized and made explicit in the subsequent Acts of 1878 and 1927. Under these, the state was allowed to demarcate valuable tracts of forests and its exclusive exploitation.

The inhabitants of these areas—mostly the indigenous people or tribal communities—were deemed to derive their customary usage of the forest and its products not from a right of ownership but from a limited and contingent privilege. The state, in this framework, was thus able to assert its rights to absolute ownership, and this was done through the reservation of certain forest areas. Therefore, in this context, it is essential to understand the meaning of property. "Property is a right to a benefit stream that is only as secure as the duty of all others to respect the conditions that protect that stream. When one has a right, one has the expectations in both the law and in practice that their claims will be respected by these with duty" (Bromley and Cernea, 1989). Hence it is the use of land or some other resource in relation to others that is central theme in property definition. The bare fact of ownership, then, is not as critical as the relationship with, and the expectation of, others who are associated with it. The right to use or not to use a property, or resource, implies inclusion and exclusion, *i.e.* rights of access. As evident, resources are a fundamental aspect of property use and property rights.

The forest area is shrinking considerably causing further poverty and misery for the indigenous communities. While the scale of deforestation has in the recent period emerged as a matter of widespread national concern, the substantive measures that have been initiated for reversing this trend have been limited in scope and efficacy. Therefore, there is a considerable debate as to whether forest area has to be covered as state property or as a private property or as a property of indigenous people.

The case for state ownership or, at least, state management of forests is hinged on a number of factors. Firstly, forest management is associated with a wide range of externalities that impinge on the economy not just of proximate producers but also of the economy as a whole, as with the relationship between forest cover and climate. In general, it can be said that forests provide, if maintained, external benefits to the rest of the eco-system. Any loss in the value of the benefit—a function of the rate of depletion—would therefore tend to exceed, often substantially, the loss in inter-temporal benefits experienced by the person or institution controlling the actual forest resource. Secondly, it can be argued that the management of forests requires a level of professional training and scientific competence that lies outside the capacities of potential private owners or indigenous people. Thirdly, the time horizons for forest management and the spatial requirements for an efficient, conjoint exploitation of the resource through harvesting and replanting favour state ownership and investment. Private rights would either be too fragmented and hence inefficient or else would need to be too large, thereby running counter to the general policy regarding land ceilings. Fourthly, the ecological variety of Indian forests is only likely to be preserved in context of state management. Private entrepreneurs would tend to replace diverse stock by fast growing varieties. Fifthly, state ownership allows for major economies of scale and a longer-term planning framework. Lastly, state ownership ultimately allows for a wider and more just distribution of revenues derived from forest products through the overall structure of Government spending. Although this effect could be achieved through the taxation of private returns, this would imply major revision of the basis of public finance in the country, let alone a more satisfactory control over 'leakages'.

Although each of these arguments contain attractive features and, in summation, would appear to offer a strong case for state ownership, that case remains strongly dependent on the degree to which these attributes can be fulfilled and sustained. After all, state ownership is largely argued for as a more efficient outcome, rather than in terms of any supposedly ethical superiority to private ownership. In this regard, all available evidence points unequivocally to the fact that state ownership has been unable to sustain the basis of India's forest resources. While some would argue that this has been because of the weakness in the construct of state ownership, consolidation of state monopoly would appear to run into difficult, probably insoluble problems.

To that extent, the very same issue that necessarily predominates in any discussion of the demand for timber by indigenous communities comes to the fore in the general discussion of the relative virtues of state ownership. For although it could be argued that both in terms of research and actual management practice, the Forest Department's monopoly has yielded poor and very limited results, the nub of the question of state ownership remains the degree to which the necessary conditions for an efficient utilization of exclusive rights can be consistently met.

Tenurial Rights for Indigenous Communities

If state control over forests has proven to be an inefficient means for their management, let alone retention, attention needs to be given to the processes by which a set of different economic signals get transmitted to potential exploiters of the resources. This requires above all a radical approach to the system of property rights itself. As the aim of any reform must be to harmonize to the greatest extent possible the social and private rates of return from forestry activity where time-preferences are the key issue, this implies a more graded and subtle use of controls and contingent rights. In the era of globalization, one argument would be to say that private property rights and a market in land and trees would be the most simple and efficient outcome. There is plentiful evidence from Europe and elsewhere that forests can be maintained in a private ownership context and that the privatization of rewards ensures the satisfactory enforcement of rights. The state, precisely because of its amorphous and disparate nature is inherently a weak vessel for the physical, let alone psychological, enforcement of exclusive control.

This argument runs into a number of problems in the Indian context. Firstly, private management of trees has customarily been associated with plantation or specialized husbandry. Secondly, given the political difficulties of establishing properties outside the usual land reform parameters, there are problems associated with the wrapping of rights. Forest management clearly has considerable potential for scale of economies and, given the ecology of most remaining Indian forests, the working areas is relatively large. Thirdly, there remains the problem of the forest communities. They lack, in general, both capital and expertise. Even if forestland was sold or leased to outside agencies, this would still raise the problem of what to do with forest communities. Both practical and ethical considerations strongly suggest that the latter must be actively included in any reform of the current system.

This is clearly evident in the case of Madhya Pradesh where forest area is substantial and tribal population also is substantial. Wherever there is good forest cover there is also heavy concentration of tribal people. Consider the following demographic feature of Madhya Pradesh:

Tribal Life Revolves Around Forest in Madhya Pradesh

Total population of M.P.	:	6.038 crores
Villages	:	51,806
Forest Area	:	32.3%
Forest Fringe Villages		20,000 approximately
Tribal Population		22% (of this 90% live in these villages)
Population below Poverty line	:	44% (80% live in forest areas)
Cattle Population	:	3.3 crores
Forest dependent Livestock	:	1.5 crores.

Source: Govt. of Madhya Pradesh & Provisional Population Tables of Census 2001.

Consider the characteristic resource endowments of most *adivasi*/indigenous forest based households. Each household in M.P. roughly commands on average between 2-10 acres. Although such holdings are large by Indian Standards, the soil quality is often low and the terrain hostile to successful husbandry. In some areas, such as in Orissa shifting cultivation (*podu*) remains the norm, although with continuously decreasing fallow periods. In almost all cases, the cultivated land is rain-fed and the intensity of land use is low. Most commonly, a single monsoon crop of paddy (*dhana)* is raised and this generates intense demands for household labour in the months of June/July and September/October. For the remaining nine months of the year household labour is normally employed on Forest Department work, in the collection of non-timber forest produce (particularly *Tendu Patta* collection) and work for other Government Departments, especially the P.W.D. Much of this non-farm work is also seasonal and the result is that under-employment levels remain high. With the exception of a limited amount of mining sector employment or else work in the urban industrial centres—such as Rourkela, Jamshedpur or Bhilai—job opportunities in the proximity of the forest areas remain limited. In some tracts, such as in much of Chotanagpur this disequilibrium has become so profound that out-migration has for long become a major recourse for household members of these indigenous communities.

Income from wage employment—largely from the Forest Department—can thus be complemented by a combination of remittances and other transactions. These latter are mostly through the sale of wood, either to urban traders/dealers or else at the periodic *hats* (markets). Despite a long history of indebtedness to local *sahukars* (money-lenders), low household income levels and high rates of under-employment, the tribal economies have generally been marked by the relative affluence of basic requirements—principally fuel and food—than by the chronic income constrained conditions of many poor rural and urban households outside the forest areas. Yet, the denudation of the forest cover gravely undermines this condition of 'primitive plenty'. Loss of fuel wood and tree cover is accompanied by a parallel loss of employment, either in Forest Department work or through the collection of non-timber forest produce.

If we consider the development indices in the selected tribal areas of Madhya Pradesh the picture is dismal, as revealed by Table 7.1.

Table 7.1: Forest, Tribals, Poverty and Development Correlations in Selected Districts of Madhya Pradesh

District	*Forest Area (in %)*	*Tribal Population (in %)*	*Tribal Literacy (in %)*	*HDI Rank*
Betul	39.0	37.5	17.2	41
Chhindwara	37.0	34.5	21.3	17
Mandla	43.0	60.8	27.2	38
Seoni	37.0	37.0	26.6	25
Shahdol	39.0	46.3	17.6	24
Sidhi	39.0	30.4	12.5	26
West Nimar	33.0	46.2	14.1	44
Dhar	16.0	53.5	16.2	16
Jhabua	19.0	85.7	10.9	45

Note: HDI—Human Development Index & M.P. has 45 districts.
Source: Madhya Pradesh Human Development Report, 1998.

It is evident that the indigenous communities or tribal people who are heavily dependent on forest resources, their development is inadequate and further loss of forest will impoverish their conditions.

Conclusion

From the foregoing discussions it is evident that there has to be reform of property rights in forest management for poverty alleviation among the indigenous people. Sustainable forest management is the key to the sustainable development of indigenous people.

Even in the age of liberalization and globalization it has to be understood that there can be no financial assets if there are no ecological assets. Sustainable development is increasingly linked to environmental conservation. Here, it is apt to quote a Tribal Chief who said:

Only after the last tree has been cut down
Only after the last river has been poisoned
Only after the last fish has been caught
Only then will you find that money cannot be eaten.

Therefore, there has to be a harmonious balance between conservation of forests and development of indigenous communities through livelihood security.

In this context, it is important to note that the National Forest Policy of 1988 recognized that "the life of tribals and other communities living within and near forests, revolves around forests. The rights and concessions enjoyed by them should be fully protected. Their domestic requirements of fuel-wood, fodder, minor forest produce and construction timber should be the first charge on forest products" (NFP, 1988). Conservation and indigenous people's livelihoods are integral part of sustainable development.

The NFP, 1988 has been further strengthened by the 1st June 1990 circular of Ministry of Environment and Forests, Government of India. It has highlighted both the need and process for involving village communities and voluntary agencies in the protection, development and management of forests.

This facilitated the formation of village level committees known as village forest committee or forest protection committee. This strategy is known as Joint Forest Management (JFM) where Government and people are partners in forest protection. Though by the end of 1999, in India, 22 States, which have 80 per cent of country's forestland and 92 per cent of tribal population, have adopted JFM as main strategy (Biswas, 2000) the empowerment of indigenous communities is a far cry.

The Panchayat (Extension to Scheduled Areas) Act, 1996 also has provision wherein communities to have ownership of NTFPs. And yet the tribal communities are deprived of the rights for management of forest products, which determine their socio-economic existence.

In keeping with the philosophy of decentralized governance, people's involvement in decision-making process and consequent empowerment is crucial. Therefore, tenurial rights for indigenous people must be secured. The following factors may be considered for effective indigenous/local management control systems. The main institutional issues are:

- The provision for secure tenure rights to indigenous people.
- The development of systems of regulation and enforcement based on local decision-making.

There is a greater need to formalize community based management systems both at the local and state level. Culture of indigenous people and dynamics of social processes have to be understood properly. Sociological/Social Anthropological insights, perceptions and knowledge are, therefore, instrumental and essential for bringing reform in property rights for sustainable development of indigenous people.

REFERENCES

Biswas, P.K. (1988), Sociological Issues in Forestry, *The Indian Journal of Social Sciences*, 1 (2).

Biswas, P.K. (2000), *Joint Forest Management for Sustainable Rural Development*, IIFM, Bhopal, Mimeographed.

Bromley, D.W. & Cernea, M.M. (1989), *The Management of Common Property Natural Resources: Some Conceptual and Operational Fallacies*, World Bank Discussion Paper 57, Washington D.C., US.

Chowdhry, Kamla (1983), *Social Forestry and the Rural Poor*, Discussion Paper Series No. 10, Ford Foundation, New Delhi.

FAO (1979), *Forestry for Local Community Development*, FAO Forestry Paper No. 7, Rome.

Government of India (1988), *National Forest Policy*, New Delhi.

Government of India (1999), *National Forestry Action Programme—India*, Ministry of Environment and Forests, New Delhi.

Government of Madhya Pradesh (1998), *M.P. Human Development Report*, Bhopal.

8

Changing Status of Common Property Resources in Tribal Areas

V.N.V.K. SASTRY

Two of my experiences basically serve as background for this article.

Experience I

In the year 1968, immediately after completion of my Masters Degree in Anthropology from Andhra University, Visakhapatnam in Andhra Pradesh, I started my research work for the Ph.D. degree in the tribal areas of West Godavari District in Andhra Pradesh. While working there, many Koya tribals became my friends. One of the Koya key informers was Erra Kannayya (Kannayya with a fair skin to be differentiated from his brother with the same name who had a black skin—Nalla Kannayya). During the discussions one of those days, he said, "you people (plains men) befooled us by showing our faces in the mirror". I could not understand the significance of his statement and asked him to elaborate on what he said. He explained that the tribals were living in forests and were having their own way of life since generations. But when they came into contact with the outsiders, especially the money-lenders and traders, the first thing that was introduced by them was cosmetics, after showing their face in a mirror and convincing them that how they could look smarter by using cosmetics.

Further, the forest contractors, their clerks, lorry drivers, etc. have enticed the tribal women by taking them in their lorries and jeeps to the nearby towns to show movies. This is the starting point of downfall of the tribal domain, he said. The wants increased without commensurate increase in the means. The tribal women were lured and kept as concubines by non-tribals with an eye on their property. The money-lenders alienated tribal land by charging exorbitant rates of interest by manipulating/creating records. Rich black cotton soils and common properties of the tribals were also encroached upon by the outsiders. Some of his observations can be directly related to the changes in the tribal areas while other changes that occurred there are due to policy changes by the government. However, his point that the outsiders have encroached into the tribal life, property and domain by exploiting gullible tribals is undisputable. Tribal societies, which are very conscious about their territorial integrity and cultural identity all over the world, and also in India, have been resisting outside interference for several decades. In one of my articles I have discussed in detail the course of tribal discontent in Andhra Pradesh for the last 200 years because of the migration of non-tribal populations into their territory and exploiting them to the extent of transforming them as beggars in their homeland.

Experience II

In the year 1993, nearly after 25 years of my last encounter with the Koya, I came across similar incidents, but with a more forceful argument from a Koya tribal of East Godavari District (adjacent to the West Godavari District and inhabited by the same tribe mentioned in Experience I). This was when I accompanied a team of Work Bank Consultants, most of whom were non-Indians. Besides collecting information on my own, I also acted as an interpreter for the foreign consultants. The consultants were insisting on participatory approach during the discussions with the tribals. The discussions went on a number of issues relating to culture, present and future development needs, etc. Suddenly an old man in his 70s got up and expressed his desire to speak. He was encouraged to speak as we were already in the participatory mood. He narrated how the tribals of his area under the leadership of Shri Alluri Seetaramaraju fought against the British rule in the 1920s. He also narrated how they opposed payment of taxes, free labour, etc. inflicted on them by the British. The country got its independence in 1947 and for the last 50 years they had been waiting for development to reach their areas, but in vain. In his opinion, the independence should have brought development to them first, as they were the most backward and fought against the British. No road was laid, no bus was coming, no electricity was provided, no doctor was available and no school was functioning—he complained. Yet they were patiently waiting for the benefits of freedom to trickle down to them. But to their shock, the white-men were brought back into their areas. He yelled at the author (as he accompanied the team) "why did you bring back the white men"? Everybody was shocked. By the time everybody recovered from the shock, the old man left the meeting in disgust, murmuring something. The strong feeling of independence was still alive among the old generation tribals, while the educated were again falling prey to the machination of the white men, was his worry.

These two instances prompted me to study the losses occurred to tribal domain. The request to write an article provided me the opportunity to recapitulate from my notes. Some of the observations are as follows:

Land and Forest

Land and forest are two principal sources of livelihood for the tribals. From the food gathering to settled agriculture stage of economy, the dependence on forest varies. The tribal societies have evolved a culture of their own around these activities. Several values, beliefs, ownership patterns are part of this culture. These were handed down from generation to generation; the concepts changed over the period but more rapidly, ever since the tribal societies were exposed to the outside societies. The interference or imposition of outside values on tribal culture through legislation, market interventions, etc. also created problems for them.

Traditionally, each of the tribal villages had a culturally defined territory, the boundaries of which were identified by natural objects like hill streams or hill ranges or trees, etc. They were called by different names as Haddu, Sivaru, etc. All the natural resources within the territory belonged to the village community (common property). The boundary gods protected the villagers and the village from evil forces, wild animals etc., they believed. The natural resources like forest and land were allocated to the villagers by the village community and they had 'usufruct' right over the resources, the *de jure* ownership remaining with the community. If any of the members of the community could not utilize the common resources allocated to him, the community could re-allocate them to any other needy person. The grown up and married children of the families who established a separate household of their own could also approach the community to allocate some resources out of the common property. Thus the community ensured that all the interests of all members of the community were taken care of and there was no feeling of destitution. Changes have come about on the ownership patterns over the years. Declaration of all natural forests as Reserve Forests by the British through the first Forest Act transferred the legal ownership from community to the state. Initially there was no problem, as forests were in plenty and inaccessible. The representatives of the state like the forest guards could not reach the interior villages frequently and thus there was no threat to the traditional ownership patterns and social organization of utilization of resources. However, there were some instances like Rampa Bhupati of Rampa area in East Godavari District where the Zamindar exploited the tribal chiefs by levying taxes on forest produce and they had to revolt in despair. Similarly in Adilabad District tribes revolted against the Nizam's Government under the leadership of Komaram Bhimu.

After India attained independence, the hold of the government over forest increased, while certain concessions were also given to the tribals, especially for collection of Minor Forest Produce (MFP) for livelihood, timber for construction of houses, etc. As Dhebar Commission, the first Commission appointed in 1960 by Government of India after 10 years of existence of the Constitution of India, noted that the rights of tribals were taken away and concessions were given. The effect was that the 'lords of forest' had to be at the mercy of a forest guard who could impose fines by falsely implicating them.

The tribals who were free to select a hill slope for shifting cultivation using slash and burn technique could no more do so, as the forest now belonged to the government and the practice was banned. No alternative occupation was planned by the government till the 1980s when these lands were converted into Joint Forest Management lands after the amendment to 1980 Forest Act was made in 1988. The period from 1960-90 was a period of turmoil for the tribals as the Joint Forest Management activities really took off after 1990. The welcome aspect of this policy was that the tribals, who became strangers earlier in their own land, were then officially became joint partners with the government in the management of forests. However, even now, the ownership is with the government with joint management with the tribal communities and the benefits to the tribals as provided in the orders of the government are yet to flow to the communities in a substantial manner.

As a part of the state policy, the government has declared state monopoly over the procurement of Minor Forest Produce (MFP) from the tribals in Scheduled Areas. For this purpose, the government have recognized the Girijan Cooperative Corporation (GCC) as the sole agency and notified 27 items of MFP for monopoly procurement. This was done with a good intention of protecting the tribal interest from usurious private traders. Over the years, the trade of Minor Forest Produce (MFP) became a commercial proposition changing from the original welfare objective. The profit motive of GCC, perhaps as a part of the liberalization policy, has slowly driven it to concentrate on a few items like gum. No doubt, this approach helped the gum pickers in earning more initially. The trees in forest, which were common property, became individual properties. Due to lack of knowledge, the tribals thought that by making deeper cuts into the trees, they would get more gum. The eagerness to earn more ultimately killed many trees. Realizing the loss of a large number of trees, the government started training the tribals to carefully tap the gum and also collect it without any contamination. Had this process been started earlier, in anticipation of the problem, things would have been different.

Slowly the concept of individual property percolated to other items of Minor Forest Produce (MFP), which are having market value. In a recent survey by the author in Mahboobnagar upper plateau forest areas, it is found that a variety of ownership patterns by the individual families have emerged gradually. The tamarind tree or a honey comb on the tree located in the premises of a house now belongs to the house owner while those located in the forest still belonged to all members of the community. The other important aspect of this changing ownership pattern is that the married children are inheriting the trees from their parents. This is in contrast with the concept of common property resources existing earlier.

The *beedi* (country cigar) leaves trade has become one of the lucrative trades in the recent years. These leaves (*tendu*) are mostly available in the forest areas inhabited by the tribals. As a part of the traditional concept of territory, the *beedi (tuniki)* leaves are also part of the common property. In one of the studies made by the author in Tuniki Cheruvu near Bhadrachalam in the Khammam District, it was found that this common property was being encroached upon by the outsiders from the tribals, who were the original collectors of *beedi* leaves. The quality of leaves in Bhadrachalam area is good and therefore, they fetch higher rates compared to the leaves collected from other areas. The forest contractors in the earlier period and the Forest Department in recent years are opening 'kallam' (procurement centre) to purchase the leaves. There is no rule that they should purchase only from the tribals. Therefore, the aggressive non-tribals have started driving away the tribals in the collection season from the villages for a week or so and collecting the entire quantity for selling to 'kallam'. When the procurement target gets over, the kallams are closed. The tribals are at loss. A policy on par with the GCC policy that kallams would collect *beedi* leaves only through tribal cooperatives and from the tribals only could help them economically and restore the common property rights of the tribals to some extent.

Earlier, the Rajah of Jeypore, informer, Vizagapatnam Agency, supported by the tribal chiefs, Zamindars in Godavari Agency and Gond tribal chiefs in Adilabad District were the *de jure* owners of the entire land, but the *de facto* ownership continued with the village community. However, the British appointed Muttadars (also from the tribal communities), Zamindars (mostly non-tribals) and Mansabdars, etc. to collect taxes, while the Nizams appointed Deshmukhs and Deshpandes. There were also villages or lands given as *Inams* (gift) to the outsiders by the Nizams. Later on, to collect land revenue and maintain the records, Patels, Patwaris, Municiffs and Karnams as village officers were appointed. This only strengthened the hold of the British/Nizams and those appointed by them over the common property of the tribals. The village officers cornered most of the land in tribal areas and passed them on to their family friends or relatives.

The Muttas, Mahals, Malguzaris, etc. were treated on par with Zamindaris in independent India and in course of time, they also were abolished. The survey and settlement operations, which were taken up later on mostly, helped conferment of titles for the non-tribal settlers. It made no difference to the tribals, who were already enjoying lands as per the recognition of the community. The conferment of individual titles for lands to tribals only furthered land alienation, as individuals who had only usufruct right of ownership earlier could not alienate community owned land to outsiders. It is not surprising to note that as many as 2.5 lakh acres of land in the Scheduled Areas are now under the possession of the non-tribals. As a contrast, in Chenchu inhabited areas in the Nallamala forests in Prakasam District, where the Forest Department allotted lands (called as enclosures) for cultivation by the tribals by keeping the ownership with it could not be alienated to others by the tribals. They are at best given by the tribals on crop sharing lease to non-tribals on an annual basis.

The common property land in tribal villages also included grazing land, mostly located in the adjacent forest areas. While grasslands disappeared due to forest degradation in general, permitting cattle in large numbers from far away rural villages for grazing has only reduced the availability of grass to the local livestock populations. Even some of the tribals are also engaged by the outsiders to tend their cattle. As the grazing land in the forest belonged to the Forest Department of the government legally, tribal ownership pattern does not work any more. Outside the reserve forest areas, grazing land is converted by tribals into agricultural land due to the increase in their population. In either case, the common property resources are slowly going out of control of the community.

Thus the changes in common property resources in tribal areas brought about several problems for them. As these changes are irreversible, a detailed examination of all policies is required to suggest protective and promotive policies for the tribals in the changing context.

REFERENCES

Sastry, V.N.V.K. (1984), Institutionalized Encroachment on Man-Nature Relationship and Impact on Primitive Tribal Groups, In *Development Strategy for Primitive Tribal Groups*, Hyderabad: Tribal Culture Training and Research Institute, Government of Andhra Pradesh.

Sastry, V.N.V.K. (1985), The Three Tribal Villages in Andhra Pradesh, Mimeo, Hyderabad: Tribal Culture Training and Research Institute, Government of Andhra Pradesh.

Sastry, V.N.V.K. (1991a), Role of Gum in Primitive Chenchu Tribal Economy, Paper presented at the National Seminar on Gum Karaya, Hyderabad.

Sastry, V.N.V.K. (1991b), Evolution of Scheduled Areas and Changes in the Muttadari System, Hyderabad: Tribal Culture Training and Research Institute, Government of Andhra Pradesh.

Sastry, V.N.V.K. (1992), Evaluation of Loaning Programme of the Girijan Co-operative Corporation, Visakhapatnam: Girijan Co-operative Corporation Ltd., Government of Andhra Pradesh.
Sastry, V.N.V.K. (1993), Chenchu Food Gatherers and Hunters of Nallamala Forests—Problems of Transition, *Man & Life*, 19 (1 & 2).
Sastry, V.N.V.K. (1996), *Forests and Tribals in Andhra Pradesh*, Hyderabad: Tribal Culture Training and Research Institute, Government of Andhra Pradesh.

9

Tribal Economy and Collective Management of the Village Common

A Case Study from a Drought Prone District of Rajasthan

BINAY SHARMA, AMOL BHOLERAO and AMITABH PANDEY

Introduction

Poverty in the rural areas is linked with the ill management of the common resources available in the village (Beck, 1994; Jodha, 1986). The resources poor region has more poor population. It becomes even more important when the community is a tribe, since the tribal community has more dependence on the common resources for their livelihood. The rural development approach of the country adopted a new strategy of converting the open access resources of the village into common and encouraging collective management approach for the resources by the directly dependent population on it. Unlike in other places where the commons were privatized by dividing them into small land holding of the landless population, here the resources were collectively managed by the communities.

In the drought prone state of the country such programmes were launched, where the local NGOs were to assist the communities in the management of village commons and derive the economic benefits from the produce of the common. Such an approach was aimed at developing the degraded resources and managing them more effectively and efficiently. This was during the year of 1986 when the approach of common property resources was gaining significance in the natural resource management and advocating the involvement of the community in the resources management (Malhotra and Poffenberger, 1989; Chopra *et al.*, 1989; Singh, 1994). This paper looks into the economic and social impacts of collective management of village commons in the village economic system.

Methodology

The State of Rajasthan was selected for its endemic drought prone nature. Through the help of the NGO involved in assisting the communities in collective management, the Patedi village was identified for the study. The criteria of selection of the village were the duration of the programme, *i.e.* 15 years as well as community composition. With the help of schedule the general information of the households were collected. The information on management of the common was collected by means of interview of committee members, key persons like executive members, etc. Focus group discussion was also conducted to know the conflicting issues, participation issues and benefit sharing mechanism.

Study Area

Patedi village is in the Bichhiwara block of Dungarpur District of Rajasthan. The village is at a distance of 20 km from Dungarpur town and a tar road connects it. The village comes under Balwara Panchayat. It consists of approximately 80 households. Over 90 per cent of the population of the village is tribal with a few SC families. The total population of the village is 341 (according to 2001 census). This village is divided into three falas: Katara fala, Navgaraha fala and Sukhamuda fala. The Bhil Tribe has three sub-castes, namely: Katara, Koted and Manar. The division of falas has been done according to the sub-castes. The village is known all over the district for its high literacy. This village has the credit of having several teachers, nurses and engineers also in the district. The major occupation of villagers in this village is agriculture but due to high literacy rate villagers prefers permanent jobs. The village has a unique feature: it is a Gram Dani village. In the Gram Dani all the works of the Panchayat is carried out by the President who is elected along with seven other members, except for the development work which the statutory Panchayat carries out.

Village Common

The community pastureland, the use right of which belongs to all the villagers was lying barren in the year 1985. There was no grass for the animals to graze and only a few trees were present. Under the DPAP programme, the State Government with the local Panchayat constructed a boundary wall in the drought years of 1985-86 to provide employment to local people. According to the villagers, the people of adjoining village, Balwara, wanted to encroach upon this plot of land. There was a quarrel between these two villages over this land, which was later solved by the local police. There were around 42 households in 1985 and out of these 38 households who spent money and fought for their common land from this village and hence, it was decided that only these families would have rights on the common land. These families then approached PEDO (People Education and Development Organisation), a locally based NGO to start plantation works. PEDO started its works on the promise of the people that the plantation will be properly managed and protected. In 1986 PEDO initiated physical works of digging trenches and pits and later planting of saplings (Table 9.1).

Table 9.1: Amount Spent on Patedi CLP

S. No.	*Name of the Activity*	*Length/Nos.*	*Quantity*
1.	Pit digging	14,768 Nos.	907.01 cum
2.	Stone fencing	91 Mt.	61.02 cum
3.	Planting	14,768 Nos	–
Mandays—1,050		Total Amount—Rs. 14,459	

Source: Secondary data.

Results and Discussion

Collective Management of Village Common

Management and protection are the two major aspects of any plantation. Keeping this concept in mind Patedi CLP (Common Land Plantation) management committee was formed in the first year of plantation. The members of the committee have not changed over the years and only if a person dies then only there is a replacement. The new member is elected by consensus of all the people in a meeting. There are a total of seven members in the management committee (Table 9.2). One of the seven members is the treasurer who keeps all the records of the grass cutting and the total expenditure related to the plantation. There is no common fund and whenever some work for the plantation has to be done the committee members call for a meeting of all the beneficiaries. Everybody is told that this work needs to be done and everybody has to pay a fixed amount decided by the committee. Whenever the watchman needs to be paid every beneficiary has to pay ten or fifteen rupees as decided by the management committee.

Table 9.2: Management Committee Members of Patedi CLP

S. No.	*Name*	*Sex*	*Post*
1.	Vijay Pal Katara	M	President
2.	Ramchandra Navalji Koted	M	Vice-President
3.	Dhaneshwar Hera	M	Treasurer
4.	Kaluram Kuber	M	Member
5.	Amri Arjan	F	Member
6.	Rupali Shivlal	F	Member
7.	Ramlal Vijaydas	M	Member

Source: Management Committee Records.

The executive committee along with the beneficiaries has decided that the plantation will be closed for grazing on the onset of monsoon (just after the first rains). This will remain closed till the cutting of grass is over, which takes place in November. After this they open it for free grazing but due to drought since last three years they keep it close after cutting and then open for grazing in the months of March and April when there is a severe shortage of fodder. It is kept open for a minimum of two months, as all the grass and fodder is finished in these two months.

The beneficiary families do protection in Patedi CLP and there is no hired watchman from January 2001. Every family is assigned duty for one-day and a male member has to go to the plantation early morning and stay there till evening. A stick is rotated in the village, which means that the particular house with the stick has to keep a watch that day and in the evening it is passed to the next house. Earlier the watchman was paid Rs. 550 per month for the last three years. As the boundary wall of this plantation has broken from all sides, protection becomes a difficult task, as the area of plantation is big. The protection is more difficult during the season when there is free grazing, during which people also have to be seen so that they do not cut the trees. The committee has also decided a fine for cattle grazing. There has not been any incident when a person is actually fined. A few times the committee has left the charged person with a warning.

Ecological Status of the Common

The net survival rate of the plantation is 60 per cent, which compared to other plantations is considered to be good. This is because of the literacy and good decision-making of the management committee and the village as a whole. The Patedi CLP has a rich growth of *Acacia catechu* (Khair) and *Acacia nilotica* (Desi babul). According to the villagers these two species are most useful as their leaves are used for feeding the cattle and the wood can be used for different purposes, like making of ploughs, bullock carts and for construction purpose. The bushes are also used for fencing. The CLP is also rich in Eucalyptus (nilgiri) species, which according to the villagers, can be sold for high rates when they are felled. *Prosopis julioflora* (Julioflora) is another species, which is abundant in the plantation (Table 9.3). *Acacia leucopholea* (Rijhwa) is the major species, which has grown naturally in this plantation (Table 9.4).

Table 9.3: List of Trees at Present in Patedi CLP

S. No.	*Botanical Name*	*Local Name*	*No. of Trees*
1.	*Eucalyptus*	Nilgiri	3523
2.	*Pithecolobium dulec*	Jungle Jalebi	637
3.	*Prosopis julioflora*	Juliflora	5143
4.	*Dalbergia sissoo*	Shishum	468
5.	*Azadirachta indica*	Neem	416
6.	*Acacia catechu*	Khair	7461
7.	*Dendrocalamus strictus*	Baas	56
8.	*Leucaena leucocephala*	Subabul	513
9.	*Acacia nilotica*	Desi Babul	7435
10.	*Acacia holosiricea*	Acacia	782
Total trees at present			26434

Source: Management Committee Records.

Table 9.4: List of Trees Naturally Grown in Patedi CLP

S. No.	*Botanical Name*	*Local Name*	*No. of Trees*
1.	*Zuzyphus jujuba*	Ber	442
2.	*Dichrostrachy cinrea*	Emna	743
3.	*Acacia leucopholea*	Rijhwa	2136
4.	*Procopis cinararia*	Khejri	256
5.	*Ficus religisa*	Piplo	12
6.	*Butea monosperma*	Khakara	812
7.	*Tectona grandis*	Sagwan	36
8.	*Tamarindus indica*	Khati Imli	2
9.	*Gmelina arborea*	Adusa	25
10.		Kartar	82
11.		Ghatobri	1829
Total No.Trees			6375

Source: Management Committee Records.

Benefit Sharing

The distribution of grass is done equally among the 38 beneficiary families. Every year after *Diwali* or in November there is a meeting and a date is fixed for grass cutting. The meeting is convened by a field worker from PEDO. Two members from each house are required to cut all the grass and then this grass is collected in small bundles, which the people call as *Pula*. All the *pulas* are collected at one place and then divided into 38 parts. Each part is then numbered from one to 38 and a stone with number on it is placed in front of each part. Then in a piece of paper the number from 1-38 is written and a lucky draw is taken out. Every beneficiary family gets one part, which they can take home. After this there is a sub-division in family. For example, if a father has two sons it will be divided among all three of them equally. This year the total grass production was 6840 *pulas* (180 *pulas* per beneficiary) (Table 9.5), which was half of last year's production. The reason for this decrease is said to be due to some sort of insect attacking the grasses in the plantation. In the first year after plantation the total production of grass was 200 *pulas*.

Table 9.5: Timeline Showing Benefits Incurred from the First Year of the Patedi Plantation

Year	*Employment*	*Fodder*		*Fuel Wood (cost)*	*Tim (co*
		Pula (bundle)	*Cost (per Pula)*		
1984–85	*				
1985–86	**				
1986–87		200	200 (600)		
1987–88		1000	1000 (3000)		
1988–89		5000	5000 (15000)		
1989–90		5500	5500 (16500)		
1990–91		6000	6000 (18000)		
1991–92		7000	10000 (21000)	1900 (3800)	5
1992–93		8500	14000 (25500)		
1993–94		9000	18000 (27000)	3800 (7600)	
1994–95		11000	22000 (33000)		6
1995–96		10000	25000 (30000)		
1996–97		–	–		
1997–98		10260	30780 (30780)	5000 (5000)	
1998–99		11500	34500 (34500)	4600 (4600)	
1999–2000		12385	37155 (37155)	6000 (6000)	
2000–01		6840	20520 (20520)	8000 (8000)	200
			29655 (312555)	29300 (35000)	211

* Cost of fodder in bracket is calculated at present market price of fodder.

** Employment generated for the villagers during first two years of planting process.

Source: Records maintained by the management committee.

After the grass is cut and distributed then all the families again assemble for the cutting of dried branches along with the dead, decaying and diseased trees. Big logs and small branches of trees are divided into 38 parts and distributed similar to the grass. This is the only time the trees and branches are cut in the whole year.

Conflict Resolution

In the village meeting conflict arising within the village is resolved by the village elders and once the decision is taken in the meeting, both the groups have to agree to it. In case of benefit sharing if any conflict arises regarding the CLP, the beneficiaries call the meeting of the management committee and all the beneficiaries take part in the decision-making process. The decision taken in this meeting is final and binding on all the members. If any one doesn't heed to the decision made in the meeting and works against it, then the whole village socially boycotts him. Therefore, the village has a strong mechanism of conflict resolution and this keeps the whole village bound cohesively. PEDO's intervention has led to increased cohesiveness between the villagers. With the meeting of CLP being held every month and every villager participating in the decision-making process, it has enhanced the trust of the people in the decision-making and conflict resolution.

Women's Role in CLP Management

Women in the region have subordinate status compared to the men, but they play an integral part in running the programme successfully either through their participation in its activities or through their presence in the meetings. Although most of the members said that women participate in the activities of CLP, but it was observed that their attendance was poor. Barring two or three women who do raise their voice while deciding about management, planning, utilization and conservation of resources, most women agreed that they were not active participants but merely present as observers most of the times.

The reasons given by the women for non-participation was their inability to take time out of the household responsibilities to sit and attend meeting, lack of interest in the programme as they are unable to identify themselves with the programme. With the intervention of PEDO in these villages participation of poor tribal farmers in village meetings has enhanced significantly. The decision making process has now percolated down to the lowest stratum economically and not confined in the hands of a few influential rich villagers.

Case Study

Rupali Bai is one of the two women members of the management committee. At the beginning she was unable to say anything in the meeting or speak out her mind, but now she is an active member of the committee and participates in every meeting of the committee and takes part in the decision-making process. Her association with the CLP committee has helped her to get out of the male dominance not only in the society but also in her house. Now every decision that is taken in her house is taken in consultation of both husband and wife, which was not seen 15 years ago. Her participation in the committee has completely changed her and now she is an active member of not only the CLP but also a member of the SHG run by PEDO in the village.

Economics of the Common

Estimation of benefits of a CLP involves identification and quantification of both direct and indirect benefits of afforestation. The direct benefits accrue to the villagers in the form of fuel wood, small wood, timber, fodder and employment. These benefits can be measured fairly accurately. The indirect benefits include protection of soil, water and wind erosion, addition of organic matter to the soil, improvement in the micro-environment, etc. Valuation of these benefits is very difficult. Social benefits are extremely difficult to estimate correctly, so we limited our objective to determining the financial benefits of the CLP to the villagers.

Fodder Supply

In dry land system where ploughing and sowing have to be compressed into a short rainy season, the number of animals needed are considerably higher than can be sustained from the fodder produced within the farm system, which can only be maintained if the farmer has access to grazing or fodder off-farm. Forests, common woodland and areas of scrub are often the principal complementary source and arboreal fodder is often the main source of livestock feed in the dry season and in periods of drought. It is a matter of concern that animals—both milch and draft animals are extremely important in the economy of the village community particularly in drought prone areas.

It has been argued that in some situation fodder shortages can become more critical than fuel wood shortages, in the sense that there are no alternative sources of livestock feed available to the poor. Shortages of fodder means that the poor farmers are unable to maintain higher quality animals needed for dairying. Sometimes shortage of fodder also forces the poor to dispose of their livestock, except goats for distress selling.

Fodder availability is an important factor for the rural poor and their economy depends on the availability of fodder. From Table 9.6, we can see that in Patedi CLP, the villagers faced moderate problem regarding fodder availability in a normal year prior to CLP. To fulfil the need of fodder (during Pre-CLP) the villagers of Patedi had private pastureland. Now with fodder being available throughout the year (Post-CLP) some of these private pasturelands have been converted to agricultural land. So from this finding it can be stated that there has been considerable increase in fodder availability from pre-common land plantation stage to post-common land plantation in normal year.

Table 9.6: Fodder Availability Scenario During Pre- and Post-CLP

Scenario	*Patedi (CLP)*	
	Normal year (Pre-CLP)	*Normal year (Post-CLP)*
(*a*) No problem (fodder is available throughout the year)	No	Yes
(*b*) Moderate problem (fodder was available till April)	Yes	–
(*c*) Problem (fodder was available till January-February)	–	–

Availability of Fodder during Drought

In this situation we are comparing availability of fodder during normal situation and drought situation, once common land plantation has been established, and for this comparison we have also taken a non-common land plantation village as a control village. Table 9.7 shows that Patedi did not have any problem of fodder in normal years, whereas Temba village had problem of fodder in a normal year. In a normal year Temba village had to depend on outside purchase of fodder, as fodder from private pasture land and crop residue was available only till January-February. Therefore, even during the drought years the CLP helped the villagers sustain their economy and fulfil the requirement of fodder.

Table 9.7: Fodder Availability Scenario in CLP Village and Non-CLP Village

Scenario	*Patedi (CLP)*		*Temba (control village)*	
	Normal Year	*Drought Year*	*Normal Year*	*Drought Year*
(*a*) No problem (fodder is available throughout the year)	Yes	Yes	No	No
(*b*) Moderate problem (fodder was available till April)	–	–	No	No
(*c*) Problem (fodder was available till January–February)	–	–	Yes	No
(*d*) Severe problem (fodder was available till Nov.–Dec.)	–	–	–	Yes

Intermediate Benefits

From the common land plantation, the villagers got a number of products after the planting activities were completed. These included grass, wind blown twigs, dead and dry fuelwood, timber, etc. The villagers freely collected these materials. The intermediate benefits worth Rs. 2,80,055 accrued to the villagers free of charge from the CLP. These benefits accrued to the beneficiaries during the last decade. The benefit during the plantation phase was in the form of employment and the villagers started getting fodder from the third year onwards.

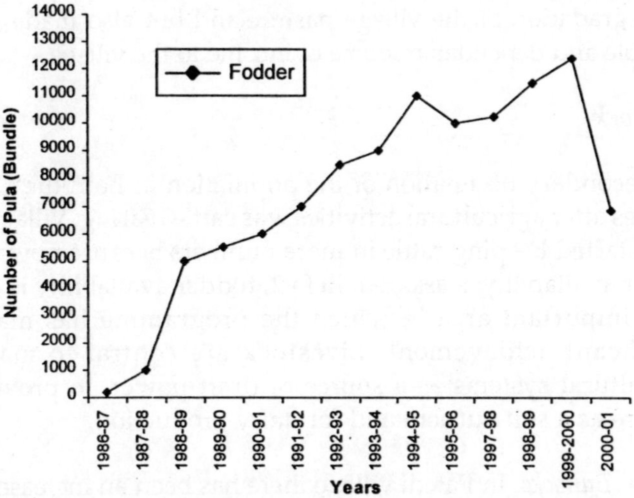

Fig. 9.1: Fodder Availability During Last 15 Years in Patedi CLP

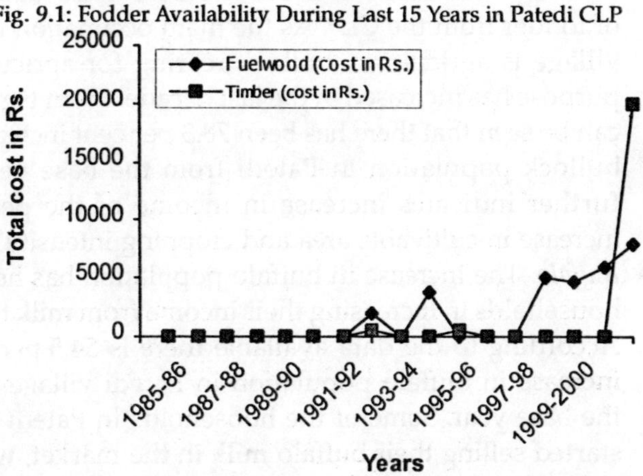

Fig. 9.2: Benefits Incurred in the Form of Timber and Fuelwood

The benefits realized by the villagers of Patedi in the form of grass, fuelwood and timber were estimated to be about Rs. 2,80,055 (3,68,655 current market price) over the 15 year period (Figs. 9.1 & 9.2). These are substantial benefits. There was no benefit accruing to the village from this land before the CLP was established and the pasture land was suffering from the problem "tragedy of commons". The NGO intervention not only halted the degradation of the village pastureland but also made it a valuable and dependable source of income to the village.

Livestock

The secondary occupation of the population in both the CLP villages after agricultural activities was cattle rearing. Villagers have started keeping cattle in more numbers because now the fodder availability is assured; in fact, fodder availability is the most important area in which the programme has made significant achievement. Livestock are central to many agricultural systems as a source of draft power, to provide manure as a soil nutrient and for dairy production.

- *Bullocks*: In Patedi village there has been an increase in bullock population. This is due to the assured availability of fodder from the CLP. As the main occupation in the village is agriculture, bullock rearing for agriculture purpose has increased in the last decade. From Fig 9.3 it can be seen that there has been 78.3 per cent increase in bullock population in Patedi from the base year. It further indicates increase in income of the people, increase in cultivable area and cropping intensity.
- *Buffalo*: The increase in buffalo population has helped households in increasing their income from milk trade. According to the data available there is 54.5 per cent increase in buffalo population in Patedi village from the base year. Some of the households in Patedi have started selling their buffalo milk in the market, which is an added source of income for them.
- *Cow*: There has been considerable change in cow's population from the base year, which can be attributed to the availability of fodder throughout the year in the village. From this it can be seen that there has been 64.3 per cent increase in cow population in Patedi Village from the base year (Table 9.8).

- *Goat*: Goat rearing has been the traditional source of livelihood for the tribals. In Patedi there has been a considerable decrease in goat population, it has decreased by 28.2 per cent from the base year. This is due to open grazing being allowed only for a month and being closed for the rest of the year. Secondly, importance for stall feeding of the cattle has increased.

Table 9.8: Population of Livestock in Patedi

Livestock	*Number in Sample Patedi*		
	Pre	*Post*	*Percentage Change*
Bullock	23	41	78.3
Cow	28	46	64.3
Buffalo	11	17	54.5
Goat	103	74	–28.2

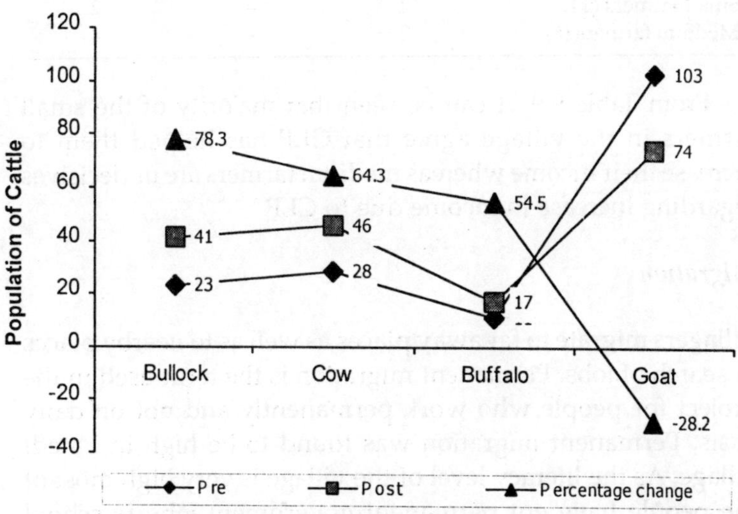

Fig. 9.3: Change in Cattle Population in Patedi

Income Rise

The common land plantation programme does not yield benefits in such surplus quantity that products can be marketed for money. The yield from the plantation during its last 15 years has been fodder, fuelwood and timber, which suffice the home requirement. Indirectly, however, it has helped in increasing the economic status of tribals by curtailing expenses on livestock feeding, because previously they had to purchase fodder from the market to sustain their livestock. Now around Rs. 1000-2000 is saved which previously was used to purchase fodder. Income derived from the CLP is in the form of fodder, fuel wood and timber. To get information regarding impact of CLP on their income 14 small farmers and 6 medium farmers were interviewed.

Table 9.9: Rise in Income in Patedi

Criteria	*Patedi*		
	Yes	*No*	*Can't Say*
Small farmers (14)	12	–	2
Medium farmers (6)	2	–	4

From Table 9.9, it can be seen that majority of the small farmers in the village agree that CLP has helped them to increase their income whereas medium farmers are undecisives regarding increase in income due to CLP.

Migration

Villagers migrate to far away places as well as to nearby places in search of jobs. Permanent migration is the term used in the project for people who work permanently and not on daily basis. Permanent migration was found to be high in Patedi village. As the literacy level of the village is very high most of the people have got permanent government jobs as school teachers and other jobs in nearby cities. Temporary (Distress) migration is the term used in this study for people who go out to work when there is no work in the village or they cannot till their land due to unavailability of water. Most of the people in this category go to work for about a couple of months and return back during agriculture period.

Table 9.10: Temporary Migration in Patedi

S. No	*Scenario*	*Patedi*	
		Normal Year	*Drought Year (1997-2000)*
(*a*)	No Migration	18	13
(*b*)	Low Migration (3 months)	03	06
(*c*)	Moderate Migration (3-6 months)	04	04
(*d*)	High Migration (6-9 months)	–	02
(*e*)	Very High Migration (9-12 months)	–	–

Table 9.10 shows the pattern of migration during normal and drought years, in case of Patedi village out of 25 respondents only 7 migrate that also for a maximum of 4 months in a normal year, whereas 12 respondents migrate in search of labour work for a maximum of 3-9 months during drought year. So comparing both the normal and drought year for Patedi distress migration has not increased drastically in this village.

Conclusion

The approach of transfer of management of village commons to the village community, with an aim of supplementing their economy, has showed positive result. The indication it gives is that the tribal communities can manage the resources efficiently as well as effectively if the resource is given the common status, by which the excludability factor can be applied into the use of the resource. In this study in a drought prone region, it is found that the common plays a vital role in supplementing the tribal economy and reduces their stress on the agriculture as well as livestock management. Due to certain factors like homogenous nature of the community, nearness to the common, literacy level of the village and high level of dependency the common was effectively managed.

Acknowledgements

We would like to thank PEDO for sponsoring the project as

well as providing all the necessary help in doing the project. We would like to thank the Director of our institute for encouraging us to take up such research work.

REFERENCES

Beck, Tony (1994), Common Property Resources Access by Poor and Class Conflict in West Bengal, *Economic & Political Weekly*, Vol. XXIX (4), pp. 187-197.

Chopra, K., Kadekodi, G.K., and Murty, M.M. (1989), *Participatory Development—People and Common Property Resources*, New Delhi: Sage Publications.

Jodha, N.S. (1986), Common Property Resources and Rural Poor in Dry Regions of India, *Economic and Political Weekly*, Vol. XXI (27), pp. 1169-1181

Malhotra, K.C., and Poffenberger, M., (1989), *Forest Regeneration through Community Protection: The West Bengal Experience*, Calcutta: West Bengal Forest Department.

Singh, K. (1994), *Managing Common Pool Resources—Principles and Case Studies*, Delhi: Oxford University Press.

10

NTFP in Economic System of Traditional Communities

A Study from Three Districts of Madhya Pradesh

AMITABH PANDEY and DEBASIS DEBNATH

Introduction

Common Pool Resource (Ostrom, 1990), like forest, provides a substantial portion of economic goods to the traditional communities. In general, the traditional communities share multiple resources from the surrounding ecosystem for different needs ranging from the economic to social and cultural. Capitalistic economics views every resource from the market point of view and suggest privatization or nationalization of resources for efficient management and optimum use. Forest resources have been initially perceived as single resources only providing timber for commercial purposes (Fernandes *et al.*, 1988). But with the depleting forest cover due to unplanned extraction of timber, led the forest managers to shift the importance to NTFP or Non-Timber Forest Produce (Mahapatra and Mitchell, 1994).

Forests provide us wood and non-wood, which are harvested separately, simultaneously and sequentially, though they are not mutually exclusive. The value of wood and non-wood varies monetarily and number of benefits they provide to the people. NTFPs in the broadest sense include all other tangible outputs including fuel and fodder, bio-mass, bamboo, cane, grasses, fibres, oils, dyes, gums, resins, medical herbs, barks, etc. (Shiva & Mathur, 1996; Tewari, 1998). NTFPs play a significant role in the life of the people living in and around the forest, who depend upon these products for their economy, cultural value and aesthetic sense (Tewari, 1994).

On the basis of the use of natural resources, the whole rural economy can be divided into peasant and primitive economy. The peasant society has the traditional social organization in the form of a caste structure with a definite social hierarchy at the local level. They mainly depend upon land resource by using it for cultivation and fulfil their requirement of forest products such as fuelwood, fodder and other materials, such as honey, seeds, etc., through self-collection or employing labours (belonging to other communities who are socially and economically backward) on hired basis. They collect NTFPs as per their daily requirement from their own, privately owned land or from the common pool resources, namely forest. It is estimated that 15-20 per cent of the rural economy is supported by NTFPs collected from their common pool resources (Malhotra *et al.*, 1991).

Primitive economy always pertains to the people that directly depends on the forest resources, who are specially referred to as the indigenous people in the global context or tribal groups or tribes in the Indian context. NTFPs are a major source of livelihood for the poor tribals, who number approximately 55 million in and around forest. Thirty-five per cent of the income of a tribal household in India comes from the collection of unprocessed NTFPs (Tewari and Campbell, 1996). Forest provides the tribal with seven 7 'F's (forest products), *viz.* fuelwood, fodder, fruits, fibre, flosses, food, and fertilizer to meet their day-to-day requirements and the seasonal employment through a number of forestry based operating scheme (Saigal *et al.*, 1997). Forest moulds the tribal way of life and culture. It offers a number of NTFPs, *viz.* leaves, roots, fruits and flowers collected from the forest nearby to invoke their tutelary deities and propitiating or controlling gods and goddesses. Thus the following ways show the tribal dependency on forest—collection and consumption, dependence for income, dependence for employment, satisfying cultural, religious and festival needs, dependence for shifting cultivation and dependence on pastoral activities.

The tribal societies have vast knowledge of the surrounding forest near their place of settlement. For instance, they know huge number of medicinal plants. They collect different parts of these medicinal plants for their health care and treatment of various diseases. They also pass the knowledge or wisdom to the next generation. The ethnic utilization of NTFPs differs due to their variegated cultural and historical backgrounds. In this paper the attempt has been made to find out the role of NTFPs in the tribal economy as well as in the cultural practices of the traditional communities. This chapter also emphasizes on cultural and socio-economic variability among three tribal communities in Madhya Pradesh as a case study.

Methodology

The methodology for this study was primarily based on an ethnographic approach with comparative analysis of economic dependence on NTFPs for tribal livelihood. The comparative analysis was designed from the level of dependence of three different communities on the NTFPs. The selection of three communities was made from the typology of economy of the tribal communities: first, hunting and gathering-cum-shifting cultivators; second, those who were equally dependent on agriculture as well as NTFPs; and the third, those who primarily depend on agriculture. Three districts were identified for this study in Madhya Pradesh based on the distribution of communities and resources. From the three-selected districts, one village was selected from each district based on the location of forest, the density of the tribal population and economic activities. The sample size at the village level was 20 per cent of the total population; basically all villages selected were homogeneous in community composition. At the village level data were collected from household through a general schedule and key informant interviews, PRA exercise for resources mapping, use pattern, annual seasonal calendar, utilization pattern and cultural pattern. The emphasis was on the qualitative aspect of the study, where the embeddedness of economic and social systems was analyzed.

Study Area

The state of Madhya Pradesh has rich forest cover, which act as sources of NTFPs for the communities living in and around it. Madhya Pradesh has 15.45 million ha. of forest area, which is nearly 35 per cent of the total area of the state. The forest of the state comprises roughly about 30 per cent of Sal, 30 per cent of Teak and about 40 per cent of mixed forest. The state (undivided) has the largest Scheduled Tribe population in India. From the tribal context it can be divided into five divisions. The eastern and southern division, which is largely inhabited by the Gond group of tribes, encompassing the Vindhyachal, Chattisgarh and Dandakaranya regions. The Gond and Korku tribes inhabit the central division covering the Chindwara and Betul districts. The western division, mainly Malwa, is inhabited by the Bhil group of tribes. The Grid region has another tribe known as Saharia. The three-selected districts were Mandla in the east; Betul in the south and Khargone in the west for this study.

Study Districts and Tribes

Mandla

The Mandla District is located in the eastern corner of the state. It covers eastern portion of the Satpura hills and has three rivers in the region, namely, the Narmada, Budnar and Halon. This district has 29 per cent of forest cover. The tribals constitute 61 per cent of the total population of the district. The forest of Mandla is of moist deciduous type having two sub-types, namely eastern Sal and the western mixed forest with Teak. Baiga and Gond are the main tribes inhabiting the district. The main NTFPs collected from the forest are firewood, poles, grasses, and edible fruits, fruits, flowers, leaves, fodder and herbs. The village selected for the study in this district is Sathia. The village Sathia is situated in Mawai block in this district. One can reach the village travelling by bus for a distance of 80 kilometres from the district headquarters. From the Mawai bus stop it is at a distance of 10 kilometres. The village is situated on a plane land and surrounded by Sal forest. The soil of the village contains mostly black soil. The forest area adjacent to the village is 2994.6 ha. The population of the village is 40, living in 11 household. The main ethnic community is Baiga. Their main livelihood is collection of NTFPs.

The Baiga tribe is known as the Panda, the term Baiga means priest. The Baiga resides between Maikal ranges and the catchment of Narmada river, which includes district of Balaghat, Bilaspur, Mandla, Rajnandgaon and Shahdol. The Baiga are divided into three sub-groups, namely, the Bhinjhwar, Bharoti and Nahar or Narotia, and these are further divided into various clans like Kukadia, Bania, Samdadia, Markam and Dhurwey, etc. Agriculture and forest produce are the main source of their economy. They collect NTFPs like fuelwood and bamboo, char, amla, bibirang to sell in the market, from where they buy their daily needs. Selling of hen, cock, goat also adds to their income. Their staple food consists of Kodo, Maize, Kutki, Jawar, Paddy, Wheat and Masoor. Mahua liquor is an important item of their diet. For the Baiga, Badedev, Dulhadev are the supreme deities worshipped during Chaitra Navami and Dussehra at the family level. They also worship their ancestors. The village deities are worshipped by the Baiga Priest (Singh, 1998).

Betul

Betul was the second district selected for this study. It is located in the southern part of the state. This district lies almost wholly on the Satpura Plateau. Betul District has 41.5 per cent of forest cover. The forest is divided into five types, moist deciduous teak (with or without bamboo), dry deciduous teak (with or without bamboo), mixed, salai and bamboo. The NTFP species comprise of mahua flower, tendu leaves, char, amla and many medicinal plants. The district has 35-40 per cent of tribals. Korkus is the main tribe in the district. The village selected for study in this district is Karanjidal. The village Karanjidal is in Bheempur block of Betul District. One can reach the village travelling by bus for 50 kilometres from Betul upto Adarsh Danora and then walking on foot for 9 kilometres on a non-motorable road. The village is situated on a hilly area and surrounded by teak mixed degraded forest. The soil of the village is constituted mostly by laterites. The village has the forest area of 186.96 ha, which is 0.5 kilometre away from the village. Total population of the village is 506 in 122 households. The main ethnic communities are Korku (70%) and Gond (30%). Their main livelihood is agriculture.

The name of the Korku tribe has been derived from combination of the word koru meaning man and ku, which makes it plural (Russel and Hiralal, 1991). The groups within the Korku are Bopachi, Bawaria, Mouasi, Nihal, Nahul, Bondhi and Bondeya, each of which is endogamous. They are concentrated in the district of Betul, Chindwara, Khandwa, Hoshangabad and Dewas of Madhya Pradesh. The Korku is second most populous tribes of the district. Their staple food consists of kutki, jawar, rice and wheat. Mahua flower is an important item in their diet. They prepare and consume mahua liquor. The Korkus are primarily cultivators, but they also depend upon forest resources for their subsistence. Some of them work as farm labours on daily wages or on an annual contract basis, and some work in various government and non-government agencies. The Korkus are influenced by Hinduism, but have not given up their traditional religious beliefs altogether.

Khargone

The third district selected for the study is Khargone District, which is located in the south-western corner of the state. The district is drained by the Narmada drainage system. The local black cotton soil contains 50 per cent silt. The forest cover is 11.40 per cent of the total geographical area of the district. The main timber yielding species are Teak, Saja, Bija, Tinsa, Haldu, Shisam, and Arjun. NTFP species are bamboo, grasses, tendu leaves, mahua flowers and fruits, lac, gum, and medicinal plants. The district has 35-50 per cent of Scheduled Tribe population. The tribes inhabiting the district are: the Bhil, Bhilala, and Barela, which comprise 90 per cent of the tribal population. The village selected for the study in this district is Khumbhi. The village Khumbhi is situated in Bhagwanpura block in the Khargone District. One can reach the village travelling by bus for 75 kilometres from Khargone upto Sirwell, and then walking on foot for 9 kilometres on non-metal road. The village is situated on a hilly area and surrounded by mixed degraded forests. The soil of the village constituted mostly of black and red soil. The village has the forest area of 325.77 ha, which is 1.2 kilometre away from the village. Total population of the village is 857 in 90 households. The main ethnic groups consist of 95 per cent Barela and 5 per cent others. The main livelihood of the people is wage work.

Bhil communities are distributed in the districts of Khargone, Khandawa, Hoshangabad and Narshingpur of Madhya Pradesh. A legend among them says that they have migrated from Gujarat. They have separate language called Rathi or Barel, which is spoken with their own community members. Hindi and Malvi are spoken with others. Actually, Barela is the sub-tribe of the Bhil. The Barela are divided into two sub-divisions, *i.e.*, Barela and Routhia Barela. They have fourteen clans such as Sastia, Jamria, Sulia, Bahelia, etc. Marriage is strictly prohibited within a clan. Polygamy is allowed. The marriage symbol for a Barela woman is a waist belt. Bride price is paid and marriage is performed at the bride's residence. They drink local alcohol, which is made from mahua. The Bhil in the past earned their livelihood from forest, forest produce, and games. The major requirements of the Bhil are wood and bamboo, which they use for various purposes. The Bhil make use of bamboo and wood for house construction. They need more and more houses because of nuclear family system and raise partition even during the period when the family head is alive. Their major occupation is agriculture and daily wage labour. Their children also get employed as wage labour. They are Hindus by religion. The tribes attend Hindu fair and festivals. Ghinshri is one of the clan Gods.

In this study total 3 tribes were studied in 3 villages in 3 districts of Madhya Pradesh. Table 10.1 and Table 10.2 give comparative information of the three villages studied.

Table 10.1: General Profile of the Village Studied in Three Districts

Sl. No.	*Description*	*Sathia*	*Karanjidol*	*Khumbhi*
1.	No. of HH	11	122	90
2.	Population	40	506	857
3.	Ethnic Composition	Baiga	Korku	Bhil (Barela)
4.	Clan	Maravi, Dhurvey, Uikey	Dhikare, Changre, Chauhan, Baraskar, Panse, Kasde, Mawase, Dhote	Nigwake, Dabur, Sulia, Khartia, Jamria, Sastia, Bahedia
5.	Litrate	16 (40%)	113 (22.3%)	258 (30.1%)
6.	Illitrate	24 (60%)	393 (77.7%)	599 (69.9%)
7.	Civic Facilities	Primary School, Angan Wadi	Primary School, Electricity	Primary school

Table 10.2: Economic Profile of the Village Studied in the Three Districts

Sl. No.	*Economic Profile*	*Sathia*	*Karanjidol*	*Khumbhi*
1.	Main Occupation	NTFPs	Agriculture	Agriculture
2.	Agri. land	244 ha.	170 ha.	204.344 ha.
3.	Land Patta Holder	3	16	22
4.	Agri. Crops	Paddy, Kodo, Kutaki Maize	Paddy, Kodo, Maize, Wheat, Gram	Maize, Jawar, Soybean, Wheat, Gram
5.	Livestock			
	Cow	8	90	109
	Ox	14	130	198
	Buffalo	-	24	54
	Goat	-	80	85
	Calf	1	-	-
	Bull	-	-	-
6.	Forest area of the village	2994.6 ha.	186.96 ha.	325.77 ha.
7.	Income Source	NTFPs, WW	Sale of NTFPs, WW	Sale of NTFPs, WW
8.	Average Annual Income (Rs.)/HH	12272	4959	7333

Discussion and Results

The CPR (common pool resources) has a substantial role to play in traditional communities' economy and culture. NTFP, a common mode of production-cum-procurement, has its own pattern of division of labour, residual ownership, and cultural pattern. In traditional communities, resources are mostly of multi-purpose utility, so is the case with the NTFP. The trend of lessening of the timber extraction from forest and enhancement of NTFP procurement has enabled the traditional communities to utilize forest for economic development. The communities living on the fringe of forest, primarily to supplement food and economic needs use the NTFP. The type of economic activities they practise is directly linked to the intensity, utility of NTFP from forest to supplement their food need as well as other livelihood needs. The collection of NTFPs varies as per availability of the product in the forest and also dependency on the product for survival. The season of availability of NTFP is mostly during the period when the demand for agriculture work is low. This is mostly after the sowing season and after the harvest.

NTFP as Common Pool Resources

The three communities studied utilize the adjoining forest as common pool resource, as they belong to the fringe community group and have the right to collect NTFP for their economic and cultural needs. Generally the trend is that each village has a range of forest for its use. The Baiga community has 2994.6 ha of forest adjoining the village to use for NTFP collection. The condition of the forest is good and is rich in diversity of the species. Besides, collection of NTFP from the forest the community has developed a tenurial system of owning certain trees like mahua, which the community recognizes. Each household has some trees owned, from which it collects flowers and seeds, other households acknowledge its right. For NTFP, the use rule is on the basis of first come first use. Korku community has 186.96 ha of forest to use for their NTFP needs.

It is located at a distance of about ½ kilometre form the village. This village also recognizes the tenurial right of certain trees. Barela community has 325.77 ha of forest located at a distance of 1½ kilometre from the village, from where the NTFP is collected. Here the NTFP is mostly collected for economic and domestic needs. The individual families own mahua tree and it plays an important role in their social system.

Level of NTFP Usage in Three Traditional Communities' Economic System

The tribal economic system primarily has significant contribution from the NTFP. But the dependency of the community on NTFP is inversely proportional to the economic activity the community is engaged in. The Baiga, for example, is primarily shifting cultivators and are totally dependent on the forest products for their livelihood. NTFP has a very important place in their economic, social and cultural system. Table 10.3 shows that NTFP contributes 46 per cent to the household economy of the Baiga, while the Korku of Betul has less use of NTFPs in their economic and cultural system. They are having agricultural land for cultivation purpose; therefore, they devote more time in the agriculture work, which is a family affair. This prevents them from contemplating more on NTFP collection. The community collects NTFP when they are free from agriculture or the economic gain from NTFP is substantial (for example collection of achar provides them good earning). From Table 10.3 it is evident that only 13 per cent is contributed by the NTFP to the household economy of the Korku. In the case of the Bhil, contribution of NTFP to the tribal economy has gone down substantially to 5 per cent, which is probably the minimum. They are basically agriculturists and their agriculture is rain-fed. Once the agriculture season of kharif is over, they migrate to the adjoining towns in search of wage labour. The contribution from wage labour in their annual income is substantial.

The dependency on NTFP is linked with the kind of forest the community lives in and makes use of. In the case of Baiga and Korku the forest is basically Sal with mixed forest. Here the availability of NTFP is round the year. But in case of the Bhil, forest is dry deciduous with teak as main crop, where the availability of NTFP is low, as well as the number of NTFPs available is also less. Therefore, the community looks for other options to generate income. Only the NTFPs with commercial importance like tendu patta and mahua are collected. Mahua plays an important role in the Bhil life; it provides them with the material to make their traditional liquor.

Table 10.3: Annual Income of the Villages Studied

Sl. No.	Activities	Income (Rs.)		
		Sathia	Karanjidol	Khumbhi
1.	No. of HH	11	122	90
2.	Agricultural output	45,000	2,20,000	2,98,000
3.	Sale of NTFP	60,000	67,000	34,000
4.	Wage work	25,000	2,60,000	3,00,000
5.	Livestock	4,500	58,000	2,80,000
6.	Total Annual Income	1,34,000	4,95,000	6,60,000
7.	Average Annual Income	12,272	4,959	7,333
8.	Percentage of NTFP to Income	44.6	13.5	5.15

Collection Pattern of NTFP in three Traditional Communities

The NTFP collected can be classified into different categories such as, NTFP used for food, fodder, fuelwood, and medicinal and cultural needs. The NTFP for food includes mahua flower, which is used as a substitute for sweets and its seeds, from which oil is extracted. Grasses are used for fodder as well as rope making for both domestic use and for the market. The NTFP is collected for the domestic needs are those used for construction of houses, fodder requirement of livestock. For economic needs, NTFPs like achar, gum, and tendu patta are collected for sale in the market to generate additional income for the household economy. The fuelwood is collected to meet the energy requirements of the family as well as used to generate income from its sale. The third type of NTFP collected is to meet medicinal requirements. Knowledgeable persons like the medicine man of the village collect these NTFPs. These include harra, akau, maida, neem etc. The NTFPs for cultural use are mostly collected at the time of rituals and religious ceremonies and include semar bole, chiraita, kaliyari flower, etc., which do not have much commercial value.

Table 10.4: Collection Pattern of the NTFPs in Sathia Village of Mandla District

Sl. No.	*Tribe*	*Species (Local Name)*	*Botanical Name*	*Collector*	*Collection Month*
1.	Baiga	Mahua	*Madhuca indica*	M/F	April-May
		Safed Musali	*Chlorophytum borivillium*	M	Jan.-April
		Tendu patta*	*Diospyrous mealanoxylon*	M/F/C	May
		Banjeera	*Apluda mutica*	M/F	Feb.-April
		Bibirang	*Embilica robusta*	M/F	Nov.-Jan.
		Bantulsa	*Ocimum sp.*	M/F	Feb.-July
		Baichandi	*Dioscorea sp.*	M	As per need
		Bamboo	*Dendrocalmus strictus*	M/F	Entire year
		Bel	*Aegle marmelos*	M/F	Feb.-May
		Mahul Patta	*Bahunia vehilli*	M/F/C	Aug.-Dec.
		Maida	*Litsae glutinosa*	M/F	As per need
		Neem	*Azadirachta indica*	M/F	As per need
		Mango	*Mangifera indica*	M/F	As per need
		Kekad	*Garuga pinnata*	M/F	Oct.-May
		Palash	*Butea monosperma*	M/F	Oct.-May
		Girachi	*Casearia graveoleus*	M/F	Oct.-May
		Dhawada	*Anogeissus latifolia*	M/F	Oct.-May
		Saja	*Terminalia tomentosa*	M/F	Oct.-May
		Sagone	*Tectona grandis*	M/F	Oct.-May
		Moya	*Pennistum hohenachkeri*	M/F	June-Sept.
		Kans	*Saccharum spontenium*	M/F	June-Sept.
		Sukla	*Hetropogan contortus*	M/F	June-Sept.
		Kandi		M/F	June-Sept.
		Chichari	*Hetropogen sp.*	M/F	June-Sept.
		Muradi		M/F	June-Sept.
		Semar	*Bombax ceiba*	M	As per need
		Bhelwa	*Semecarpus anacardium*	M	As per need
		Kaliyari	*Gloriosa superba*	M	As per need
		Charaitia	*Swartia chirata*	M	As per need
		Blackberry	*Zyzyphus nummularia*	M/F	As per need
		Umar		M	As per need
		Amla	*Embilca officinalis*	M/F	As per need
		Char	*Buchnania lenjen*	M/F	As per need
		Salya	*Boswellia serrata*	M	As per need
		Jogilati	*Desmodium ferjunium*	M/F	As per need

M = Male, F = Female, C = Children.

The Baigas, who are shifting cultivators but forced to become sedentary agriculturalist, directly depend on NTFP for their livelihood. They collect as many as 35 species of NTFPs from the forest for their economic, cultural, health and religious requirement (Table 10.4), while the Korkus collect 24 species of NTFPs from the forest for economic, cultural and health needs (Table 10.5). The Bhils collect about 15 species of NTFP for their economic and cultural needs (Table 10.6). There is a wide diversity in the collection of the NTFP species; it ranges from food needs to those of religion and health. The variation is also seen in the collection pattern among the 3 communities in 3 different regions.

Table 10.5: Collection Pattern of the NTFPs in Karanjidol Village of Betul District

Sl. No.	*Tribe*	*Species (Local Name)*	*Botanical Name*	*Collector*	*Collection Month*
1.	Korku	Mahua	*Madhuca indica*	M/F/C	April-May
		Tendu patta	*Diospyrous mealanoxylon*	M/F/C	May
		Char	*Buchnania lenjen*	M/F/C	May
		Amla	*Embilca officinalis*	M/F	Nov.-Dec.
		Palash	*Butea monosperma*	M/F	Oct.-May
		Karai	*Saccopetalum tometosa*	M/F	Oct.-May
		Amaltash	*Casia fistula*	M/F	Oct.-May
		Akau	*Calotropis gigenita*	M/F	Oct.-May
		Harra	*Terminalia chebula*	M/F	As per need
		Neem	*Azadirachta indica*	M/F	As per need
		Mohin	*Lannea caromandelica*	M/F	As per need
		Behada	*Terminalia belirica*	M/F	As per need
		Jarramatadi		M/F	As per need
		Dhawada	*Anogeissus latifolia*	M/F	As per need
		Tinsa	*Oiegenia oojenensis*	M/F	Oct.-May
		Saj	*Terminalia tomentosa*	M/F	Oct.-May
		Sagone	*Tectona grandis*	M/F	Oct.-May
		Sukla	*Hetropagan contortus*	M/F	June-Sept.
		Kans	*Saccharum spontenium*	M/F	June-Sept.
		Tikadi		M/F	June-Sept.
		Sunher	*Terneda quadrivalvis*	M/F	June-Sept.
		Salya	*Boswellia serrata*	M/F	As per need
		Blackberry	*Zyzyphus nummularia*	M/F	As per need
		Bamboo	*Dendrocalmus strictus*	M/F	March-May

M = Male, F = Female, C = Children.

Table 10.6: Collection Pattern of the NTFPs in Khumbhi Village of Khargone District

Sl. No.	*Tribe*	*Species (Local Name)*	*Botanical Name*	*Collector*	*Collection Month*
1.	Bhil	Tendu patta	*Diospyrous mealanoxylon*	M/F	May
		Mahua	*Madhuca indica*	M/F/C	April-May
		Tinsa	*Oiegenia oojenensis*	M/F	Oct.-May
		Saj	*Terminalia tomentosa*	M/F	Oct.-May
		Sagone	*Tectona grandis*	M/F	Oct.-May
		Ponia	*Schima sulcatum*	M/F	July-Sept.
		Sedhi		M/F	July-Sept.
		Lalsukali		M/F	July-Sept.
		Sadad	*Pterocarpus marsupium*	M/F	Oct.-May
		Kekad	*Garuga pinnata*	M/F	Oct.-May
		Behada	*Terminalia belirica*	M/F	Oct.-May
		Anjan	*Hardusckia binala*	M/F	Oct.-May
		Bhatodi		M/F	Oct.-May
		Bamboo	*Dendrocalmus strictus*	M/F	March-May
		Dhawada	*Anogeissus latifolia*	M/F	Nov.-May

M= Male, F= Female, C= Children.

The primary unit of collection of NTFP is the family. The entire family contributes to the collection with a distribution of work on the basis of age and sex. The men mainly collect the species required for the religious and cultural purposes. The collection of NTFPs varies from regular collection like tendu patta, mahua flowers, seeds, etc. to their occasional collection like the medicinal herbs. The collection pattern also varies from one NTFP to another. Men collect the NTFPs located in the distance and unsafe places, which may be difficult for women and children to go and safely collect them. Women and children are sometimes denied access to specific places, which are only visited by men for collection of NTFPs. Sometimes NTFPs, which are difficult to identify or differentiate from the other species, are collected by men, like safed musli in Mandla due to its specific location of availability as well as identification factors. Fuelwood is mainly collected by women, as the forest department staff is lenient towards women. Similarly women collect the fodder as it is easily collected and requires less energy and strength to cut and carry. The children are used in those NTFP collections, which are to be collected in shorter time and are location specific, where men and women can keep a watch on them. For example, children along with the men and women collect flowers, seeds, char, tendu patta or mahua leaves. The women play an important role in processing of NTFPs, like washing and drying of safed Musali and mahua flower. Similarly women and children contribute much to the making of leaf plates, in which the leaves of palash trees are used by the Bhils in Khargone District.

NTFP in the Cultural System of Traditional Communities

The NTFP is found to play an important role in the cultural system of the Baiga community of Mandla. The use of forest species is for festivals like Holi, where the semar tree bole is collected and pruned and erected at the centre of the village akhara. Similarly joglati climber is used at the time of Haryali festival. It is put on the door to ward of the evil eye. In Rishi Panchami festival, kaliyari and chiraita flowers are offered to the deity during the rituals. Bamboo and mahua leaves are important species used in almost all the ceremonies of the village. Bamboo is used for preparation of the shed used for rituals and making of basket and other bamboo utensils used in the rituals. Similarly, mahua and char leaves are used to make plates and cups in which offering is made to the deity as well as for distribution of prasad to the villagers. Species like bamboo, mango, blackberry, umar, palash, salai and number of grasses are used in making the altar for the marriage ceremony..

In the Korku village of Betul, species like mohin, salai, blackberry, bamboo and tendu are used in marriage for making the shed. In Bhil society, sagone plays an important role in the rituals as it is in abundance in the area. The community depending on NTFPs has more number of species used in their cultural activities, while the community engaged in agriculture has lesser number of NTFPs used in rituals.

NTFP in Health System of the Traditional Communities

The Baiga of Mandla uses more number of NTFP species for treatment of their health problems. It has specialists, called as

Ojha, to cure the diseases, who makes diagnosis of the cause(s) of illness. After that he gives the traditional medicine, either collected or prepared by him, or advises the patient to do it on his own. For example, maida tree bark is used to curing dysentery in the village. The bark of the tree is crushed to extract the sap, which is mixed with water along with the whey and given to the patient. Neem tree bark is used for curing fever. The bark is crushed and sap is mixed with buttermilk and given to the patient. The fruits of Banjeera, another bush, are used in curing malaria. The fruits are crushed and mixed with water and given to the patient a number of times to cure the disease. The sorcerer uses mango tree branch to exercise the spirit and cure jaundice.

In Betul District, the Korkus use a number of species collected from the forest for treatment of different ailments. Some of the species used are delineated here. For example, they use the leaf of amaltas and karai tree, make a paste and add to water, which is used to cure abscess and boils. Similarly, the latex of akau, a bush, is used to remove the thorn pierced into the foot of a person. Harra and behra fruits are used to cure cough and cold. The fruit is roasted and chewed to cure the problem of cough and cold. Neem and mohin tree bark are crushed and mixed in water and is consumed to get rid of fever. Similarly, dhawada tree bark is crushed and is taken after mixing it with water for curing cough.

The Bhils do not take any species from the forest for the treatment purpose and depend on the modern medical facilities for their health problems. Since they work as migrated wage labourers mostly in near by towns, availability of medicinal species there is extremely rare. Secondly, the type of forest there is dry deciduous, which becomes dry after the rainy season and does not contain the diversity of species, as it is available in other two forest areas described above.

NTFP Used by the Three Traditional Community for Economic Purpose

The next major use of NTFP is for meeting fodder, fuel and house construction needs of the communities. Table 10.7 shows

Table 10.7: Fuelwood, Fodder and Bamboo Species Used in Mandla

Sl. No.	*Tribe*	*Species*	*Season of Collection*	*Who Collect*	*Quantity (qt.)*	*Use Pattern*
1.	Baiga	Kekad	Oct.-May	M/F	2000	Fuel wood
		Palash	Oct.-May	M/F	–	Fuel wood
		Girachi	Oct.-May	M/F	–	Fuel wood
		Gunja	Oct.-May	M/F	–	Fuel wood
		Dhawada	Oct.-May	M/F	–	Fuel wood, HC
		Saja	Oct.-May	M/F	–	Fuel wood, HC
		Sagone	Feb.-May	M/F	–	HC,
		Moya	June-Sept.	M/F	–	For SC
		Kans	June-Sept.	M/F	–	Rope making SC
		Sukla	June-Sept.	M/F	–	Fodder
		Kandi	June-Sept.	M/F	–	Fodder
		Chichari	June-Sept.	M/F	–	Fodder
		Muradi	June-Sept.	M/F	–	Fodder
		Bamboo	Jan.-Dec.	M/F	–	Basket, Mkt., HC, Fencing
2.	Korku	Dhawada	Oct.-May	M/F	800	Fuel wood, HC
		Tinsa	Oct.-May	M/F	–	Fuel wood, Agricultural implements
		Saj	Oct.-May	M/F	–	Fuel wood, HC
		Sagone	Oct.-May	M/F	–	Fuel wood, HC, Wheel of Cattle
		Char	Oct.-May	M/F	–	Fuel wood
		Sukla	June-Sept.	M/F	–	Fodder
		Kans	June-Sept.	M/F	–	Fodder
		Tikadi	June-Sept.	M/F	–	Fodder
		Sunher	June-Sept.	M/F	–	Fodder
		Pola Bamboo	Mar.-May	M/F	–	HC, Fencing
3.	Bhil	Dhawada	Oct.-May	M/F	–	Fuel wood, gum
		Tinsa	Oct.-May	M/F	–	Fuelwood, Agricultural implements, HC
		Saj	Oct.-May	M/F	–	Fuel wood, HC
		Sagone	Oct.-May	M/F	–	Fuel wood, HC
		Ponia	Jul.-Sept.	M/F	–	Fodder
		Sedhi	Jul.-Sept.	M/F	–	Fodder
		Lalsukali	Jul.-Sept.	M/F	–	Fodder
		Bhatodi	Jul.-Sept.	M/F	–	Fodder
		Sadad	Oct.-May	M/F	–	Fuelwood
		Kekad	Oct.-May	M/F	–	Fuelwood
		Baheda	Oct.-May	M/F	–	Fuelwood
		Anjan	Oct.-May	M/F	–	Fuelwood/Fodder
		Bamboo	Mar.-May	M/F	–	HC, Fencing/Holi

M= Male, F= Female, C= Children, HC = House Construction.

the number of species used by the traditional communities as fuelwood, fodder and making of house as well as agricultural implements. Grasses are used apart from fodder for making of rope; bamboo is used for making basket and other storage containers. From Table 10.2, the livestock dependency of the Korkus and Bhils is evident. They meet their fodder requirements basically from the common pool resources of forest. Secondly, the livestock composition suggests the subsistence economic management strategy of these

Table 10.8: Utility Stage of the Collected NTFPs in Studied Districts

S.No.	Tribe	Name of the Village	Local Name of Species *	Which Part
1	Baiga	Sathia	Mahua	Flower
			Safed Masali	Root
			Tendupatta	Leaf
			Banjeera	Fruit
			Bibirang	Fruit
			Bantulsa	Fruit
			Mahua Seeds	Fruit
			Maida	Bark
			Neem	Leaf
			Mango	Bark
2	Korku	Karanjidol	Mahua	Flower
			Mahua Sedds	Fruit
			Tendupatta	Leaf
			Amla	Fruit
			Palash	Root
			Karai	Leaf
			Amaltash	Leaf
			Akau	Milk
			Harra	Fruit
			Neem	Bark
			Mohin	Bark
			Baheda	Fruit
			Jarramatadi	Root
			Dhawada	Bark
3	Bhil	Kumbi	Mahua	Flower
			Tendupatta	Leaf
			Kalakuda	Bark
			Mahua Seeds	Fruit
			Kahu	Bark
			Mango	Bark

* The Botanical name is given in species list.

communities and vulnerability aspect. The species mix of livestock provides different benefits at different time. Like goat is used in distress selling, ox is used for agriculture, while cow and buffalo for meeting the milk requirements. Less number of buffaloes suggests that relationship between fodder availability and cost of management of the animal in fodder deficient period, whereas other species can survive from the fodder available from the CPR.

Table 10.8 shows different parts used by the traditional communities of the species collected from the forest. Different parts like leaf, root, stem, bark, bole, fruits, flower are made use of for different purposes by the tribal communities for food or medicine or for selling them in the market for economic gain.

NTFP Processing and Marketing by the Traditional Communities

The tribal communities process some of the NTFP species collected from the forest to get an additional income. This process is considered as value addition activities. The main aim of processing is to get good remuneration for the NTFPs from the traders. The Baiga, for example, process tendu patta, collected in the month of May-June. Green leaves of tendu patta are collected, cleaned after removing the bad leaves, which are then are made into bundles of fifty each, and tied with rope, made of the roots of the palash tree. The safed musali are roots, which are collected and cleaned in water to remove the mud and dried in the sun. By this process the rate available to the person increases three to five folds. Banjera, bantulsa and bairang fruits are collected and dried in sun before selling it to the traders. Mahua flowers are collected, washed and dried in sun before selling in the market. Mahua seeds are crushed to remove the kernel; the seed is used for extracting oil.

The Korkus process the following NTFPs for selling in the market. Tendupatta, mahua flower and seed are processed in similar manner as done by the Baiga of Mandla District. Here char is the prime NTFP collected which provides them with good additional income. The char fruits are collected and ground, then washed in water to remove the outer skin. The fruit is then dried in sunlight. The traders give them good rate for the processed achar. Amla is another NTFP the villagers' process before selling it to the traders. The fruit of amla are collected and boiled, the flesh are then collected in separate containers and dried for three-four days in the sun. The pharmaceutical companies pay good rate for the processed amla.

The Barela of Khargone District process tendu patta and mahua flower and seed in the same manner as done by other two tribal communities. Here they collect dhawada, from which they collect gum, which used by the pharmaceutical companies in the preparation of medicine. This NTFP after processing fetches the villager good earning. The gum collected from the tree is washed in water to remove the dirt; later on, it is dried in the sun, before selling it to the traders.

The processed NTFPs are sold in the near by market or to a trader, with whom the tribals have established a relationship for quite some time. The Baigas have two market places: one is the village itself where the trader comes and collects the product from the collector. The second is the Mawai town where regular *hat* is held and the villagers go to sell their collected NTFPs, and some use them for exchange for household requirements. The villagers even use the NTFPs for distress selling. The Korkus have three market places for their NTFPs: one is Chikhli, second is Karnjidol, and third one is Bheempur. The Bhils have two market places; one is the village itself other is the town of Sirwell. In the case of nationalized NTFPs the Madhya Pradesh government fixes the rate, while in case of non-nationalized products the traders fix the rate, and there is huge variation of prices from market to market and from trader to trader.

Conclusion

From the study it is found that the traditional communities survive and earn much from the NTFPs. Their earning is dependent on the resource potentiality. The variation is seen in the use and importance of NTFPs in the economic system of the studied communities. The community that is primarily agriculturist, like the Korku and Bhil depend less on NTFPs compared to the Baiga, who are shifting cultivators, and who dependence on NTFP is more to supplement their food and domestic needs. The knowledge and use of species vary in the similar pattern. The communities have local techniques, which they apply for processing of the NTFPs before selling in the local market. The traditional communities have a number of ritual practices at the individual and communal levels, where NTFPs are used. The forest dwelling communities have sufficient knowledge of species and utilization of various parts of the species. These tribal groups collect and process number of medicinal plants and their various parts in the treatment of acute and chronic diseases.

The economic system of the fringe communities depends on NTFPs. Therefore, when planning for proper NTFP management, these aspects of community-wise variation in use should be taken into cognizance and put into application. The knowledge about NTFP by the communities should be utilized for better management of resources. In the era of increased community role in common resource management, the dependency on resources by the community can provide better information on whether the collective management be fruitful or not.

REFERENCES

Fernandes, W., Menon, G. and Viegas, P. (1988), *Forests, Environment and Tribal Economy*, New Delhi: Indian Social Institute.

Mahapatra, A., Mitchell, C.P. (1994), Sustainable Development of Non-Timber Forest Products: Implication for Forest Management in India, *Forest Ecology and Management*, 94, pp. 15-29.

Ostrom, E. (1990), *Governing the Commons: The Evolution of Institutions for Collective Action*, New York: Cambridge University Press.

Malhotra, K.C., Deb, D., Dutta, M., Vasula, T.S., Yadav, G., and Adhikari, M. (1991), *Role of Non-Timber Forest Products in Village Economy: An Household Survey in Jamboni Range, Midnapore*, Calcutta: Indian Institute of Bio-social Research and Development, Calcutta.

Russell, R.V., and Hiralal (1991), *The Tribes and Castes of Central Provinces of India*, Vols. 3 & 4, Delhi: Low Price Publication.

Saigal, S., Chetan Agrawal and J. Y. Campbell (1997), "Food, Fodder, Fuel, NTFP can Sustain JFM", *Wastelands News*, Aug.-Oct., pp. 46-55.

Shiva, M.P. and R.B. Mathur (1996), *Management of Minor Forest Produce for Sustainable Development*, New Delhi: Oxford and IBH Publishing Co. Pvt. Ltd.

Singh, K.S. (1998), *India Communities*, Delhi: Oxford University Press.

Tewari, D.D. (1994), Developing and Sustaining Non-Timber Forest Products: Policy Issues and Concerns with Special Reference to India, *Journal of World Forest Resources Management*, 7, pp. 151-178.

Tewari, D.D. (1998), *Economic and Management of Non-Timber Forest Product*, New Delhi, Oxford & IBH Publishing Co. Pvt. Ltd.

Tiwari, D.D., Campbell, J.Y. (1996), Increased Development of Non-Timber Products in India: Some Issues and Concerns, *Unasylva*, 47, pp. 26-31.

11

Tribal Participation in Joint Forest Management

A Study in Visakha Agency Area of Andhra Pradesh

V. SUBRAMANYAM

Introduction

A large majority of the tribal population in India lives in the forest areas of the Eastern Ghats, Western Ghats, Central, North-Eastern, and the Himalayan mountainous regions. The State of Andhra Pradesh is inhabited by 33 Scheduled Tribes with 4.2 million tribal population, constituting 6.3 per cent of the total state population. A large chunk of tribal population in the State of Andhra Pradesh lives in the Eastern Ghats region. The district of Visakhapatnam has about 4.69 lakh of tribal population. About 90 per cent among them lives in the agency area, which is a part of the Eastern Ghats. The tribals are otherwise known as forest dwellers and have developed symbiotic relations with the forest. Forest, not only provides them with food, shelter and even clothing, but is also very much related to and intertwined with their socio-economic and religious life. According to an estimate by the Ministry of Environment and Forests (MoEF), Government of India, even today about 23 million tribal population are totally dependent on forest for their livelihood (1995). Due to large-scale commercial exploitation of forests over a period of time, an alarming situation of deforestation has resulted, creating the problem of natural imbalance. This eventually causes critical problems for the livelihood of the tribals. According to the National Remote Sensing Agency (NRSA) estimates, India has lost about 9.17 million hectares of its forest in about 40 years of time with the conversion of 4.24 million hectares of forestland into non-forest wasteland. Demand and supply deficit of 3 Fs—Fuelwood, Fodder and Forage, besides timber, has increased manifold due to stagnant production, viewed in the context of increasing population pressure.

The National Forest Policy, 1988, stressed the importance of people's participation in protection, conservation and development of forest areas in the country. The main objective of the policy has been that the forest communities should be motivated to identify themselves with the development and protection of forests from which they derive considerable benefits. The State of Andhra Pradesh has taken up the Joint Forest Management (JFM) programme since 1994. It is one of the 22 Indian states initiating JFM to regenerate degraded forests and improve the economic condition of the forest dwellers. JFM programme is one of the 3 major components under the World Bank aided "Andhra Pradesh Forest Project" (APFP), the other two components being Production Forestry Scheme and Community and Private Forestry Scheme. APFP is funded for a period of 6 years initially. The main objective of this programme is the protection and management of 173000 hectares of forestland through the Vana Samrakshna Samitis (VSS), which are village-level people's institutions.

In this study an attempt has been made to understand the importance of forest on tribal life, the implications of recent forest policies on forest communities, tribal participation in World Bank aided JFM and the role of anthropology in understanding the whole process of tribal-forest nexus.

Study Area

Visakhapatnam District in Andhra Pradesh has two distinct regions of contrasting ecological and topographic features: one with plain landscape extending from the sea coast up to the foothills of the

Eastern Ghats with moderate temperature, and the second, covered by thick forests atop elevated Eastern Ghats with cold climate. The latter forms the Agency Area of the district. This study was conducted in Vanabhasingi, Jerrela and Kondapada villages of Munchingput Mandal and Karakaput village of Paderu Mandal, which fall under Paderu Forest Division of the Visakha Agency Area in Andhra Pradesh. The study villages were selected by purposive sampling. Out of these villages, Kondapada and Karakaput have VSS, which were formed way back in 1996 under JFM programme. The major tribal groups in the villages include Bagata, Konda Dora, Konda Kammara, Kotiya, Mali, Porja, and Valmiki. Table 11.1 indicates the population in the study villages.

Table 11.1: Tribe-wise Population in Study Villages

Tribe/Caste	*Vanabhasingi*		*Jerrela*		*Kondapada*		*Karakaput*	
	HH	*Polulation*	*HH*	*Population*	*HH*	*Population*	*HH*	*Population*
Mali	41	188	–	–	–	–	–	–
Kotiya	3	10	–	–	–	–	–	–
Bagata	4	20	–	–	34	141	–	–
Porja	1	4	45	190	1	5	–	–
Konda Kammara	1	6	–	–	–	–	–	–
Valmiki	3	8	6	24	–	–	–	–
Konda Dora	–	–	–	–	–	–	52	256
Sindi	1	5	–	–	–	–	–	–
Tamil Muslim	1	4	–	–	–	–	–	–
Total	55	245	51	214	35	146	52	256

Forest Area

The total geographical area of India is just over 328.8 million hectares. In 1987, the recorded forest area in the country was 75.18 million hectares or 22.8 per cent of the total geographical area. Table 11.2 shows the classification of area under forest, as per the State of Forest Report (1987) prepared by the Forest Survey of India, MoEF, Government of India. The National Forest Policy of 1952 aimed at maintaining one-third of the total geographical area under forest in plains and 60 per cent in hilly regions. But the reality is somewhat different.

Table 11.2: Forest Types in India

Forest	*Area in Million Hectares*
Legal Status:	
Reserved Forest	40.18
Protected Forest	21.73
Unclassified Forest	13.27
Total	75.18
Actual Forest Cover:	
Dense Forest	36.14
Open Forest	27.66
Mangrove Forest	00.40
Total	64.20
Types:	
Tropical Forest	52.00
Sub-tropical Forest	05.77
Temperate Forest	04.57
Alpine Forest	01.86
Total	64.20

Source: Government of India, Ministry of Environment and Forests, Forest Survey of India, Dehradun, The State of Forest Report, 1987.

The State of Andhra Pradesh has a total forest area of 61613.63 km^2. Forests in the state cover about 22.4 per cent of the total geographical area. Of the 3 regions of the state, Telangana has the largest share of forest area (10.16%), followed by Coastal Andhra (7.12%) and Rayalaseema (5.86%). In each of these regions the share of the area under forest to their respective local areas is broadly similar (*viz.* Telengana 24.24%, Rayalaseema 23.84% and Coastal Andhra 21.11%) and almost equals the share of forest area at the state level. At the district level, only 8 of the 23 districts have areas about 25 per cent under forest. Of these, 3 are in coastal Andhra (Visakhapatnam 41.40%, East Godavari 29.90% and Prakasam 26.10%), 2 in Rayalaseema (Cuddapah 32.40% and Chittoor 30.30%) and 3 in Telangana (Khammam 47.80%, Adilabad 36.50% and Warangal 29.90%). All the 23 districts in the state are classified into 10 territorial forest circles, such as Ananthapur, Kurnool, Guntur, Rajamundry, Visakhapatnam, Khammam, Warangal, Adilabad, Hyderabad and Nizamabad (Annual Administrative Report, Forest Department, Government of A.P., 1981-82). Of these 10 territorial forest circles, Visakhapatnam has the forest area of 4698.56 km^2, which constitutes 41.40 per cent of the total area of the district. The present study was carried out in the Paderu division of Visakhapatnam forest circle. Table 11.3 shows the Mandal-wise distribution of forest under Paderu division.

Table 11.3: Distribution of Forest Area in Paderu Division

Mandal	*Total Area in hectares*	*Forest Area in hectares*
Paderu	48400	9519.31
G. Madugula	54400	18229.27
Hukumpeta	62300	6037.91
Pedabayalu	50900	18935.10
Munchingput	56100	22539.84
Dumbriguda	26700	17735.36
Araku Valley	26100	11865.33
Total	324900	103862.12

It is evident from the Table 11.3 that Munchingput Mandal has the largest forest area in the whole of Paderu Forest Division and therefore, 3 study villages; Vanabhasingi, Jerrela and Kondapada belonging to this Mandal have been selected. The fourth village, Karakaput, falls under Paderu Mandal, which has a considerable forest area.

Forest in Tribal Life

From early writings by the British administrators, it is evident that nearly half of the areas in India were under forest once upon a time. Capt. Forsy in his study of the highlands of Central India in 1860 has given a comprehensive account of the stretch of forest that existed in the Meykel and Satpura ranges. Sir W. Grigson fully realized the importance of forest in the tribal life of India and paid much attention to the improvement of forest in the Bastar region of the present day State of Chatisgarh. Dr. Verrier Elwin, who worked among the Murias of Bastar described how the Murias explored the fauna of the region and achieved a harmony between the life of the region, the life of the hunter and the institutional life of the Ghotuls or youth dormitories. The legends of the Gonds of Adilabad reveals that their imaginations linked up vividly with their greatest gods. The forests are associated with the worship of the dead, and also worship of some of the oldest trees, which help in their survival for centuries.

In most of the countries, of late, humans have been improvident by destroying forests to make way for their homes, hearths and industries for comfort. This has resulted in significant environmental changes, eventually influencing the normal life of the forest dwellers. Most of the countries in the world have realized now the great importance of forests for not only human survival, but also as a vital contributory factor to the growth of human culture and civilization. Nevertheless, the present approach and outlook of the urban leadership, economists and legislators are inadequate to protect, preserve and utilize forests for their own sake, as well as for the preservation of natural wealth and for the welfare of those who live in or near them.

In the Visakha Agency area a large majority of tribal people continued to live in forests and hills. The Porja, Khond, Gadaba, Konda Dora, Nooka Dora, and other tribes continued to use the forest as their homeland in spite of stress, strain, invasion and defeat. Subsequently, these tribes have adjusted themselves to the fluctuations of the new developments in agricultural economy. They could very well face the problems of adaptability as long as they were not disturbed by the complications of political developments, legislation and encroachment of new economic and market forces.

Tribals and Forest Flora and Fauna

Social organization of the tribals is generally based on totemic clans. Various tribal groups claim mythical affinity with different species of natural animate or inanimate objects, which they believe as their ancestors. This belief system and associated practices are called totemism. The totemic objects are invariably considered as sacred, and killing or eating these objects are strict taboos. In case, a totemic animal dies, the concerned clan members observe death rituals and bury it as if their own kith or kin is dead. The tribes of Visakha Agency have the totemic clans, such as *korra* (Sun), *ontala* (snake), *pangi* (kite), *kello* (tiger), *kimudu* (bear), *gollori* (monkey), *chelli* (goat), *matya* (fish), etc. Tribals in the agency believe that their gods and goddesses take aboard in forests, and therefore, they consider hills and forests as their sacred complexes. They observe annual rituals and ceremonies in honour of these gods and goddesses. They have a strong belief that many spirits wonder in the forest and take shelter on certain trees, water points, caves and rocks. They consider some trees in the forest as sacred and keep their deities under the shades of such trees. Some of the sacred trees for the tribes of Visakha Agency are: Ippa (*Madhuka longifolia)*, Jammi (*Prospers cinararia*), Marri (*Ficus bengalensis*), Konda Juvvi (*Ficus juberculate*), Ravi (*Ficus raligrosa*), Dondera (*Butia frondosa*), Neem (*Margosa indica*), Neredu (*Myrtus cyneinum*), Jalli (*Araclus futecosa*), Andugugu (*Strychnos photatorum*), etc.

It is customary that the tribals do not eat new fruits or flowers, either produced or collected from the forest, unless they are ritually offered to their gods and goddesses. They also conventionally share the first fruits with the members of their community. Marrying with the fruit bearing trees is very popular among the tribes of the Visakha Agency. Ceremonial eating of first mango fruits is always preceded by mock marriage with the *mamidi* (mango) tree. The tribal who planted the mango tree will have to tie *pothus* (marriage badge) to a branch of the said tree, when it first starts bearing fruits.

Tribes and Forest Resources

The tribals collect many Minor Forest Produces (MFP) for self-consumption as well as for the market. They collect firewood for fuel, timber for construction and making agricultural implements, furniture and other articles for domestic use. The use *adda* fibre for rope making. Sometimes, firewood is collected and sold in the market. It is the primary source of income for some families of the Primitive Tribal Groups (PTGs). Forest is used for grazing of their domesticated animals. *Mohwa* flowers are used for the preparation of country liquor through the traditional method of distillation. They also extract toddy from the sago palm tree (*jeelugu chettu*). Forest is considered as the storehouse of herbal medicinal plants, about which the tribes are well aware. The tribes in the Visakha Agency still practice shifting cultivation or *podu*. This form of cultivation appears to have been well established during the Neolithic period, more than 10000 years ago. This form of cultivation is mostly suitable for the humid tropical forests, where the rate of vegetation regeneration is high.

Forest Policies and Tribes

During the British rule in India and after Independence, spate of forest legislation restricted the tribals from entering into the reserved forests for the exploitation of forest resources. Large-scale deforestation and degradation of the environment created a critical condition for their survival. With a view to protecting forest, the first ever Forest Act was promulgated by the British in 1865. The provisions of this Act dealt with the details of forest conservancy, namely the procedure to be followed for creating "Reserved Forests". Commenting on this Act Stebbing recorded, "In the more backward provinces, the more or less civilized jungle tribes had to be gradually weaved from views which were the natural outcome of their immemorial usage of forests, and educated up to a realization, even if only a dim and hazy one, of the value of the protection, it was desired to give to the forests in the interests of the latter ...". However, forest conservancy remained the focus of the forest policies ever since the first forest policy was implemented in 1894, which gave precedence to permanent agriculture over forestry and offered classification of forests as protection, production, minor and pasture lands, and considered forests as "reservoir of valuable timber".

After Independence, the National Forest Policy was first formulated in the year 1952. The salient features of this policy was the classification of forests into 4 categories: (1) Protection forests—those forests which must be preserved or created for physical or climatic considerations, (2) National forests—those which needed to be maintained and managed to meet the needs of defence, communication, industry and general purposes of public importance, (3) Village forests—those which have to be maintained to provide firewood, to yield small timber for agricultural implements, and other forest produces for local requirement and for grazing, and (4) Free lands—the areas that come outside the scope of ordinary forest management, but are essential for improvement of the physical condition of the country.

The Forest Policy of 1952 observed, "If the following two considerations are given undue weight, it would result in the destruction of the national well-being. They are: (1) Neighbouring areas are entitled to a prior claim over the forest and its produce, and (2) Agricultural requirements have a preferential claim over forestlands" (The National Forest Policy, 1952: 28-29). In a sense, the tribals' claim over forest resources began to skew since then. "This attitude restricted the tribal claims on the one hand and did not give more importance to cultivation at the cost of forests on the other". The fact that the city dwellers naturally got higher advantage of urban facilities from which forest dwellers are permanently deprived, was completely neglected by the policy of agriculture and the latter established their industries in the sylvan surroundings of the forests (Hundred Years of Indian Forestry, 1961).

In the year 1988, the Government of India again promulgated a new forest policy to replace the 1952 document. The objective of this forest policy is considered to be more useful for conservation and regeneration of forests, but it affects the livelihood of certain tribes, which are exclusively dependent on shifting cultivation. Commenting on the new forest policy, Walter Fernandez says, "Policy that affects the very life support system of the tribals and other rural poor has been formulated without their participation. This perhaps is indicative of the attitude of the decision makers towards these marginalized groups" (1989: 37). In this policy, it is heartening to observe that the tribal relationship with forests is revived in different modes for the mutual benefit of the tribals as well as the forests.

Yet another significant development in dealing with the tribal problems has been the sensitization of the forest administration through planned education during the initial orientation in the Forest Academy (Ramesh Chandra, 2000: 14). The concepts like "Joint Forest Management" and "Joint Forest Participatory Management" could take shape only as a continuing endeavour of the latest forest policy and recognition of the people's concern and stake in the forest resources.

The forest policies prevent the tribals in many ways, even from utilizing the concessions extended to them. The declaration of wildlife protection zones in the dense forest region of Nallamalai in Andhra Pradesh resulted in the displacement of thousands of Chenchus (one of the PTGs in the state), who lived there over generations. Those of them, who are rehabilitated in the colonies, have been facing the problem of adjustment to the new environment, in addition to the usual subsistence crisis. The primitive tribal groups like the Khond, Gadaba, Porja, and the shifting cultivators are scared of the forest officials to prepare new *podu* plots in the forest. There is hardly any viable subsistence alternative for these groups to eke out their livelihood. Table 11.4 explains the implications of the forest policies in the study villages.

Table 11.4: Tribal Problems Due to Forest Policy

Nature of the Problems Faced	*No. of Respondents*	*% of Total Respondents*
To prepare new podu plots	118	61.14
Preventing entry of cattle into the reserved forest	25	12.95
To encroach into reserved forest lands	32	16.58
Fear against forest officials	18	9.33
Total	193	100.00

Features of JFM

As mentioned earlier, the Forest Policy of 1988 issued guidelines for regeneration and protection of degraded forests with people's participation. Considering the importance and problems due to forest degradation in the vicinity of human habitations and the need to regenerate the same, JFM was implemented in all the districts of Andhra Pradesh. The salient features of the programme are:

1. Local people's interest to be considered before starting the programme at a given location,
2. To lay emphasis on places where good leadership is available or the NGOs are active enough to facilitate interface between the government and the people,
3. To associate an officer not below the rank of a Range Officer to ground and monitor the programme,
4. To provide for local people's requirements and wishes in the planning process, and
5. To provide for constant and frequent review of the programme and to amend the rules and regulations, if necessary, to steer the course of events in a positive direction.

Based on these points the State Governments have been directed to constitute local village communities into "Vana Samrakshana Samithis" (VSS) to carry out the forest programmes jointly with the State Forest Departments as per the rules annexed to the Government Order and the guidelines issued by the Government of India as per the 1988 National Forest Policy. The Forest Department in Andhra Pradesh has started a campaign called "Vana Samrakshana Udyamam" (VASU) since 1996 on the same lines as APFP. This programme is not covered by the World Bank aid, though efforts are being made to mobilize funds by the State Government. Thus with the same theme and concepts, JFM in Andhra Pradesh is being carried out under two streams—JFM (APFP) and JFM (VASU). The Forest Department and the NGOs are playing key roles in these programmes.

Rights and Benefits to VSS

The VSS protecting the forests is entitled to the following shares from the forest:

(*a*) All Non-Timber Forest Produce (NTFP), except those for which the GCC holds the monopoly rights. However, the right to collect shall remain with the members of the VSS, if they so desire. The members shall be paid collection charges upon delivery of the produce as per the rates fixed by the government.

(*b*) VSS shall be entitled to 100 per cent share in timber and bamboo harvested from the regenerated degraded forests as prescribed in the approved micro-plan, subject to the following conditions.

(*c*) Expenditure incurred on harvesting shall be deducted from the total income. However, the harvesting work will be done by the members of the VSS only as far as possible.

(*d*) Expenditure necessary to sustain the productivity of forests, like raising plantations, carrying out other silvicultural operations as per the micro-plan shall be deducted from the total income. This amount will be retained in the joint account of the VSS and the Forest Department for ploughing back in the forests under the management of VSS (this amount should ordinarily be 50 per cent of the net income after deducting harvesting and transportation costs, and in case the required amount is more than 50 per cent of the income, the proposal needs approval of the general body of the VSS).

(*e*) Balance income shall be equally distributed among all the members of the VSS.

Some of the regulations that govern the VSS are:

(*a*) Access to forestland and usufructuary benefits will be allowed only to the members of the VSS.

(*b*) Cutting of trees should not be permitted before they are ripe for harvesting. The Forest Department also should not cut trees on the forestland being protected by the members of VSS, except in the manner prescribed in the approved JFM plan. In case of emergency, the needs of the members of the VSS and the managing committee should be taken into account.

(*c*) The areas to be selected for treatment under JFM should be free from the claims (including existing rights, privileges and concessions) of any person, who is not a beneficiary under the scheme.

(*d*) Wherever voluntary agencies are available with experience in forestry programmes, they may be associated to play the role of facilitator and as an interface between the Forest Department and the community. They can articulate the views of the community. The members of the voluntary agencies would not however be entitled to any remuneration, rights or benefits under the JFM programme.

(*e*) The village falling within the watershed as identified by OPAP may be given preference. I introducing JFM programmes so as to enable to integrate with the holistic activity.

(*f*) The Divisional Forest Officer may supercede the VSS for sufficient reasons only after the approval of the District Forestry Committee.

(*g*) The JFM programme will be reviewed after a period of 10 years, but the government reserves the right to do so even earlier, if circumstances so warrant.

JFM in Paderu Division

It is estimated that about 38000 hectares of forestland have been degraded in Paderu Forest Division alone to meet an enormous demand for forest resources due to biotic pressures, such as fuel requirements, grazing land for livestock, and land for agriculture. In order to conserve and regenerate the forest, the Division has taken up JFM since 1993-94. The programme has been in operation in 7 Revenue Mandals in the Division. Between 1993 and 2001, about 296 VSS were formed in the Division and Table 11.5 lists the details of the operationalization of the programme.

Table 11.5: JFM in Paderu Forest Division

Scheme	*No. of VSS*	*Total Members*	*Land Brought Under JFM (ha)*
APFP	93	18686	15677.14
CSS/AST & RP	8	1299	728.55
CSS (NTFP)	4	342	488.64
NABARD-V	65	8277	6340.89
VASU (EAS)	111	11702	10476.31
CSS (Medicinal)	8	304	350.00
AOFFP	7	295	553.00
Total	296	40905	34614.53

People's Participation in JFM

In order to understand the tribal participation in JFM and other programmes of afforestation, an in-depth empirical study was conducted in 4 study villages mentioned earlier. A total of 193 households were covered and 193 head of the households in 4 study villages were interviewed. Of these 4 villages, VSS were found in Kondapada and Karakaput villages.

In Kondapada village, an amount of Rs. 3,29,793 was spent between 1996 and 2000. The tribal residents of the village are found actively participating in JFM programme. They informed that the programme was definitely helpful for their economic betterment as well as for the regeneration of the degraded forestland. They reported that they have stopped clearing new *podu* plots in the reserved forests. A large number of the residents showed interest in horticulture and planting trees having commercial value around their settlements. In fact, the villagers expressed their eagerness to be supplied with the saplings of silver oak, eucalyptus, jofra, neredu, kagu or ganuga, usiri, jack, mango, etc. by the Forest Department. They have a feeling that afforestation is helpful in receiving higher rainfall and reducing soil erosion. The villages where JFM is not in operation, the people participate in the afforestation programme undertaken by the ITDA, although the villagers feel that it is not as effective as JFM, as the latter is funded by the World Bank.

Table 11.6: Awareness about JFM in Study Villages

Village	*Respondents Aware of JFM*		*Respondents Unaware of JFM*	
	No.	*%*	*No.*	*%*
Vanabhasingi	27	13.99	28	14.51
Karakaput	52	26.94	–	–
Jerrela	24	12.44	27	13.99
Kondapada	35	18.13	–	–
Total	138	71.50	55	28.50

Table 11.6 reveals the awareness of the tribals about the JFM. It is found that about 71.5 per cent of the respondents in the study villagers are aware of the JFM, while 28.5 per cent are not aware. If this programme is extended to the non-implemented villages within a year or two, it is felt that it would yield good results and some more degraded forestland could be regenerated.

In Visakha Agency, large number of tribal villages are still not covered by the JFM programme. From among the 4 study villages, 2 do not have VSS and not covered under JFM programme. Table 11.7 details the beneficiaries from the other 2 villages, which come under the JFM programme.

Table 11.7: JFM Beneficiaries in Two Study Villages

Village	*No. of Families Benefited*	*% of Total Families*
Vanabhasingi	52	26.94
Karakaput	35	18.13
Total	87	45.07

Conclusion

Since generations, tribals have established symbiotic relations with the forest. They regularly interact with the forest for their livelihood. It is an established fact that the mankind would live as long as the forests live. In general, forests are the most valuable heritage of mankind. Since long tribals have continued to live in the forest and adapted to the forest ecosystem in such a way that one cannot be conceptualized without the other. Therefore, the tribals should be allowed to utilize the forest resources for meeting their basic requirements.

Shifting cultivation in the tribal areas is an age-old practice. In fact, the existing ecological condition forced them to practice this crude method of cultivation for their subsistence and survival. Of course, this is one of the causative factors of deforestation in the tribal areas. But it must be understood that the damage caused due to shifting cultivation is comparatively less than the damage due to the interference by other agencies, such as timber merchants, smugglers, industrial houses, mining, hydro-electrical projects, etc. Anthropological studies reveal that the tribal families practicing shifting cultivation need to be given alternative agricultural land for growing paddy and cash crops. Totemic and sacred trees should be identified and planted under the JFM programme. Fruit bearing trees should be supplied to the tribals under this scheme. Constant follow up action is essential for the success of the programme. Periodical evaluation is also needed to assess the progress and to identify the lapses of the programme.

The forest policies are at least good in so far as the protection and conservation of the forests. But these policies restrict the entry of the tribals into the forest for grazing their cattle and collection of firewood. The forest policy of 1988 is totally against the practice of *podu*, which has created the problem of survival for those, who are exclusively dependent on this kind of cultivation.

The JFM programme in the study villages has received good response from the tribal people with the VSS members actively getting involved in the programme. However, creation of awareness, community forestry, farm and agro-forestry and social forestry should be intensified in the tribal areas to make them participate in these programmes. The psychology and culture of the tribal people should be properly understood to implement these programmes effectively. If they understand the evil effects of deforestation and importance of conservations, they can come forward voluntarily to take up afforestation.

Anthropological studies are much helpful to understand the indigenous methods of conservation, the role of forest in tribal life and the problems associated with deforestation. Anthropological methods and techniques are useful to persuade the tribals to participate in the JFM programmes. The integrated empirical observation of an anthropologist and the practical knowledge of the forest officials and other government and non-government agencies seem to be much useful for tribal development in the desired direction.

REFERENCES

Agarwal, Anil and Sunita Narain (1986), *The State of India's Environment, 1984-85*, New Delhi: Centre for Science and Environment.

Biswas, S.K. (1988), *Forest Administration in India*, Allahabad: Chugh Publications.

Brandis, D. (1997), *Indian Forestry*, Oriental University Institute.

Fernandes, Walter (1989), The Forest Policy and the Forest Conservation (Amendment) Act, 1988, *Lokayan*, Jan.-Feb.

Government of India (1995), *State of the Forest Report*, Dehradun: Forest Survey of India, Ministry of Environment and Forest.

Indurkar, Pushpa (1992), *Forestry, Environment and Economic Development*, New Delhi: Ashish Publishing House.

Rameshchandra (ed) (2000), *Environment, Forest and Tribes*, New Delhi: Himanshu Publications.

Roy-Burman, B.K. (1968), Forests and Tribals in India, In L.P. Vidyarthi (ed) *Applied Anthropology in India*, Allahabad: Kitab Mahal.

Subramanyam, V. (2001), Forest Resource Management of Tribals in Visakha Agency Area, UGC Minor Project Report (Unpublished), Andhra University, Visakhapatnam.

12

Upholding the Rights of the Indigenous People

A Study of the Autonomous District Councils in Northeast India with Particular Reference to the Khasi Hills of Meghalaya

SUDHIR JACOB GEORGE

Introduction

At the time of Independence the framers of India's Constitution grappled with the problem of incorporating a vastly diverse population into a single political entity. India's tribes comprising about 8.08 per cent of the total population, hundreds of languages within four language families, and countless tribal divisions and religious practices proved to be problematic issues of this overall challenge. India's founding fathers demonstrated a necessary sensitivity towards the needs of the tribal groups, particularly those inhabiting the Northeastern part of the country, as these tribal groups' relationship to the governing institutions under the British rule was especially fragmented and indirect. To correct this and also in recognition of the special characteristics of the region, the Autonomous District Councils (ADCs), governed by the Sixth Schedule to the Constitution was provided. The Committee on Tribal Areas headed by G.P. Bordoloi submitted a report in accordance with the directions of the Advisory Committee on the Fundamental Rights of Minorities, Tribal Areas, etc. of the Constituent Assembly of India. The Bordoloi Committee opined that while it is in everyone's interest to incorporate all Indians into a single representative system, a period of substantial autonomy at the district level in the tribal areas would enhance that process, while at the same time offer a reasonable compromise for those people in the Northeast who sought complete independence from India as well as Britain. The Bordoloi Committee crafted an institution to ensure maintenance of the distinct social customs and tribal organizations of different peoples as well as their religious beliefs, as also to ameliorate the fear of tribal exploitation by the people of the plains on account of their superior organization and experience in business. It also sought to ensure that the specified regions would have sufficient financial autonomy to make the political, social and economic autonomy meaningful. This paper attempts to analyze the working of Autonomous District Councils (ADCs) in the tribal areas of Northeast India, under the Sixth Schedule of the Constitution with particular focus on the working of the Khasi Hills Autonomous District Council and its role in upholding and protecting the rights of the indigenous people of Meghalaya.

Fifth and Sixth Schedules of the Indian Constitution

In India a major transition took place at the time of independence and this was reflected in the debates of the Constituent Assembly regarding the Fifth and Sixth Schedules of the Constitution. The influence of Nehruvian liberalism and nationalism was applied to the British administration's excluded and partially excluded areas. The areas remained, but were re-named as "Scheduled Areas", excluded from normal post-Independence legislative and political processes. The discourse of exclusion however differed; it no longer advanced the colonial state project of state detached from society, but rather promoted the new state project of forging a national identity. In the mid-1800 the British Government in India designated certain areas as non-regulated areas, codified in the Scheduled Districts Act of 1874. In the early 20th Century, the nomenclature was changed to excluded areas, with some areas being "partially excluded" (Hasan, 1988: 28-29). The excluded and partially excluded areas tended to be at the fringe of the colonial empire at its frontiers. In these frontier areas "the boundaries of the British power.... were in fact always moving, always in a flux, right up to its last days in India" (Guha, 1977: 2). Paternalism appeared to be another reason. These areas were backward tracts and the natives of these areas were susceptible to moneylenders and manipulators coming from the more settled, urban, "advanced" areas of the Raj. Some felt that these areas should be kept in seclusion as museum specimens (Hazarika, 1966: 78; Elwin 1960: 8). While discussing about the Northeast Frontier, some members of the Constituent Assembly claimed that the British wanted the Nagas to remain as they were. For the British, then, paternalism and the creation of difference overlaid the dissection and categorization of the native society (Metcalf, 1997). The colonial state was the rational modern father; not only would it demarcate its offspring (the Indian nation), but it would draw boundaries among the siblings, shut up in the attic, prohibited and excluded from familial interaction (Fernandes, 1993: 13). In the immediate post-Independence experiment, exclusion helped define the "we" of the Indian nation. The frontier areas needed to be treated differently, not because they abutted other imperial (*i.e.* territorially aggrandizing) states, but because the loyalty of those in the areas to the new Indian state was in question. Would the Nagas in the Northeast agitate to join Burma or Tibet through irredentist movements rather than imperial designs of Burma or Tibet? (India was upstaged in 1962 by China's aggression on its Northeast border). Was the integration and assimilation of the Nagas or winning their loyalty through granting them self-government the solution to this problem? These options were debated over and over in the Constituent Assembly. There was tension in liberalism between preferring assimilation of minorities and respecting minority cultures, apparent at the time of independence and constitution building, *vis-à-vis* the walling of the liberal nation-state. The assimilationists argued against Scheduled Areas and Autonomous Councils. They adverted to national unity stating, "We should proceed in such a way that all different communities may vanish and we may have one nation, the Indian nation" (Constituent Assembly Debates, 1949: 985). They swore allegiance to the concept of equality: "We have declared at the top of our voice that every person in India, be he male or female irrespective of class, creed or community or race, shall be equal and shall have equal citizenship rights.... After all this, are we justified in creating cleavage and gap with partially excluded areas and Tribes and Councils and the rest?" (Constituent Assembly Debates, 1949: 994). The assimilationists enlisted freedom and opportunity. There was the urge to assimilate the tribals. This was denied during the British rule. The tribal people, however much they liked, did not have the opportunity of assimilation. Non-tribals had no right to purchase any property in the tribal areas. Interaction between the people of the plains and the tribals was difficult. During the British days, it was not permissible to introduce mainstream culture among the people living in the periphery. Even after the British have gone, the same conditions prevailed in the new Constitution (Constituent Assembly Debates, 1949: 1015).

The Nehruvian liberals in response argued that national unity is reinforced through accommodation not imposition; that certain tribal cultures are more egalitarian than the dominant mainstream culture, and that arrogance and disrespect underline blanket statements regarding "our culture". The Nehruvian liberals dominated the Constituent Assembly and won the debate and the Sixth Schedule, providing for the establishment of Autonomous Councils, was adopted. But in reality there were no clear-cut sides to such debates. Each side brought into at least partially, the other side's arguments (just as both sides brought into to some degree, the colonial state's justifications). This is clear in the juxtaposition of the Fifth and Sixth Schedules, both passed by the Constituent Assembly. The Fifth Schedule was much more acceptable to the assimilationists than the Sixth, because it was perceived as a temporary measure with the ultimate goal being tribal assimilation into the economic mainstream of the nation. In the meantime, paternalism and the emerging development ethos would guide implementation of the Fifth Schedule provisions. Tribals, not knowing their own economic self-interests, would have to be protected from land grabbing outsiders; the areas under the Fifth Schedule would become, in fact, special development zones. In reality, even in development terms, there has been sparse application of the provisions of the Fifth Schedule.

The Fifth Schedule did not provide for self-government, which the Sixth Schedule allowed for the establishment of Autonomous Councils. These then are to be governed by predominantly elected district and regional Autonomous Councils, which can set up their own laws and which have legislative jurisdiction over land, forest, water, agriculture, education, health, and social issues. The Councils are also responsible for internal adjudication. The Councils have their own budgets and can levy and collect taxes and receive royalties from mining leases. They can also impose restrictions on outsiders owning property or engaging in economic activities in the district/region. The Fifth Schedule is rather modest, investing all executive and legislative powers in the State Governor, who can consult the appointed Tribal Advisory Council, that is, the Governor is able to exclude the Scheduled Areas from state legislation as well as decree legislative provisions (such as external protection from outsiders). In the Fifth Schedule it is stated, unless the context otherwise requires, the expression 'State' does not include the State of Assam (Thakur and Thakur, 1994: 2). The Sixth Schedule was limited to the Assam region and the Northeast Frontier Agency. The Assam region was more "other" than other tribal areas. It was more excluded under the British; it was more peripheral geographically, culturally and linguistically from the Hindi core (Young, 1976). Even Nehru agreed that the frontier breeds a different type of people, though he found such frontiers both physically and intellectually exciting. There was a practical reason as well for the distinction between the Fifth and Sixth Schedules: only the tribes on the southern flank of the

Brahmaputra in Assam got Autonomous Councils because that is where the opposition to integration into the new Indian nation-state thrived. The Sixth Schedule is the result of delicate negotiations between these tribals and the post-Independence Government of India (Constituent Assembly Debates, 1949: 1017).

Constitution of Autonomous District Councils

The Autonomous District Councils (ADCs) governed by the Sixth Schedule of the Constitution are a comprehensive indicator of the integrationist approach in India. The population of the areas that came under the ADCs was around 80 per cent tribal. ADCs were intended to be a mechanism whereby distinct tribal practices could be supported simultaneously, such that those communities secured access to individual oriented political institutions. The sub-committee led by G.P. Bordoloi of the Sardar Vallabhbhai Patel Advisory Committee on the Fundamental Rights of Minorities, Tribal Areas, etc. of the Constituent Assembly of India, which went into the needs and requirements of the tribes of the Northeast, while opining that it is in everyone's interest to incorporate all Indians into a single representative system, felt that a period of substantial autonomy at the district level in tribal areas would enhance that process, while at the same time offering a reasonable compromise for those people in the Northeast, who sought complete Independence from India as well as Britain (Hansaria, 1983: 183-229). The Bordoloi sub-committee report included detailed provisions for Autonomous District Councils in the erstwhile 'excluded areas' of Assam. The proposal for the Sixth Schedule of the Constitution of India was presented to the Constituent Assembly on the 5th September, 1949 and it was ratified on the 7th September, 1949.

As compared to all other institutions of Indian national incorporation, ADCs were closest to the pure integrationist position. Council members were to be freely elected, but as the population was essentially tribal, it was but natural that the majority of members would also be tribals. In addition, the

Chief Executive Member, elected by the council members, was mandatory to belong to a Scheduled Tribe. To offset this predominance of the tribals, the Governor was to nominate two members and they were to be non-tribals.

The District Councils for the Khasi, Jaintia and Garo tribes of the Northeastern State of Meghalaya are corporate bodies having perpetual succession with the right to own and dispose of property and with the right to sue and be sued. The compositions of the Councils vary from time to time and from place to place. They consist of both nominated and elected members. Each District Council has a Chairman and a Deputy Chairman with designated statutory functions. Election of members to the District Council is direct. The base of election is adult franchise, single member constituency and simple majority. Only registered voters can contest and also vote. A non-tribal has to possess residency tenure of 12 years to secure the right to vote in the District Tribal Council elections. The term of office of the members is for five years. There is a provision of the extension of the term of the District Council by one year at a time.

For the implementation of the policies and programmes approved by the District Council, a cabinet system of government exists. The Executive Committee consists of the Chief Executive Member and two others. The District Council from among its members elects the Chief Executive Member (C.E.M.). The Governor on the recommendation of the C.E.M. appoints other members. When the C.E.M. resigns, other members cease to be members of the committee. The Executive Committee is collectively responsible to the District Council. The Council may remove the Executive Committee at any time without assigning any reason. However, it has to elect a C.E.M. within 48 hours from the date of the removal of the committee. If it fails, the Governor may appoint any member of the Council to be the C.E.M. and two other members of the Council to be members of the Executive Committee. Such an Executive Committee shall hold office until the election of the C.E.M. by the District Council (Rao, Pakem and Hazarika, 1984: 160-161).

Powers and Functions of the District Council

The powers and functions of the District Council are four-fold: Legislative, Executive, Financial and Judicial. The District Council has the power to make laws on certain subjects, enumerated in the Sixth Schedule of the Constitution of India. These being, to make laws on the allotment, occupation or use of, or the setting apart of land, other than reserved forests for the purpose of grazing, residential or other non-agricultural purposes; the regulation of the practice of *jhum* or other forms of shifting cultivation; the establishment of town and village councils and the determination of their powers and functions; village police; public health and sanitation; the appointment or succession of chiefs or headmen; money-lending and trading by persons other than the Scheduled Tribes; the inheritance of property; marriage and divorce; and social customs.

As regards the executive powers, the District Councils are authorised to establish, construct or manage primary and middle schools (however, during the 1990s the State Government took over the management of primary schools as the District Council could not run them efficiently), dispensaries, markets, cattle pounds, forests, road and waterways, and determine the language to be used as the medium of instruction in schools.

The District Council has the power to assess and collect land revenue, levy taxes on land, buildings, tolls, and taxes on professions, trades, callings and employment. It can also levy taxes on the entry of goods carried on ferries, taxes on the maintenance of schools and dispensaries.

The Council has also the right for a share in the royalties received by the State Government from licences or leases granted for the purpose of prospecting or for extracting minerals. This has of late become a contentious issue with the new liberalization policy of the Government of India. Besides, the District Councils and indigenous tribal organizations are demanding the right of contracting directly with external agencies to improve the economy of their respective areas.

The Council has the power to constitute village courts for the trial of suits and cases in which both the parties are tribals. In addition to the village courts, it may constitute subordinate district and additional subordinate district council courts and also district courts. It may appoint suitable persons as judges of these courts.

Besides these functions, the State Government can entrust certain functions to the District Council. Under this proviso the development departments transferred to the control of the Councils in Meghalaya are agriculture, public works, flood control, irrigation, soil conservation, animal husbandry and veterinary services, fisheries, forests, community development, cottage industries, education up to middle school, health and family planning and development.

The officers and staff of the entrusted departments are under the immediate administrative control of the District Councils. However, they are appointed and disciplined by the State Government. They are responsible to the State Government for the implementation of the schemes entrusted to the District Councils.

The District Council can constitute committees, both *ad hoc* and standing, and determine their powers, functions and their composition.

Revenue Sources of the District Councils

The District Councils in the Northeast, particularly in Meghalaya, derive their income from various sources, *viz.*, taxes on animals, vehicles, boats; taxes on professions, lodges, callings and employment. Government grants, loans and advances and subventions from the Government are important sources of revenue. The major source of income is, however, from the forest, which is more than 65 per cent, and taxes on goods brought to the market for sale. Besides these incomes, there are grants-in-aid for various purposes. Substantial amounts are given as grants-in-aid. From this it is evident that the income from taxation is not much. In fact, the Councils are not courageous enough in levying taxes. Even if they do, they do not collect them vigorously. As a consequence, substantial amounts from this source lapse.

The Sixth Schedule attempted to give ADCs the legislative, judicial, administrative, and financial capacity—within a context of central and state interests—and needed to establish and enforce their own social and developmental priorities. These priorities are expected to be community-driven, but the institutional processes by which these priorities are to be pursued are as modern as the Indian Constitution.

Autonomous District Councils (ADCs) in the Northeast and Economic Development

Economic development of the Northeast has been faster than the rest of the country. ADCs can however share little of the credit for this success. Despite the facilities for direct economic administration as provided in the Schedule, these have considerable difficulty in both fund raising and project administration. In this light, the analysis of ADC's development effectiveness has to be critical. However, the record is not entirely bleak. The Schedule by providing an additional level for political discourse and an additional outlet for expression and resolution of local grievances has made ADCs improve on the level of social and political stability compared with what would be in their absence. Such stability improves the effectiveness of all economic initiatives regardless of the political level at which they are directly administered.

In Meghalaya, which attained the status of a full-fledged state in 1972, the ADCs are in a peculiar situation. In fact, the Khasi, Jaintia and Garo Hills were provided with District Councils as a part of the State of Assam. But the ADCs are weak agents of economic growth and development in Meghalaya for the following reasons:

(*a*) They are ineffective in lobbying at the State Government and shaping the State development budget. Influence at the state level is important not only because State Governments have the largest development budgets, but also because the States administer several Federal government-sponsored development projects. The Sixth Schedule requires the State Governments to place relevant portion of spending bills relating to ADCs in time merely for discussion. This limits their power to advise or direct the State Government. Thus in practical terms, the Khasi Hills ADC has no direct role in state budget preparation, even in the matter of grants-in-aid for small development projects.

(*b*) ADCs have been unable to influence state budget processes indirectly through members of the State Legislative Assembly (MLAs) elected from constituencies in the ADC territory. In Meghalaya, the entire area of the state falls into one of the three ADC territories. However, MLAs have tended to find themselves in an adversarial rather than cooperative relationship with ADC leaders.

(*c*) ADCs have relatively small development budgets.

(*d*) Within the context of their limited budgets, ADCs face annual budget difficulties, as the State Government is always late in providing its required disbursements.

(*e*) The ADCs are ineffective at tax collection on their own. Local and State Governments collect less taxes and fees than they can, since taxpayers as voters frequently punish ambitious tax collectors at polls (depending upon who asks, this is either a political choice or a political compulsion).

(*f*) ADCs are ineffective agents of development, as they do not deploy their meagre budget in a way that can promote economic growth.

Forest and mineral royalties finance 40 per cent of the Khasi ADC budget and this rises to 60 per cent, if State and Central Governments' block grants are excluded. This extensive reliance on resource royalties places undue pressure on Meghalaya's environment. The increased demand for government sanctioned timber felling boosts ADC royalties, but unscrupulous producers and government officials also collude to facilitate illegal felling practices.

Limestone and coal are the most important minerals in the state. Too frequently, limestone quarrying leads to environmental degradation by which the land is twice ravaged. First the trees are cut, and then soil washed away as limestone is removed from the open quarries. Though the area is declared as forestland, much of it is unredeemable wasteland. The annual production of 3 million tonnes of coal in the state, mostly from open cast coal mines, have their own set of environment related problems and other difficulties. The states' coal supply is slated to last another century but the costs have already begun to tell in the form of increasingly acidic water, and further about 40 per cent of those employed in the coal mining areas are the school drop-outs. Meghalaya's three ADCs have no role in regulating coalmines but they receive royalties; thus they have to cope, in one way or the other, with the social and environmental dilemmas presented by the mining industry.

Notwithstanding the above drawbacks in economic development, in an important sense however, ADCs play a significant developmental role. Their substantial staffs are actively involved in community outreach and provide regular opportunities for villagers to voice economic, political, and social grievances to the extent that the ADC's institutionalisation of political discourse dissuades communities from greater violent presentations of their political concerns, it enhances the stability that any effective economic development operation requires.

Social Impact of Autonomous District Councils

The main function of the ADCs has been integration of tribal communities into the Indian political system without undue external pressures on well-functioning social systems. The substance of tribal culture need not change as a result of instituting ADCs but tribal processes were expected gradually to become more consistent with broader Indian political institutions. ADCs are granted the powers to design primary school curricula, run schools, try cases in district courts, and codify customary laws through legislation. Each of these powers has left its mark on the tribes, ADC and the State. The Khasi ADC has used schools for political socialization. Teachers are important links between villagers and the modern society. Their advice is sought regarding legal, medical, and most important, political voting questions. However, most often, ADC selects teachers on political convictions rather than on merit. In both cases familial, clan, rather than tribe are the most important community units. Over a period of time in view of the mismanagement of the primary education sector in mid-1990s in Meghalaya, the three ADCs lost the cultural, social, political and economic benefits of administering primary education, as the State Government took over the administration of primary education in the state.

Another area in which the ADC does have a significant social impact is the administration of justice. The Sixth Schedule is ambiguous about the relationship between the state, ADC and tribal courts. Para 4 authorizes the ADCs and regional councils within ADCs to constitute district courts, village councils and courts, and the procedures to be followed by such courts regarding the conduct of cases, appeals, and enforcement of court decisions and orders. Para 5 authorizes the Governor to extend the authority of the ADC courts to try cases that would carry a sentence of more than five years in prison, including a death sentence. The Sixth Schedule, then, provides the opportunity for the ADC to administer the judicial disputes ranging from the smallest village quarrels to capital offences. However, in practice, it has not worked out that way. There has been not a single instance anywhere in the Northeast that the Governor has authorized an ADC court to try a major crime.

The final area in which the ADCs have a social impact is through their legislative capacity. ADCs have not passed many laws and only a portion of these has received the constitutionally required assent of the State Governor. Those passed, however, have had complex effects on Khasi social relations. They have begun the process of codifying customary laws, but have also crafted laws that are quite inconsistent with the customs. Though it has clarified traditional tribal political processes, but by doing so has changed those very processes.

Several of the laws the ADC attempted to enact have been contrary to the interpretations of Khasi tribal custom. In particular, the ADC has essayed to weaken the customary power of women in an essentially matrilineal society. Customarily, Khasi lineage follows matrilineal practice with the male moving into his wife's family home, all property devolving to the youngest female in the wife's family. However, a 1980 Khasi ADC bill labelled "Inheritance of Self Acquired Property would have enabled every Khasi male to bequeath possessions and property purchased with money he himself earned". Similarly, a 1997 Bill would have limited the rights of children of a Khasi woman who married a non-Khasi man to receive government benefits directed exclusively towards Khasis. These Bills clearly aimed at changing customary relations between genders. For this reason, the Governor refused to give his constitutionally required assent to the Bills, but the fact is that the ADC, which is charged with representing the Khasi people and codifying Khasi customary laws, attempted to pass them into laws in the first place. Another set of laws has codified traditional Khasi political process. The ADC in Meghalaya also codified its constitutional rights to manage markets and forests and to collect revenue from both. It also established a parallel town-level administrative body, the town committee.

These legal rights had a limited impact, especially in the early years, because the ADC lacked practical enforcement ability; tribal chiefs were in fact in control at the village level. Even today, the tribal chiefs collect and keep most market revenue. Rather than competing with tribal institutions, the ADC regulations have induced those institutions in conformity with modern expectations. There are periodic disputes regarding elections, but the ADC, which has established processes by which disputes are resolved, runs these elections. Instead, the direct influence of the town committees waned, as village *durbars* began to conduct themselves more and more according to the two-committee rules. Tribal politics continued by and large to proceed according to customary law, yet crucial links with modern political and judicial institutions were established from early in the Khasi ADC's career. Institutional competition has led to an evolution of tribal political processes in the direction of ADC role models. District level autonomy has facilitated social change in tribes through the process of political dialogue among the main protagonists, thereby reducing the incidence of more violent alternatives.

Conclusion

Though functionally weak, ADCs have a substantial and positive impact on the deepening of the democratic process. In addition to its effect at the village level—both through ADC created village councils and town committees, and through its indirect shaping of change in traditional tribal political processes—a new layer in India's federal democracy has increased the number of positions available to those aspiring to political leadership. For some, the ADC is an end-point. Such modest aspirants help to ensure that at least a portion of the competition within the ADC territory remains between political combatants in that arena, if the ADC represents the interests of its citizens with a single voice, which is created through a pluralist political process. Other ADC leaders use the experience gained at the ADC level as a springboard to higher political office. Here again pluralist political analysis explains the competitive framework in which such aspirants operate. Both as a political institution and as a formal link to state political institutions, the ADC eases pressures by ethnic communities to resort to violence in pursuit of their political objectives.

The ADC in addition to being a source for party penetration and community dialogue has provided an opportunity for upwardly mobile leaders to have their political apprenticeship. Thus by fostering an additional layer of political participation, the ADCs have broadened the net from which the state and national political leaders are selected. The calibre and competence of the elected leaders has over time improved and concomitantly, the ability of all levels of the state political institutions, to resolve conflicts without the disputants resorting to violence. ADCs, the third tier in India's federal system, enable political representation and debate to take place in a more comprehensive manner than would have possible at the state level *per se*.

REFERERENCES

Elwin, Verrier (1966), *The Adivasis*, Delhi: Ministry of Information and Broadcasting, Government of India.

Fernandes, Walter (1993), *The Indigenous Question: Search for an Identity*, New Delhi: Indian Social Institute.

Government of India (1949), *Debates*, Constituent Assembly, Delhi.

Guha, Amalendu (1977), *Planter Raj to Swaraj: Freedom Struggle and Electoral Politics in Assam, 1826-1947*, New Delhi: ICHR.

Hansaria, B.L. (1983), *Sixth Schedule to the Constitution of India: A Study*, Guwahati: Ashok Publishing.

Hasan, Amir (1988), *Tribal Administration in India*, Delhi: B.R. Publishing.

Hazarika, J. (1966), *Geopolitics of North-East India*, New Delhi: Gian Publishing.

Metcalf, Thomas R. (1997), *Ideologies of the Raj*, Cambridge: Cambridge University Press.

Rao, V.V., Pakem, B., Hazarika, N. (1984), *A Century of Government and Politics in North-East India, Vol. II, Meghalaya 1874-1983*, New Delhi: S. Chand.

Thakur, Devendra and D.N. Thakur (1994), Tribal Life in India, in *Tribal Law and Administration*, New Delhi: Deep and Deep.

Young, Crawford M. (1976), *The Politics of Cultural Pluralism*, Madison: University of Wisconsin Press.

13

Study of Tribal or Rural Health in the Context of Globalization

An Anthropological Framework

N. SUDHAKAR RAO

Introduction

The main objective of this paper is to develop a conceptual framework to study health culture in the holistic perspective. This framework provides a theoretical background that enables an anthropologist to undertake specific case studies. However, particular issues of health can also be located within the same framework either for comparison or in-depth understanding of the problem. The earlier anthropological attempts of 'world distribution theories of illness', 'systemic approach' and 'ecological approach' of studying illness shall be placed in the perspective so that anthropological understanding of health culture would be meaningful. This broader framework, it is hoped, will be of great help meeting the challenge of comprehensive understanding of the health status of the Indian rural or tribal population in the changing scenario due to the process of globalization.

First, this paper attempts to provide a background for the present study. Then, it will focus on the consequences of globalization and the New Economic Policy of the Government of India implemented since 1991. It follows the anthropological perspective on the study of health and illness, and finally, the holistic study of health culture.

Background

Either in small and pre-literate or in large and post-industrial society, health care assumes great significance. In the recent past, the slogan 'Health for All by 2000 AD' emerged from the debate on health among intellectuals, administrators, medical personnel, social scientists and social workers of all the countries. But the call 'health for all' is yet to see the day despite multi-pronged attacks on the health problems which have been enmeshed intricately with the socio-cultural practices, availability of infrastructural facilities, perspectives of the governments, public participation, and so on. In an effort to achieve this goal of 'health for all' the Alma Ata Declaration has placed health services to those inhabiting in hilly terrains, far flung or remote areas, precisely the tribal/ethnic and rural populations, on the first priority. It covers all endemic disease-affected populations and other vulnerable sections of the society (Jose, 1998).

Though health is a matter of concern and it is critical in every society for long-term development of individuals and society at large, it has been argued that health care is often times beset with problems due to undue priorities given on gender and age lines. Thus, it is argued that women have long been neglected in several patriarchal societies and also by policy framers and executors, especially in these societies. The health status of women and men is different in almost all countries, and it is a fact that women live longer than men. But in reality women maintain poor health due to biological, social and cultural reasons. Female disability is especially high in Asia according to World Development Report, 1993 (Devi, 1998: 2). The social and cultural reasons of gender bias have been well documented in several research reports and publications around the world. In Indian context, it is said that the story of indifferent attitude towards women starts from the moment it is known that the conceived baby is a girl and it runs throughout her childhood, adolescence, married life, old age and ends only with her death. In other words the 'discrimination starts from womb and ends up in the tomb' (Nigam, 1999:11). In India several researchers noted that in the male dominated society, woman's health is generally accorded secondary importance (Deodhar, 1983; Nagla, 1997; Nigam, 1999; Singh and Mohanti, 1995).

Globally, while old problems persist, new problems have been added due to environmental degradation, pollution, and the emergence of new diseases and drug resistant and mutant micro-organisms. India is no exception in this aspect also. The last two have increased burden on the medical sciences to confront with the new as well as old problems. Besides these, people of India had to face other problems as the consequences of New Economic Policies of the government. It is feared that the gap between rich and poor is on the increase; the cut in the subsidies and decreased expenditure on public health and education would seriously affect the health of the poor; and the privatisation would affect employment opportunities for dalit, tribes and women. All of these directly or indirectly would have impact on the health status of the poorer sections of the society. However, 'communication revolution' in this context, is significant, as it has provided some respite causing dramatic changes in the global scenario by removing the physical barriers between the countries and people paving way for the 'global community'. This has resulted in taking health care much closer to the common people. The health consciousness of the developed and developing countries brought forth several means of taking the health care to the doorsteps of the people. The role played by the national and international voluntary organizations in this regard will have to be recognized at this time, especially in underdeveloped countries, where infrastructure facilities are poorly developed. But one has to find out whether these developments would be of any help for the majority of the marginal people.

In the above background, the role of anthropology may be seen as having immense potentiality to serve the humanity. In this endeavour, we may find what anthropology has contributed to the health sector and what it can do in future. So far as the contribution of anthropology to health care is concerned, it has provided creditable service with the participation of anthropologists for the success of health care programmes, especially in non-western societies (Enge and Harrison, 1986; Green, 1986; Paul, 1955). The health personnel have recognized and appreciated the anthropological methods of data collection, such as participant observation, emic approach and holistic perspective, for these methods provide greater insights into the health interventions than the conventional methods followed by others (Foster, 1953; Pelto, 1978). Further, anthropological knowledge of tribal and rural society and culture around the globe has been proved vital for the health interventions. But there seems to be great contentment among the anthropologists about the appreciation and appropriation of anthropological methods and body of cultural knowledge provided by them. In fact, they should strive that the theoretical basis of anthropology to understand health system helps the health personnel and the governments to improve the health conditions of the tribal and non-tribal fellow citizens. Even a cursory look at the publications on ethno-medicine reveals nothing but a catalogue of beliefs related to health, different herbs, native pharmacopoeia and etiological and cognitive aspects of illness and curative methods (Barua and Phukan, 1998; Khatua, 1998). Some rituals of either curative or thanks giving type are also mentioned sporadically. What we really lack is sound theoretical perspective that will guide investigation and improve data collection techniques and analysis as well.

Globalization and the New Economic Policy

Though globalization process is essentially economic in nature, it has far reaching effects on the social life of the people, especially of the poor in the developing countries. Neither distance nor national borders impede economic transactions when the costs of transport and communication become minimum and the barriers created by different national states become porous in the process of globalization. Initiated by the Euro-American developed countries, it enveloped entire global communities promising great future for the third world, and was thus imperialist in nature, which had hegemonic influence on the latter. Being dependent on the International Monetary Fund (IMF) and the World Bank (WB) that are under the control of the developed countries, India had to succumb to the prescriptions of the Structural Adjustment Programme (SAP). In response to the balance of payment crisis, the Indian Government initiated a series of economic reforms from July 1991 to conform to the SAP guidelines. These economic reformations are now known as the New Economic Policy (NEP) and they paved way for privatization, which is a departure from the past policy of protectionist, welfare-oriented and socially responsible government. It is now believed that for accelerating the economic growth it is necessary that the state should encourage the private sector not only in domestic but also in international markets. Further, the state should withdraw subsidies and curtail government expenditure especially through cuts in social sector programmes and dismiss unproductive public sector employees. It also envisaged that privatization of social programmes like health and education on the principles of cost recovery. The main thrust in this new economic policy is to reduce state control over economy and to stimulate exports (Streeten, 1987: 1469-70).

Pathy (1995) believes that according to the World Development Report (1992) the emphasis on the exports to augment foreign exchange earnings has damaged the natural environment, and the adoption of SAP has invariably increased the debt burden of the signatory countries and the ecological destruction and impoverishment of the marginalized peoples (*ibid.*:17). In the SAP administered countries there is an increased poverty, unemployment, inequality and destitution. The UNDP has observed that the adoption of SAP has doubled the absolute poverty, income inequality and infant mortality (*ibid.*:17). Pathy notes some evidence of negative impact of NEP in India with large-scale retrenchment in the public and private sectors and aggravation of unemployment and poverty, which are endemic in the country.

Let me quote Pathy, though it is a bit long, for its aptness. "The trend is obviously not to increase public health infrastructure but to privatize it and levy user charges in the exiting public health sector. The World Bank Report, Investment in Health (1993), proposes to restrict the PHCs for only population control and prevention of communicable diseases and for 'user fees' to be instituted in public hospitals to recover the costs, with curative medicine being left to the private sector. As such, currently only a quarter of the health expenditure is in the public sector, amount to barely Rs. 27 per capita per year in rural areas and Rs. 100 per capita per year in urban areas. The present health policy will further aggravate the health crisis of the poor, the marginalized, the women, dalits, tribals and senior citizens. The increase in the 1994-95 budgets on health, education and rural development is largely nominal. The reduction in social sector investment and the price rise of basic necessities will increase illiteracy, ill health and poverty of the masses" (*ibid.*). Thus, we find the 'user fees' in the government hospitals, and payment of hefty amounts towards non-conventional courses opened up as self-financed courses in the universities. Perhaps this is only the beginning.

In the 'Social Logic of Liberalization' Panini (1995) echoes Pathy's views to state that economic liberalizations may have accentuated economic disparities, sharpened caste divisions and promoted patriarchy and fundamentalism. He opines that privatization has largely benefited the middle class rather than lower rung of the society. In his view, the economic liberalization is not viable in the areas of education and public health due to deficiencies in social and institutional infrastructure in the country. In the same vein George Mathew states that "the problems of child survival, health and nutrition, childhood disability, schooling and education and child labour in India are immense" (1999:68-69) in the contest of NEP. He further writes, "The evidence on child welfare in India clearly shows that IMF fundamentalism worsens the conditions of life of the children of the poor. If the experience of countries that introduced structural adjustment programmes in the 1980s is anything to go by, the current policy augurs ill for the children of the poor. That is, a substantial section of India's future society is facing a terrible disaster as a result of the new economic policy" (*ibid.*:69).

Thus, fears are evident about the chances of deteriorating public health conditions in the country and increased poverty and unemployment that affect the nutrition of children and health status of the marginal people due to NEP. Now, there is greater need to find out the changing trend of health status of people during the process of globalization. Before such an endeavour, it is necessary to review the anthropological approaches to study of health.

Anthropological Approaches to Study Human Health

In the earliest efforts to understand the health culture of the people, anthropologists have been sensitive to document their practices related to health, be it the use of herbs or magical therapy. Murdock, Wilson and Frederick attempted to analyze data from Human Area Files to find people's theories of illness. They categorized the theories into natural causation theory and supernatural causation theory that are found commonly in all the human societies (Channa, 1998). It makes clear that health is a great concern for all societies.

There is also a systemic approach where medicine is considered as a sub-system, and its relationship with other sub-systems of life. In this context, western medical system and traditional system of health are seen interacting with each other in culture contact, diffusion and acculturation process. Attempts have been made to understand treatment and health seeking behaviour through people's response to modern health practices, medical profession and relationships between institutional structures (Ahluwalia, 1974).

Ecological approach to human disease and adaptation to diseases is yet another anthropological perspective to understand health culture. In this perspective, according to Alland (1970) "behaviour strategies developed in response to pathology" form systematic anthropological study (quoted by Kar, 2000: 172). This approach undoubtedly provides scientific frame of reference, it emphasizes conceptualization of the outsider even though people develop their own notions of health, illness and curative strategies. For Kar, "Every culture, irrespective of its simplicity and complexity has its own notion regarding health and health seeking behaviour, and this is often referred to as *Health Culture*. It is an integral component of the overall culture of the community. The health of any community, particularly of a tribal community, by and large, is a function of the interaction between socio-cultural and socio-biological practices, the genetic attributes and the environmental conditions" (Kar, 2000: 172).

The Health Culture, as rightly pointed out by Kar, is universal, but it is also unique in each culture; it is a historical product and it is a complex phenomenon. It is transmitted consciously and unconsciously through the process of socialization, it undergoes the process of verification, tests, reliability and refinement. Health culture cannot be understood only in terms of health and illness; it needs a "holistic" theory, conceptual framework, method and analysis used by the anthropologists.

Health in Holistic Perspective

Health care in any society as a system may be located where society is articulated by three structures: cultural values, environment and social structure. Often anthropologists paid attention to one structure neglecting the other two, though none of the structures play a deterministic role (Leach, 1968: 3) in holistic studies. But, for understanding health behaviour none of these can be neglected. In this perspective, we find the health system in the intersection of these structures that may be represented as in the following Venn diagram.

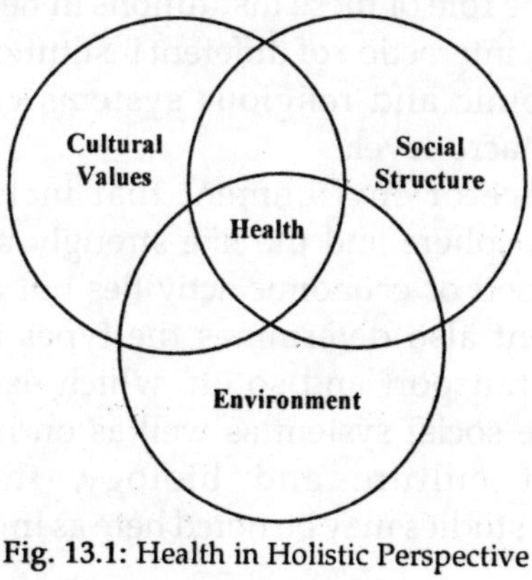

Fig. 13.1: Health in Holistic Perspective

These three structures mould the health behaviour, which may be elaborated as the following. The ideas about good health, ill health and the maintenance of good health are rooted in cultural values. These are developed and nurtured on the basis of people's conception and relationship with the divine beings, humans and natural physical environment. This system of man-god-nature relationship or the worldview provides a cultural repertoire that guides the individual and directs the family to adopt a particular strategy for dealing with the ill health or orders for health management.

Various social factors such as, family type, family size, gender relations, gender inequality, concept of person and continuity of descent, economic inequality, the role of economy in terms of importance attached to earning and non-earning members' sickness, pressure from the family or caste or tribal members, political freedom, decision-making authority, religious restrictions or compulsions, and so on, do determine the conceptions of ill health, sick roles and responsibilities of care takers and the actions one takes for treating a patient and the like. Further, the holistic study of enduring health system is concerned with the interaction of various institutions like hospital that include medical practitioners, paramedical staff, midwives, nurses and herbalists, and magico-religious institutions maintained by *bhagats, babas, ammas, sanyasis, magicians, sorcerers,* etc. that influences the health status of a community. The analysis of therapeutic procedures enable us to understand the role of these institutions in health behaviour of the people. So, interaction of different institutions intersecting political, economic and religious systems can be noticed operating at a macro-level.

The influence of environment that includes altitude, temperature, biosphere and the like strongly bears upon not only the livelihood or economic activities but also on health. The environment also determines the types and shapes of shelter, dress, transport and so on, which exert substantial influence on the social system as well as on human biology. Interaction of culture and biology, the subject of anthropological studies may be noted here as important feature at this juncture. Here, not only that the notions, perception, and cognition of the people but also the empirical studies that provide understanding of causal relations between the natural elements and diseases in specific populations become an area of investigation. For instance, less incidence of heart ailments among the hill people, perhaps, has much to do with the natural habitat and biology of the people. Thus, the three dimensions of human interactional framework from the basis for understanding of health behaviour in the holistic perspective.

Most often the research publications report ethnomedicine on the basis of observations and the curative practices that the researcher encounters during fieldwork. These reports seldom provide any comprehensive account in accordance with the paradigm considered above. They lack not only an integration of the three dimensions, but also establishment of any causal relations of three parameters with health behaviour. Nor there is systematic attempt to seek relationships between any set of variables of those mentioned. The above stated holistic approach would enable one to study and construct health behaviour and health status of a tribe or rural society at a macro-level taking into account a few variables from each sphere of interaction. A triangulation of qualitative and quantitative data and analysis require in this exercise. An outcome of it helps comparison of different social systems or their sub-strata. However, this analysis most often leads to 'etic' categorization (Pelto, 1978). Deeper understanding demands an insight from the 'emic' approach taking the categorization of the people into account. The investigation may begin with the probing of different cases of ill health or health problem through case study approach and generalization from particular cases.

To explain this, let me consider the case of barrenness or repeated miscarriages among the Yanadi of Sriharikota. According to Yanadi, ideally, the marriage should follow pregnancy, and if it does not occur, they suspect in the eruption of disharmony primarily in the relations between extra-natural and the human victim, nature and the sick person, and between nature and the extra-nature with the intervention of humans. Thus, the interaction of these three dimensions is to be examined.

The Yanadi follows trial and error method through the elimination process: disharmony among relatives, inappropriate food intake, environmental changes, and intervention of humans in the harmonius relationship between nature and extra-nature, and biological inadequacies between the male and female. Surrounding each diagnosis, there are practices buttressed by a set of beliefs that involve consultation with the specialists, observing rituals, imposing food restrictions and change of attitudes and so on. The success achieved through any of these efforts enhances the existing knowledge or reinforces the beliefs and failure casts doubt on the beliefs and practices. While the procedure adopted may be the same in each case of sickness or may be different, the order or trials and priorities may change. Yet the cognitive structure integrates all the diagnostic efforts either loosely or thickly. At the end, the Yanadi has an explanation intelligible to them in their own understanding of reproductive behaviour. It could be something wrong with the biology of individuals or the food taken by them that did not allow conception, or body of the individual failed to adapt to the environment (heat or cold), or the ancestors were not happy with them, or surviving relatives bore grudge against the victim, or the ghosts have been harming the victim, or the gods were not happy with the behaviour of the victim. Thus, examination of each case of illness unravels different cognitive structures and the ways in which they are connected to each other. If the effect is due to environment as conceived by them, relationship between the human body and environment need to be explored and similarly other relationships are to be investigated.

Further, the study should not consider the barrenness or abortions in isolation but must be studied in relation to the variables such as types of marriages (consanguineous or new alliances), family size, economic status of the family, general health conditions, natural environment of the population and others that emanate from the paradigm suggested above. This takes the investigation to the objective analysis and 'etic' categorization and analysis.

Thus task of the researcher is not to simply to categorize beliefs and list of different herbs, native pharmacopoeia, aetiology, cognitive aspects of illness, some rituals and the like, rather to construct a generative structure, on the basis of social structural, cultural repertoire, natural conditions and other variables that impinge on the health, that explains behaviour in different circumstances of the health. This is done through the analysis of various constraints, options, advantages and disadvantages, codes of conducts, character, and postulates, convictions that are found as 'symbolic' galaxies in the words of Schneider (1976) surrounding various sicknesses and curative attempts. It is also to probe into the ways people make sense of the situation.

The above paradigm provides the macro perspective that enables one to make generalizations valid for the community under study. But it requires an understanding at the micro-level and micro processes, which are often neglected or taken for granted. The micro-level perspective is the foundation on which macro structures are constructed. It considers the strategies adopted in the health management at the grassroots level.

The Place of Individual

To gain micro-level understanding of health, we shall focus on health practices from individual's point of view taking internal and external perceptions and interpretations at micro-level. As individuals are conscious of their health, they try to maintain good health and avoid to falling sick, suffering and so on. That is to say health is experiential and the experience can be understood by giving due importance to individual in society and influence of society upon the individual. Social norms and obligations immensely act upon the individual's behaviour mostly through family that mediates between the individual and society. Family socializes an individual to acquire, consciously and unconsciously, the norms, values, attitudes, and skills including acceptable health practices. Therefore, an analysis of socialization process itself provides the basic structure on which health culture rests.

The society where individual grows and interacts is not completely independent by itself. It is part of a larger system;

the state having its own ideology, goals and philosophy that provides education, legal system and health carė directly influences the society and the individual. Therefore, to some extent the behavioural pattern of an individual is shaped and moulded by the state's mandate. Therefore, when attempts are made to understand health behaviour focusing on individual we have to understand family, society and state and the interaction of which may be represented as in the following.

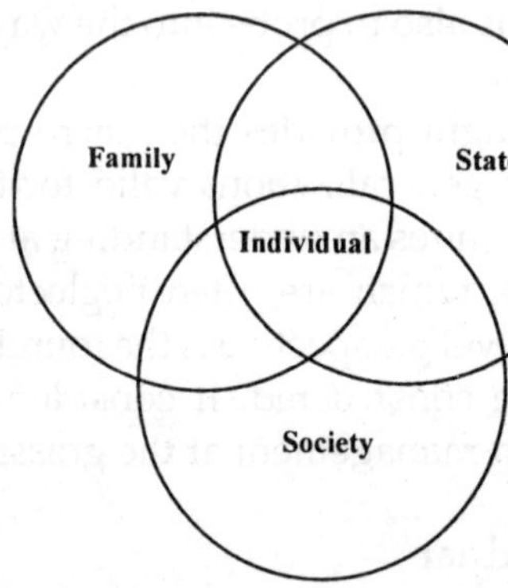

Fig. 13.2: Individual and Health

Body and Health

The micro-level study should take into account the peoples' perception of natural elements and the relationship of body with them. It concerns primarily with the body and psyche. The psychological health behaviour concerns with the up keep of body and mind. Anthropological knowledge becomes necessary for understanding the mental health, as it is closely related to social structure of the society. For instance, spirit possession is known to have relationship with the hierarchies, inequalities and antagonist elements in the society. Even there are notions of bad and good deaths, the attributes emerge from the nature of death-accidents, sudden happening, protracted struggle for survival, homicides, suicides and so on. However, as regards the body, anthropologists have identified two components; cultural construction of the body and physiology:

food and nature including extra-natural (spirits, ghosts and the like) that affect the health of an individual. So at the micro-level it is necessary to understand the food habits and relate them to health. Being warm-blooded species man adapts to heat, cold, snow and different weather conditions. Others are mainly cultural constructions interfering health. Thus, it may be represented in Fig. 13.3.

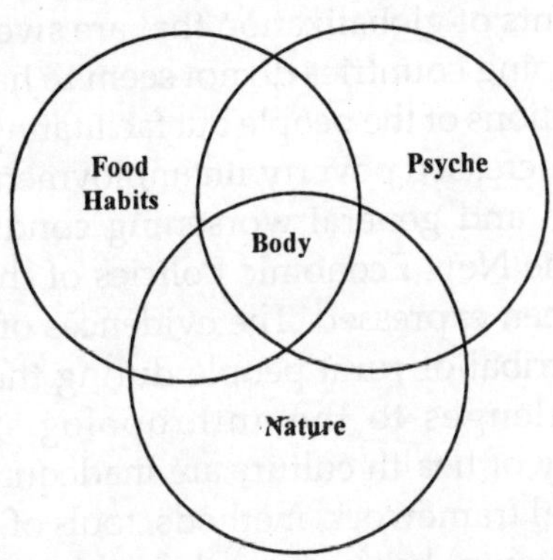

Fig. 13.3: Body and Health

Restoration of Health

The final and important aspect of health care concerns the restoration of health. It is about the strategies adopted by not only the sick person but also by those who are taking care of the sick person. It is usually the family or household members or those related to the sick person who takes the decision of treating the sick person. So the process of decision-making is important as it is contingent upon several factors such as the type of medicine one would try, the health provider, constraints of finances, conveniences of the attendants of the sick person, social status of the sick person, etc. Here, the concept of 'transaction' of Fredrik Barth (1966) will be of use. Decisions are made keeping in view certain resources, priorities and values. Individuals evaluate the situation keeping the choices available and constraints before them to maximise the benefits whatever they may be. Even though individuals and families differ in decision-making, a general pattern of the community can be discerned.

Conclusion

Health care is one of the major concerns of the third world countries and in spite of best efforts, international and national agencies were not able to achieve 'Health for All by 2000 AD'. The wind currents of globalization that are sweeping strongly over the developing countries do not seem to have augmented the health conditions of the people but facilitating deterioration. Strong fears of increased poverty, unemployment, malnutrition among children and general worsening condition of public health due to the New Economic Policies of the Government of India have been expressed. The evidences of impact on the health of poor tribal or rural people during the globalization pose new challenges to the anthropologists to conduct systematic study of health culture are inadequate and require better conceptual framework, methods, tools of data collection and analysis. Attempt has been made in this paper to develop an anthropological holistic framework to meet the challenges.

The suggested general paradigm involving the interplay of cultural values, environment and social structure form the macro-level analysis and holistic perspective of health culture. But the micro-level analysis requires focusing on the individual, body and restoration of health. One may begin with micro-level analysis to come up with the macro-level generalizations, but both are necessary for understanding the health system from an anthropological perspective. It is implied that the study envisages application of both qualitative and quantitative data collection techniques and strangulation of both types of data meaningfully.

REFERENCES

Alland, A. (1970), *Adaptation in Cultural Evolution: An Approach to Medical Anthropology*. New York, Columbia University Press.

Ahluwalia, Aneeta (1974), Sociology of Medicine, In ICSSR (ed) *A Survey of Research in Sociology and Social Anthropology*, Vol. II, Bombay: Popular Prakashan, pp. 401-430.

Barth, Fredrik (1966), *Models of Social Organisation*, Royal Anthropological Institute of Great Britain and Ireland 23.

Barua, I. and Phutan, R. (1998), Socio-Religious Aspect of Health Among Sonowal Kachari, *Eastern Anthropologist*, 51(4), pp. 351-362.

Burnet, M. and White, D.O. (1972), *Natural History of Infectious Disease.* 4th ed., Cambridge: Cambridge University Press.

Burnet, F.M. (1963), *The Integrity of the Body*, Cambridge, Mass: Harvard University Press.

Burton, L.E. and Smith, H.H. (1975), *Public Heath and Community Medicine for the Allied Medical Professions.* 2nd ed. Baltimore: The William and Wilkins. Co.

Carter, A.T. (1982), Hierarchy and the Concept of Person in Western India, In L. Fruzzetti, A. Oster and S. Barnet (eds). *Kinship Caste and Marriage in India*, Cambridge, Mass: Harvard University Press.

Channa, S.M. (ed) (1998), *Medical Anthropology*, New Delhi: Cosmo Publications.

Deodhar, N.S. (1983), The Concept of Health and Disease, In N.V. Bhave, N.S. Deodhar and S.V. Bhave (eds) *You and Your Health*, New Delhi: National Book Trust.

Devi, L. (1998), *Encyclopaedia of Women Development and Family Welfare.* New Delhi: Anmol Publications.

Dubos, Rene (1965), *Man Adapting*. New Heaven: Yale University Press.

Enge, K. and Harrison, P. (1986), The Local Fight Back When Tiomes are Tough: the Ethnography of Health Care in Peru, In Edward C. Gree (ed) *Practicing Development Anthropology*, Colorado: Westeview Press.

Foster, G.M. (1953), Use of Anthropological Methods and Data in Planning in Operation. *Public Health Reports* 68(9), pp. 841-857.

Garfinkel, H. (1967), *Studies in Ethnomethodology.* Cambridge, M.A.: Polity Press.

Green, E.C. (1986), Anthropology in the Context of a Water-Borne Disease Control Project. In Edward C. Gree (ed) *Practicing Development Anthropology*, Colorado: Westview Press.

Hobson, W. (1965), *The Theory and Practice of Public Health.* 2nd ed. London: Oxford University Press.

Jose, B.K. (1998), *Tribal Ethnomedicine, Continuity and Change.* A.P.H. Publishing Corporation, New Delhi.

Kar, R.K. (2000), Ecology of Health and Health Culture: A Case Study among the Tea Labourers in Assam, India. *International Journal of Anthropology*, 15.1-2, pp. 171-183.

Khatua, N. (1998), Sickness and Healing among the Hill Korwa. *Eastern Anthropologist*, 54(1), pp. 51:61.

Leach, E. (1976), *Culture and Communication.* New York: Cambridge University Press.

Mathew, George (1995), The New Economic Policy, Social Development and Sociology. *Sociological Bulletin*, 44(1): 63-77.

Mausner, J.S. and Bahn, A.J.K. (1974), *Epidemiology: An Introductory Text.* Philadelphia: W.B. Sunders Co.

Murdock, G.P., Wilson, F.S. and Frederick, V. (1998), World Distribution of Theories of Illness, In S.M. Channa (ed) *Medical Anthropology*, New Delhi: Cosmo Publications.

Nagla, M. (1997), *Sociology of Medical Profession: A Study of Medical Organisation and Profession of Medicine.* Jaipur, Rawat Publication.

Nigam, S. (1999), Denial of Right to Health. *Legal News and Views.* pp. 11-13.

Panini, M.N. (1995), The Social Logic of Liberalization. *Sociological Bulletin,* 44(1): pp. 33-62.

Pathy, Jagannath (1995), The Consequences of the New Economic Policies on the Peoples of India: A Sociological Appraisal. *Sociological Bulletin,* 44(1), pp. 11-32.

Paul, B.D. (1955), *Health, Culture and Community: Case Studies of Public Relations to Health Problems.* New York: Russel and Sage Foundation.

Paul, Hugh (1964), *The Control of Disease (Social and Communicable).* 2nd ed. Baltimore: The William and Wilkins Co.

Pelto, P.J. (1978), *Anthropological Research: The Structure of Inquiry.* New York: Cambridge University Press.

Schneider, D.M. (1976), Notes Towards a Theory of Culture, In Kenneth H. Basso and Henry Selby (ed) *Meaning in Anthropology,* Albuquerque: University of New Mexico Press.

Singh and Mahanti (1995), *Tribal Health in India.* Inter India Publications, New Delhi.

Streeten, Paul (1987), Structural Adjustment: A Survey of the World Issues and Options, *World Development,* 15(12), pp. 1465-80.

14

Role of Social Anthropology in the Study of HIV/AIDS in the Context of Globalization

ARAVINDA MEERA GUNTUPALLI

Introduction

AIDS is an acronym made up of the first letter of the words Acquired Immuno Deficiency Syndrome. This was first detected in 1981 in USA. No region of the world is free of infection, although some are clearly more intensively affected than the others. By the early 1990s, HIV/AIDS has been officially reported by 164 countries. AIDS first began as a disease among the male homosexuals and people of high and middle income in developed countries; it is now prevalent among poor heterosexual groups in the developing world. From a disease of affluence, HIV/AIDS has shifted to a disease of poverty (Gordenker *et al.*, 1995), at least in terms of location and most affected populations.

The HIV/AIDS epidemic represents the most serious public health problem in India. The first case of AIDS in India was detected in 1986. Since then, HIV infections have been reported in all States and Union territories. It is estimated that as on mid-2001, 3.97 million Indians were infected with the virus (NACO, 2001). Fear of AIDS has spread into existence when on April 1986, 10 prostitutes were detected as seropositive for AIDS by Centre for Advanced Research in Virology, CMC,

Vellore, and National Institute of Virology in Pune through ICMR initiated screening of high risk groups for HIV antibodies in 1985 to find out whether AIDS virus has spread to India or not.

Migration of labour, low literacy levels leading to low awareness, gender disparities, poverty and livelihood issues, lack of health facilities, and prevalence of sexually transmitted diseases and reproductive tract infections are some of the factors attributed to the spread of HIV/AIDS. While HIV/AIDS threatens all segments of society, it is poor and marginalized people, and in particular women, who are especially vulnerable. The major risk factors for vulnerability to HIV infection are social and economic dependence.

The prevalence of the infection in all parts of the country highlights the spread from urban to rural areas and from high risk to the general population. The second decade of the epidemic is marked by heterogeneity as it shifted from the high-risk population to bridge population (clients of sex workers, STD patients and partners of drug users) and then to the general population (NACO, 2001).

Global Scenario of Anthropological Research in HIV/AIDS

Global inequalities of class, gender, and ethnicity as revealed by poverty, powerlessness, and stigma propel the spread of HIV. 'Anthropologists' witness to suffering, their concern and engagement, are potent elements in the research process and in advocacy in national and international arenas. The combined strength of theory and practice in the field of international research on AIDS is a significant contribution to anthropology in the twenty-first century.

From slow beginnings in the mid-1980s, AIDS research by anthropologists has grown rich and diverse. In addition to medical anthropologists, researchers from three of anthropology's classic four fields, from numerous sub-disciplines, have examined aspects of the pandemic. By the late 1980s, however, pioneering work by anthropologists began to raise the importance of cultural systems in shaping risk behaviour relevant to HIV transmission and prevention. Since the start of the 1990s, this emphasis on cultural analysis has taken shape alongside a growing anthropological research focusing on structural factors shaping vulnerability to HIV infection. Work on social inequality and the political economy of HIV and AIDS has become especially important. Much of the current research seeks to integrate both cultural and structural concerns in providing an alternative to more individualistic behavioural research paradigms.

Increasingly, however, as behavioural research and behavioural interventions began to be developed in a growing range of diverse social and cultural settings, the relative effectiveness of both the research instruments and intervention strategies came to be questioned, notably by anthropologists. The difficulties of translating or adapting research protocols for cross-cultural application quickly became apparent in the face of often radically different understandings of sexual expression and practices in different societies and cultures and even in different sub-cultures within the same. It had become clear that a far more complex set of social, structural, and cultural factors mediate the structure of risk in every population group, and that the dynamics of individual psychology cannot be expected to fully explain.

On the one hand, particularly during the early 1990s, there was a growing focus on the interpretation of cultural meanings as central to a fuller understanding of both the sexual transmission of HIV in different social settings and the possibilities that might exist for responding to it through the design of more culturally appropriate prevention programmes. On the other hand, emerging at the same time but gaining greater attention over the mid to late 1990s, there was increasing concern with the impact of a range of wider structural factors that could be seen as shaping vulnerability to HIV infection as well as conditioning the possibilities for sexual risk reduction in specific social contexts (Farmer, 1994).

Stimulated by social constructionist concerns, an important shift of emphasis began to take place from an earlier focus on individual psychology and individual subjectivity to a new concern with inter-subjective cultural meanings related to sexuality and risk behaviour. This new wave of anthropological research on HIV and AIDS thus sought to go beyond the calculation of behavioural frequencies. The focus of much important research on HIV and AIDS over the course of the past decade has thus moved from behaviour, in and of itself, to the cultural settings within which behaviour takes place and to the cultural symbols, meanings, and rules that organize it. On the basis of such work, an important reformulation of the very notion of intervention has begun to take place. It has become increasingly apparent that the idea of a behavioural intervention may in fact be a misnomer, since HIV/AIDS prevention interventions almost never function at the level of behaviour but rather at the level of social or collective representations. Earlier notions of behavioural intervention have given way to ethnographically grounded AIDS education and prevention programmes that are community-based and culturally sensitive programmes aimed at transforming social norms and cultural values, and thus at re-constituting collective meanings in ways that will ultimately promote safer sexual practices.

Another corollary, which is more recently given credence by many anthropologists, is the national and global context of local society and culture. Anthropologists recognize that, while individual cultures are more or less internally coherent systems, they are also part of nations, which are, in turn, connected with other nations of the world. Thus local cultures are not completely autonomous, independent systems; they are influenced by international circumstances and events. So anthropologists started taking globalization and the global context also into account in the research of HIV/AIDS.

Societies may have once lived in relative isolation but now in this era of globalization this is not possible. So agents of change must be taken into account not only for which intervention is needed, but also its economic, social and political environment. This is the real complex task for all social scientists and especially anthropologists to unravel as on one side we talk about local society and culture that shapes risk behaviour of population and on the other side there is a growing need to focus on agents of change due to globalization and decreasing isolation of local cultures. Anthropologists are facing a major challenge in trying to understand HIV/AIDS epidemic in India where there are many local cultures, languages and cultures that are losing their complete isolated nature. So the change elements and their relation to HIV/AIDS have to be taken into consideration in the research of HIV/AIDS.

Objectives of this Study

This paper focus on Indian situation where this epidemic has attained catastrophic proportions reveals cultural and social regularities for the production and increase of the dreadful disease. This paper shows how anthropology can help in locating the links between globalization and this dreadful disease along with understanding the consequences of the disease. Both theory and methodology of anthropology has potential in solving this problem.

The specific objectives of this study are:

- To give an over view of different social and cultural factors that are related to the transmission of HIV/AIDS in the context of globalization.
- To explore the relation between globalization and HIV/AIDS.
- To describe the underlying principles of anthropology, indicating their application to research in HIV/AIDS.
- To propose directions for the future of anthropology in the era of HIV/AIDS and globalization.

Globalization

Globalization in this paper is understood as the expansion of economic, social, political and cultural transactions across national boundaries among people, enterprises and governments. The impact of globalization varies both within and between nations and among different regions of the world.

To some, it brings development and progress through integration of local markets into international systems; for others it results in the increased marginalization of economies or parts of economies that cannot compete effectively in the global economy.

Globalization of market economy has spread all over the world in the last decade of the 20th century. Globalization, which integrates the world economy through liberalization of trade and investment and de-regulation and privatization of business so that the world transnational corporations (TNCs) can operate freely across national boundaries. Information technology such as computers, Cell phones and Internet is playing a key role in promoting globalization.

There are different views regarding globalization. Some view globalization in optimistic way and some in pessimistic way. Some researchers strongly believe that globalization has not decreased inequality of income and wealth. Number of researchers have become aware of that fact that social differences are globally increasing in a double process of polarization within countries and among countries.

UNCTAD General Secretary Ricupero noted for example: "The big story of world economy since the early 1980s has been the unleashing of market forces...The invisible hand now operates globally and with fewer countervailing pressures from governments than for decades. Many commentators are optimistic about the prospects for faster growth and for convergence of standard of livings and incomes which greater global competition should bring. However, there is also another big story. Since the early 1980s the world economy has been characterized by rising inequality and slow growth" (UNCTAD, 1997).

A major claim of proponents of globalization is that increased internationalization of the world economy will lead to a convergence between rich and poor countries. Pritchett (1995 and 1997), senior economist at the World Bank, concluded, however, that convergence "just hasn't happened, isn't happening, and isn't going to happen without serious changes in economic policies in developing countries." This conclusion is based on extensive research, which shows: Divergence in relative productivity levels and standard of living is the dominant feature of modern economic history. In the last century, incomes in the "developing" countries have fallen far behind those in the "developed countries", both proportionately and absolutely.

Boyer (1996) concludes for example: Statistical evidence does not confirm any general and secular trend towards economic convergence in productivity levels and standards of living. Such convergence is restricted to small club of nations that have been able to invest sufficiently in productive investment, infrastructure, and education. The poor countries have been left out of the process of economic development.

Globalization and HIV/AIDS

This research paper would focus on pros and cons of globalization in the context of HIV/AIDS in India and in this context there are two major views regarding the process how globalization affects health.

1. There is a view, which sees the increased interdependence attendant upon globalization resulting in an increased willingness of nations to work together in pursuit of improved health. This offered an optimistic analysis of the health benefits of globalization to poor countries and to poor communities. These included increased trade, easier diffusion of new technologies, and at a cultural-political level—acceptance and application of common human rights throughout the world. If we see the relation between HIV/AIDS and globalization in the Indian context in an optimistic way, there should be benefits to India by the diffusion of different contraceptive methods, medicines and effective systems for the prevention and treatment of HIV/AIDS from rich nations.
2. Contrastingly, the pessimistic approach sees globalization as a phenomenon because of which there

> is increasing disparity in income and increasing inequality within and among nations. This view even stress on the increasing concentration of pharmaceutical industry that would give large profits to the rich countries for treatment of HIV/AIDS and there is less attention paid to the needs of communities and countries which have lower ability to express their needs through markets.

According to Dennis Altman, sexuality today has far more to do with global politics and economics. In an excerpt from *Global Sex: AIDS, Sex, and Globalization*, published by the University of Chicago Press, he discussed how globalization is transforming the way in which sexuality is treated around the world. Altman also explains that AIDS is both a product and a cause of globalization, affecting sexual practices, legislation, and the commercialization of sex on a large scale (Altman, 2001).

Dennis Altman also says that AIDS fits the common understanding of "globalization" in a number of ways, including its epidemiology, the mobilization against its spread, and the dominance of certain discourses in the understandings of the epidemic. Dennis Altman regarding globalization and spread of HIV/AIDS says that it is probable that the virus was spread beyond its original home through urbanization and population shifts, and that its rapid dispersion across the world is closely related to the nature of a global economy. HIV followed the huge population movements of the contemporary world, whether these are truckers moving across Zaire and India, women taking up sex work as a means of survival as old communities and social order crumbled, men seeking work on the minefields of South Africa and Zimbabwe, or tourists (for example Americans in Haiti), refugees (Haitians fleeing to the United States), and soldiers (Cubans serving in Angola; UN troops in Cambodia or the former Yugoslavia) moving across national boundaries.

Different cultural understandings of the meanings humans give to their bodies are constantly being challenged and re-made by the impact of particular 'Western notions', imported via economic, cultural, and professional influences; the AIDS epidemic has created "experts" who in turn influence perceptions of sex and gender through HIV education and prevention programmes. Such programmes further the diffusion of a particular language around sexuality and sexual identities, which depend upon particular, largely Western, assumptions. Programmes around HIV/AIDS have often made use of identities such as "sex worker" or "gay/bisexual men"/ "men who have sex with men," and thus play a part in the further globalization of movements based on such identities.

Causes for the Spread of HIV/AIDS in India

Quinn proposed following seven risk factors for the epidemic, based on a sociological model: population migration, social disruption, declining economy, STD epidemic, urbanization, poor medical services, and low status of women (Quinn, 1994). Some of the risk factors may be mere associations, linked to other factors, which are root factors. Some of the risk factors that are mentioned above may be causal and some are associative.

Poverty and underdevelopment are the key factors that contribute to the AIDS pandemic in India. Financial difficulties and economic problems force men to leave their families to find work, encourage drug usage and make prostitution a survival strategy. Most of the population depends on fishing or agriculture, which are fragile economies. Majority of the members of the sex industry in Mumbai and Chennai come from population groups subjected to crises. In the absence of coping mechanism prostitution becomes a contributory factor. In India prostitution is prescribed by law and is considered as immoral means of livelihood by society. This is for individual to disregard social mores or the law to take prostitution; the circumstances must be extremely compelling great reason to be alarmed.

Prostitution in India

The growing internationalization of trade in sex and has played a major role in the diffusion of HIV, and its rapid spread into almost every corner of the world. While it is often said that HIV is "spread through prostitution", it is also true that fear of AIDS itself changes the nature of the international sex trade.

Sex workers, the classless, and probably the most underprivileged in contemporary society has become the common subject of discussion in the light of HIV/AIDS. Devadasi system, which is a religious prostitution, is there in many parts of India. The devadasi system has a significant place in the history of HIV/AIDS in India. Today the system of devadasi might be disappearing outwardly but covertly the system still thrives and day-by-day is taking new shape.

Factors, which combine with poverty accounts for a large majority of women entering prostitution. Prostitution is not created by globalization in India directly. But the initial phases of globalization as expected by some researchers has increased inequalities between people and even the gap between rural and urban areas in terms of indicators of development. In this context, marginalized women from rural areas migrate to urban areas for survival and finally take prostitution as their survival strategy. Most of the times they fall into the trap of prostitution as they are generally promised some kind of unskilled job in urban areas and they migrate in the hope of getting work. Finally, they find that they are exploited, find no escape strategy and enter prostitution.

Another significant factor to be observed is shift from prostitution that was based on Devadasi women to prostitution based on poor and lower caste women. In Mumbai brothels along with Devadasis, prostitutes belonging to lower castes and poor communities can be observed (self-observation). Prostitution in the era of HIV/AIDS and globalization demands young women. It is well established that there is an increasing demand for younger, presumably uninfected, prostitutes, often from rural areas, which has meant an increased demand for young Nepali girls in India (and Burmese girls in Thailand). Legislation and commercialization of sex also took place in the era of globalization.

Positive impact of globalization includes improved access

to contraceptives by prostitutes, increasing sensitivity towards the prostitutes and increasing awareness about HIV/AIDS. Due to the influence of the West, AIDS and sexuality have become subjects of open discussion, which was never Indian way. In many societies more open discussion of sex is itself an enormously significant change caused by globalization. Various national and international organizations, women groups, human right groups are now have strong associations between and within nations to share their views.

It is common to hear HIV workers from different parts of India explaining the changes in social expectations, which are required to even broach the discussion of sexual behaviour. Ignorance about basic sexual and reproductive possibilities remains a huge obstacle to safe behaviour in India that started to change recently. Beyond this, the range of preventive programmes brought into existence by the threat of the epidemic has meant, at least in some limited arenas, that there have been real changes in behaviour. Reports from the many Indian researchers show a high degree of concern and interest in changing sexual norms and behaviours to the empowerment of women in the face of sexually transmitted diseases.

Hijras

India is well known for one of its unique cults in the world. It is the 'hijra cult', where males become transvestites or get castrated to gain feminity, is nothing but institutionalized homosexuality. Some of them are involved in the organization of female prostitution. Of the total 3000 hijras in Mumbai, over 60 per cent are engaged in prostitution and 50 per cent are infected with HIV (Sinha, 1999). Initially hijras were not open about revealing their sexuality as they were looked down by the society. They are now less hesitant to talk about their sexuality with the increasing heat of discussion where significant change regarding open discussion of sexuality and HIV/AIDS has occurred. They have formed their own communities (like DAI Welfare Society, Mumbai) that aims to increase knowledge and awareness about HIV/AIDS especially, to hijras who are in the prostitution.

Blood and Organ Donors and Drug Usage

Blood supply is another high-risk area for HIV transmission. They are many commercial donors who donate their blood regularly and donate their organs for the sake of money. This issue is also linked to poverty directly. Marginalized people who are less informed about modes of HIV transmission would be at high risk of getting infected when they use blood donation as one of their survival strategies.

Intravenous drug use (IDU) that is less common in India is one of the factors for this HIV pandemic. However, in states of Northeast bordering Myanmar-Manipur, Nagaland and Mizoram have large number of IDUs and HIV prevalence among them have reached to 70 per cent (Sinha, 1999). The growing internationalization of trade in drugs has played a major role in the diffusion of HIV, and its rapid spread into almost every corner of the world. It has been argued that "patterns of use of illicit drugs are becoming globalized and standardized," leading to the rapid spread of HIV in countries in both Southeast Asia and South America where the injecting practices have partly replaced traditional opium smoking.

Globalization, Movement of the People and HIV/AIDS

As an infectious disease, AIDS, like globalization does not respect borders or national authorities. The inter-relationship between globalization and the spread of HIV/AIDS, however, is relatively complex. This research paper tries to focus on the areas of key interactions between AIDS and globalization. In principle, the opening of markets and the free movement of goods and capital increase the movement of labour, which is another factor of production. Even though there are many barriers that control labour to cross international borders, the demand of labour in many parts of the world leads to constant movement. Sometimes there is a chance of illegal and undocumented migration.

In its narrow definition, the term migrant refers to individuals whose decision to migrate is taken freely, for reasons of personal convenience and without intervention of external compelling factor. This narrow definition includes migrant workers, economic migrants and seasonal migrants. Migrant is generally used to refer all groups of persons who migrate across internal and international borders. Migration is a process and it is not a fixed activity. In any migration process three basic stages origin, transit and destination are involved.

UNAIDS report by Kathleen Cravero (2000) on globalization trends and HIV/AIDS showed that HIV prevalence is highest in the region like Africa that is most tenuously linked to the global economy and says that there is inverse relation between HIV prevalence and degree of globalization in case of Africa. It also shows that some of the dimensions of globalization may favour the spread of HIV/ AIDS as in the case of Thailand. HIV/AIDS and migration are salient features of the latter half of 20th century. The movement of people that accompanies globalization forges new linkages and brings together social groups and geographical areas that previously had little contact. These new patterns of human interaction, in which different cultures, societies and income levels overlap with one another, are an integral part of globalization that is fundamental to the spread of HIV.

Globalization also affects the internal movement of labour (*i.e.*, movement within the borders of the country) in two important ways. First, the extension of transportation infrastructures intensifies rural-urban interaction. Second, the quality of human resources is enhanced thorough the extension of improvement of education services which, initially at least, are high in urban centres. These improvements in human capital facilitate the transition from labour-intensive industrialization to more capital-intensive forms of development.

Concurrently, about 100 million persons move voluntarily within or between nations each year, while almost 40 million are either internally displaced or refugees out side their own countries (UNAIDS and IOM, 1998). Human migration, whether voluntary or involuntary, may result in the spread of HIV infection both to those who migrate and to the members of the community, which receives migrants, as well as to individuals in the country of origin, if the migrant returns infected. In transit areas, migrants may have increased opportunities for risk taking behaviour as the behaviour they have always practiced in their home area may pose greater risks in the new setting. For example, in transit areas along borders where significant number of persons move between countries, sexual transactions are often made in places where alcohol and commercial sex workers are readily available. In terms of HIV what may have been a relatively low risk activity in their place of origin will become a high-risk activity in transit area, where illegal, poor and undocumented migrants have few safer alternatives available (UNAIDS and IOM, 1998).

In many instances, mobile populations are more susceptible to HIV infection because of the risk factors associated with their occupation, social status, or economic situation. It is well known that vulnerability to HIV is often greatest when people find themselves living and working in conditions of poverty, powerlessness and social instability, conditions that apply to many migrants. Separation from family and socio-cultural norms, isolation/loneliness, a sense of anonymity that offers more sexual freedom, and inadequate financial resources make migrants more vulnerable to involve in high-risk sexual behaviour. These are the factors that make migrants more vulnerable to HIV/AIDS.

Studies of certain highly mobile groups, such as truck drivers, commercial sex workers and itinerant traders, have contributed to the understanding of migration as a factor in the spread of HIV. Being a migrant, in and of itself, is not a risk factor; it is the activities undertaken during the migration process that are the risk factors (UNAIDS and IOM, 1998).

In the area of destination migrants generally face problems in adapting to the new environment. This can influence their mental and physical health, and their sexual behaviour. High-risk behaviours such as multiple partners sex and sex with commercial sex workers are not solely the result of migration itself. They are also a function of being separated from a regular sex partner, the concentration of migrants in one place and the stress and vulnerabilities associated with the migration process. The anonymity of being a foreigner, especially in transit areas, can increase sexual freedom. Often the new environment is exclusively male, resulting in sex between men. Links between prostitution and transport and other corridor pertain mainly to highways and bridges connecting cities. They serve as corridors for both sex workers to migrate and for prospective customers to have access to sex workers (Sinha, 1999).

Even without precise data on the sexual behaviour of migrants while away from home, one finds several hypotheses in the literature, which try to explain why migrants may adopt high-risk sexual behaviours:

1. One hypothesis is that migrants often have problems adapting to the new environment, which influences their mental, physical health and their sexual behaviour. The tendency of migrants to have multiple partners and to visit sex workers is the result of a process associated with migration that not only increases household separations but also concentrates migrants in one place. This affects then leads to increase in stress and vulnerability (Doyal and Pennell, 1981; Hunt, 1989; Basset *et al.*, 1993). Doyal explains that the migrant labour system has led to prolonged family separations which have had serious repercussions for all concerned and the absence of partners of male migrants are compounded by the fact that their new environment is often almost exclusively male. The resulting unequal sex ratios make it difficult for men to establish partnerships with women, and encourage contacts with CSWs.
2. A second hypothesis suggests that the migrant acts primarily as a foreigner, and that his anonymity at destination increases his sexual freedom (Hrdy, 1987).
3. A third hypothesis is that the tendency of migrants to visit CSWs arises from the fact that they are not sufficiently integrated to meet young women. Sex workers who offer impersonal relationships are easily

and rapidly accessible (Anarfi, 1993). These hypotheses have been supported by data from studies in various locations.

It is not the origin or the destination of migration, the social disruption that characterizes certain types of migration, which determines vulnerability to HIV (Decosas *et al.*, 1995). This view has received support from initial results of AIDSCAP studies, which suggested that these mobile populations encounter on their travels might be a more significant HIV risk factor than their attitudes or habits. But there are many difficulties for studying this migrant and mobile population and their risk behaviour for a range of reasons.

In Asia, AIDSCAP has studied five areas of affinity that share common cultural, economic, demographic or epidemiological characteristics. Most of these areas are linked by trucking routes, border zones or port cities with high concentrations of transport workers, business travellers, commercial sex workers, migrant labourers and other groups who may be at higher risk of acquiring HIV than more stable populations. Recognizing that the potentially deadly combination of mobile populations and a thriving sex industry drives transmission of HIV across national boundaries throughout the region, AIDSCAP and the Asia Bureau of the U.S. Agency for International Development (USAID) are encouraging development of interventions that also cross borders. Hot spot studies locations include fishing ports in Thailand and Cambodia, river trade routes on the Thai-Lao border and truck crossings between India and Nepal (South Asia UNDP, 2000).

The rapid assessment, entitled *Sexual Networking in Five Urban Areas in the Nepal Terai* was conducted by a Valley Research Group (VARG) team including an expatriate anthropologist, a Nepali physician long-associated with HIV/AIDS programming, and male/female field interviewers. The majority of clients selected for interview were transport workers. Secondary clients interviewed included migrant workers, businessmen, students, labourers and civil servants.

Due to the transient nature of men's lifestyles in a border region it was found that commercial sex is sought on both sides of the Nepal-India border. Probably the most significant finding resulting from the client research was a national road map on which transport workers were asked to designate the locations preferred for commercial sex (FHI Report, 1997).

Anthropology and HIV/AIDS

AIDS-related anthropological research are the following issues: sexual behaviours and attitudes, knowledge and perceptions of AIDS, local etiologies and treatment-seeking behaviours, social organizations, customs and norms, underlying socio-economic factors, and community strategies for coping with AIDS and its consequences. A wide range of anthropological methods is available for research on HIV/AIDS. Potential research methods include participant observation, field journals, tape recordings, interviews with key informants, narratives, life histories, questionnaires, role plays and performances, focus group discussions, peer research, classification and semantic differential rankings, non-verbal techniques, network analyses, and triangulation.

Anthropological Methods in HIV/AIDS Research

Anthropological methods imply a qualitative rather than quantitative focus, relatively long-term research, and dependence on observation and exchanges with informants. The lack of interest of medical researchers in motivations behind various behaviours, and the focus on measuring the frequency of various behaviours, distinguish their approaches from that of tradition of anthropology. Attempts to quantify behaviours that are subjective and that depend on common understanding of terms that are difficult to define exactly are likely to pose difficulties of interpretation.

In the context of HIV/AIDS and globalization, different anthropological methods can be applied and the application of the various methods used by anthropologists are discussed below.

Participant Observation

Advantages

- We can establish good relationships with people, which lead to more understanding regarding their risk behaviour and their perception regarding HIV/AIDS.
- We can get a better sense of how HIV/AIDS research topic fits into their lives as a whole.
- We can observe increasing impact of westernization and globalization on sexuality and the positive and negative effect of the same.
- We can observe firsthand the differences between what people say they do and what they actually do (ideal culture *vs.* real culture) in context of risk behaviour, discriminatory practices and care giving to people living with HIV/AIDS.
- We can actually understand situation that increases risk behaviour of various groups of population having high-risk behaviour like migrants, prostitutes etc.
- We can also learn about things that you may have never thought to ask about in relation to HIV/AIDS research.
- We can observe how information technology spread, especially, Internet is playing a role in increasing knowledge of sex (in a wrong way) in adolescents.

Disadvantages

- The sample size is going to be small because it is time-consuming.
- Our presence might affect people's behaviour.
- Our responsibilities as a participant might limit the amount of research you can do.

Interviews (Unstructured)

Advantages

- Allow informants to decide what's important for them in relation to their risk of getting or transmission of HIV/AIDS in relation to globalization.
- We receive large quantities of qualitative data.

Disadvantages

- Smaller sample compared to surveys.
- Data cannot be compared as easily as surveys.

Surveys and Censuses

Advantages

- We get a larger sample.
- Responses can be compared statistically.
- We can train other people to do the surveys for you.

Disadvantages

- The results are not as rich because we don't spend as much time with each individual or household.
- We won't know if people are telling the truth.

Permutation and combination of all the methods of fieldwork discussed may be helpful in giving clearer picture.

Anthropologists were invited to collaborate in surveys of knowledge, attitudes, and practices (KAP) sponsored by public health agencies from the mid-1980s after the outbreak of HIV/AIDS. Qualitative methods initially were often confined to focus groups and rapid appraisals. Anthropological demographers, experienced in surveys of reproduction and migration, sought to devise methods, principally studies of sexual networking, that would yield valid data to explain the spread of HIV and aid in prevention. In the 1990s a growing number of anthropologists conducted processual ethnographies that linked individuals' life worlds to global structures and processes, showing how these are involved in spreading HIV. The ethnographies make extensive use of interviews, personal documents, and cultural performances, enriched by description of the contexts of their production.

Anthropologists can construct questionnaires based on local concepts and beliefs. Unstructured interviews are excellent means of exploring new topics, exploring topics in greater depth and in designing more structures interviews; semi-structured interviews allow more directed exploration and facilitate systematic coverage of a topic; and structured interviews are best for examining the distribution of specific beliefs in population. In the recent years, anthropologists are using focused group discussions, which can be helpful in rapidly assessing a community's idea about HIV/AIDS.

Traditionally anthropological research required at least a year and some times more than two years of field study, followed by a thorough analysis and written account which is time consuming process and was criticized by many action professionals. In response to these concerns, anthropologists have formulated a variety of quicker and more focused approaches to the collection of information. Rapid assessment procedures (RAP) have been developed to survey the research setting and address health issues in one or two months, using a systematic set of questions and methods. Both RAP and a similar approach, the Focuses Ethnographic Study (FES), directed towards understanding of specific disease conditions, have been used by applied medical anthropologists in 1990s (Pelto, 1997). Networking is the new area anthropologists are working in to understand the how networks are formed between people who are having risk behaviour.

One of the basic premises of anthropology is that research as intervention is socio-cultural processes. Social relationships in any study on human beings are important. Within ones own socio-cultural setting, it may be reasonable to assume that people share some of ones values, concepts, and behavioural norms and here two social-cultural systems involve those of donor and recipients. As in cross-cultural research, there are rules of behaviour that must be recognized for affective intervention. Here it is important to know how one is regarded by the community examined in order to know-how to interpret community members' responses to an intervention. Rural urban, tribal non tribal, high low, men women, caste and permutation and combination of all the above methods can put different risk behaviours as well as different intervention strategies.

Conclusion

The relation between HIV/AIDS and globalization can be viewed in both positive and negative ways. The phase of globalization where only a few regions, especially the urban areas, are moving with high speed in terms of development create negative impact on the spread of HIV/AIDS, as only people who are highly educated and mobile would benefit and this would lead to increasing inequalities among people. When considering the impact of globalization on various societies, government and policy makers rarely think of various options to control the negative impacts of globalization on vulnerable people. This perspective incorrectly presents globalization pessimistically. But there is considerable scope for the national governments to shape and regulate the process of globalization in the country. Increasing acknowledgement of the limitations of biomedical approaches in solving the global AIDS crisis and enhanced awareness of the inadequacies of prevailing behavioural paradigms used in the design of HIV prevention programmes have highlighted the significance of the social and cultural dimensions of AIDS which must be taken into consideration in order to develop more effective means of bringing the pandemic under control. In short, theoretical models and methodological skills traditionally associated with the discipline of anthropology are becoming more and more recognized as essential to dealing with HIV/AIDS as a disease that afflicts collectivities as well as individuals, a disease of societies, cultures and nations.

The best anthropological research on AIDS refuses to reify culture, treating phenomena commonly designated as "cultural constraints to change" as the results of complexly linked aspects of social life. It shows how structural and corporeal violence result in social suffering and contribute to risk of AIDS, and demonstrates the key role of power and inequality in determining the health of populations. Anthropologists' witness to suffering, their concern and engagement, are potent elements in the research process, and in advocacy in national and international arenas.

Sydel Silverman, recently retired President of the Wenner Gren Foundation for Anthropological Research, challenges anthropologists to continue to advance anthropology's "grand vision for the understanding of humankind". She honors anthropologists' marginal status as a source of critical imagination, conferring the ability to see what others take for granted. This tradition would appear to be alive and struggling in the time of AIDS, as many anthropologists' research promotes critical appraisal of intellectual currents that affect the world's processes and problems. The combined strength of theory and practice in the field of international research on AIDS is a significant contribution to anthropology in the twenty-first century (Brooke, 2001).

REFERENCES

Anarfi (1993), Sexuality, Migration and AIDS in Ghana—A Social Behavioural Study, In J.C. Caldwell *et al.* (eds) *Sexual Networking and HIV/AIDS in West Africa*, pp. 45-68, Supplement to *Health Transition Review*, 3.

Basset, M. *et al.* (1993), Separation from Wife, High Risk Behaviour and HIV among Male Urban workers in Harare, Zimbabwe, *VIII International Conference on AIDS and STD in Africa*, Marrakech, December, 12-16.

Boyer, R. (1996), The Convergence Hypothesis Revisited: Globalization But Still the Century of Nations? In S. Berger and R. Dore (eds.) *National Diversity and Global Capitalism*, Ithaca, London.

Brooke G. Schoepf (2001), International AIDS Research in Anthropology: Taking a Critical Perspective on the Crisis, *Annual Review of Anthropology*, pp. 335-361.

Cravero, Kathleen (2000), Globalization Trends and HIV/AIDS, UNAID Report.

Decosas *et al.* (1995), Migration and AIDS, *Lancet*, 346, pp. 826-828.

Dennis, Altman (2001), *Global Sex*, Chicago: University of Chicago Press.

Doyal, L. and I. Pennell (1981), The Political Economy of Health, *Southend Express*, Boston.

Farmer, P. (1994), Aids-Talk and the Constitution of Cultural Models, *Social Science & Medicine*, p. 38.

FHI (1997), Final report of AIDSCAP Programme in Nepal, August 1993 to July 1997, Family Health International, Arlington, USA.

Gordenker *et al.* (1995), *International Cooperation in Response to AIDS*, London: Pinter.

Hrdy, D.B. (1987), Cultural Practices Contributing to the Transmission of HIV in Africa, *Review of Infectious Diseases*.

Hunt, C. (1989), Migrant Labour and Sexually Transmitted Diseases: AIDS in Africa, *Journal of Health and Social Behaviour*.

NACO (National AIDS Control Organization) web site. www. NACO.nic.in.

Pelto Perth J.(1997), Qualitative Data Gathering for the Reproductive Health Research, John Hopkins University.

Pritchett, L. (1995), Forget Convergence: Divergence Past, Present and Future, *Finance and Development*, June 1995.

Pritchett, L. (1997), Divergence, Big Time, *Journal of Economic Perspectives*, p. 11.

Pachauri, S. (1997), Reproductive Health in India: Conceptual Issues and Implementation Challenges, Jaipur: IIHMR (Indian Institute for Health and Marketing Research).

Sinha, S.P. (1999), *India Sits on AIDS Bomb*, Delhi: B.R. Publishing Corporation.

Quinn, T.C. (1994), Population and Migration and Spread of Types 1 and 2 Human Immuno Deficiency Viruses, *Proc. Natl. Acad. Sci.*, USA, pp. 91.

UNAIDS and IOM (1998), Migration and HIV/AIDS: International Migration.

UNCTAD (1997), *Trade and Development Report*, New York: UNCTAD.

15

Barriers to Eye Care in Rural Andhra Pradesh

VILAS KOVAI, S. KRISHNAIAH, B.R. SHAMANNA,
RAVI THOMAS and GULLAPALLI N. RAO

Introduction

"Vision 2020: The Right to Sight" is a global initiative to reverse the present trend of blindness and visual impairment with the aim of elimination of avoidable blindness by the year 2020 (Rao, 2000: 1).

One of the major challenges of the programme is to effect a significant increase in the uptake of eye care services. Understanding the role of treatment seeking behaviour for visual impairment especially that caused by easily treatable refractive errors and cataract in the rural areas is a crucial issue to be addressed while implementing Vision 2020 programme (Rao, 2000: 1; Dandona *et al.*, 2001: 908-916).

The Andhra Pradesh Eye Disease Study (APEDS) was conducted in the southern State of Andhra Pradesh (Dandona *et al.*, 2001: 908-916; Dandona *et al.*, 1997: 251-257). The purpose of APEDS was to obtain reliable population based epidemiological data on the prevalence and causes of eye diseases as well as those about the perceptions of people regarding visual impairment and barriers to eye care. This report analyzes the reasons for not availing eye care services by the rural people in Andhra Pradesh on the basis of the combined results in the rural areas of APEDS. The urban data has already been published in *British Journal of Ophthalmology*, 2000 (84, 22-27).

Methods

The details of APEDS methodology have been described elsewhere (Dandona *et al*., 1997: 251-157). A sample size of 7,771 subjects was selected by a multi-stage sampling procedure from 70 clusters from three rural areas in different parts of the southern Indian State of Andhra Pradesh. These three rural areas were located in West Godavari District, which has a well-off rural area, as well as Adilabad and Mahabubnagar Districts, which have comparatively poor rural areas. The aim was to obtain a study sample representative of the rural population of this state (Dandona *et al*., 1997: 251-257).

A structured schedule probing the barriers to eye care underwent a trial run on 100 subjects as a pilot, and then was refined for use in this study. The schedule had a list of personal, social and economic barriers. Trained bilingual field investigators then administered the schedule to subjects >15 years of age. Subjects were asked if they noticed any change in vision over the past 5 years. Those who said yes were asked if they sought treatment for the noticed change in vision. The barriers to regular eye check up for those who did not find any change in vision and for those who had perceived decrease in vision but had not sought treatment were particularly explored, because removal of these barriers to eye care services might determine the success of programmes for blindness prevention. The investigators documented multiple responses and marked them with a separate code for the most important reason as perceived by the subjects. Random checks were made on administration of schedules for quality control.

The subjects were then invited for detailed eye examination at a local site. Objective refraction followed by subjective refraction was conducted on all those who presented with distant or near visual acuity worse than 6/6 in either eye.

Visual impairment was defined as presenting distant visual acuity < 6/18 or equivalent visual field loss in the better eye. For distance visual acuity of <6/60, the equivalent visual field loss was considered as central visual field <20° (Dandona *et al.*, 1998: 497-504).

Moderate visual impairment was defined as presenting distant visual acuity <6/18 to 6/60 in the better eye. Severe visual impairment/blindness was defined as presenting distant visual acuity <6/60 in the better eye. The examination and inferences drawn regarding the cause of visual impairment in APEDS have been published.

Data were analyzed to assess the use of eye care services by subjects with visual impairment due to cataract and refractive errors in rural areas. The associations of use of eye care services with age, gender, education, socio-economic status, religion, level of visual impairment and cause of visual impairment were assessed. The barriers to eye care based on level of visual impairment were also assessed. For analysis, the perceived barriers were categorized as personal, social and economic. Individual perceptions (severity of problem and knowledge of eye care services) for not seeking treatment were categorized as personal. Monetary reasons (loss of wages, travelling and treatment cost) were categorized as economic. Reasons linked with lack of support of family members, for family/harvest/business were categorized as social reasons. Univariate analyses followed by multiple logistic regressions were performed. The effect of each category of a multi-categorical variable was assessed by keeping the first or the last category of that variable as the reference.

Results

Total Subjects

The interviewed and examined were a total of 7,771 (rural component of APEDS) with a response rate of 88 per cent in three selected areas of Adilabad, West Godavari and Mahaboobnagar Districts which represent rural Andhra

Table 15.1: Distribution of Subjects who Noticed Change in Vision Over the Past 5 Years and Treatment Sought by Background Characteristics

Back ground Characteristics	*Total (n = 1221)*	*Number Noticed Decrease in Vision*	*Number Sought Treatment (%)*
*Age (years)**			
16-29	29	13 (44.8)	4 (30.8)
30-39	43	35 (81.4)	10 (28.6)
40-49	158	136 (86.1)	39 (28.7)
50-59	333	295 (88.6)	71 (24.1)
60-69	453	421 (92.9)	138 (32.8)
≥ 70	205	187 (91.2)	61 (32.6)
Sex†			
Male	524	466 (88.9)	137 (29.4)
Female	697	621 (89.1)	186 (29.9)
Education‡			
I	933	835 (89.5)	229 (27.4)
II	213	188 (88.3)	68 (36.2)
III	63	54 (85.7)	19 (35.2)
IV	9	9 (100.0)	6 (66.7)
V	3	1 (33.3)	1 (100.0)
Socio-economic status$			
Extreme lower	177	158 (89.3)	54 (34.2)
Lower	675	606 (89.8)	175 (28.9)
Middle	331	291 (87.9)	83 (28.5)
Upper	18	15 (83.3)	5 (33.3)
Religion@			
Hindu	1173	1045 (89.1)	312 (29.9)
Muslim	48	[illegible]2 (87.5)	11 (26.2)
Level of visual impairment#			
<6/18-6/30	496	427 (86.1)	131 (30.7)
<6/30-6/60	517	471 (91.1)	122 (25.9)
<6/60	208	189 (90.9)	70 (37.0)
*Cause of visual impairment***			
Cataract	583	540 (92.6)	157 (29.1)
Refractive Error	504	427 (84.7)	102 (23.9)
Others	134	120 (89.6)	64 (53.3)

* p=0.000 for noticing decrease in vision and p=0.203 for seeking treatment, χ^2 test in univariate analysis.

† p=0.927 for noticing decrease in vision and p=0.893 for seeking treatment, Fisher's Exact Test.

‡ p=0.020 for noticing decrease in vision and p=0.005 for seeking treatment, χ^2 test in univariate analysis; Education categories defined as—I: no education, II: class 1-5, III: class 6-10, IV: class 11-12, V: higher than class 12 including technical courses

$ p=0.701 for noticing decrease in vision and p=0.572 for seeking treatment, χ^2 test in univariate analysis; Socio-economic status

Contd....

defined according to monthly per capita income in rupees extreme lower ≤ 200, lower 201-500, middle 501-2000 and upper >2000. Data is not available for 15 subjects on socio-economic status. (Data on socio-economic status is missing for 20 subjects in total, data not available for 17 subjects for notice in decrease in vision and data is not available on 6 subjects for seeking treatment).

@ $p=0.642$ for noticing decrease in vision and $p=0.731$ for seeking treatment, Fisher's Exact Test.

$p=0.025$ for noticing decrease in vision and $p=0.016$ for seeking treatment, χ^2 test in univariate analysis.

** $p=0.002$ for noticing decrease in vision and $p=0.179$ for seeking treatment, χ^2 test in univariate analysis.

Pradesh. 5,573 of the selected population were older than 15 years of age and 1260 subjects presented with distant visual acuity as defined (<6/18 or equivalent visual field loss in the better eye). The data was available on 1221 subjects older than 15 years of age with visual impairment (of the excluded 39 subjects, 26 subjects were children and 13 subjects over 15 years of age were blind with multiple disabilities). 1087 of the 1221 subjects had noticed decrease in vision over the past 5 years and 134 subjects had not noticed any such change. 697 (57%) were females and 1173 (96%) Hindus. Of the total 933 (76%) were illiterates and 852 (69.7%) were subjects were with lower socio-economic status. (Table 15.1).

1013 (85.3%) subjects had a level of visual acuity <6/18 to 6/60 (visual impairment) and 208 (14.6%) subjects had vision <6/60 (blindness) (Fig. 1).

The prevalence of visual impairment was 16.2 per cent CI (12.28-17.22) of the subjects >15 years of age. 68.6 per cent CI (65.93-71.45) of subjects did not seek treatment despite noticing change in vision. 71.2 per cent CI (69.31-75.21) of those with refractive errors and 36.7 per cent CI (32.84-40.66) of those with cataract did not seek treatment despite noticing decrease in vision.

The causes for visual impairment included cataract (583; 47.7%), refractive error (504; 41.2%), and other causes were responsible for 134 (10.9%).

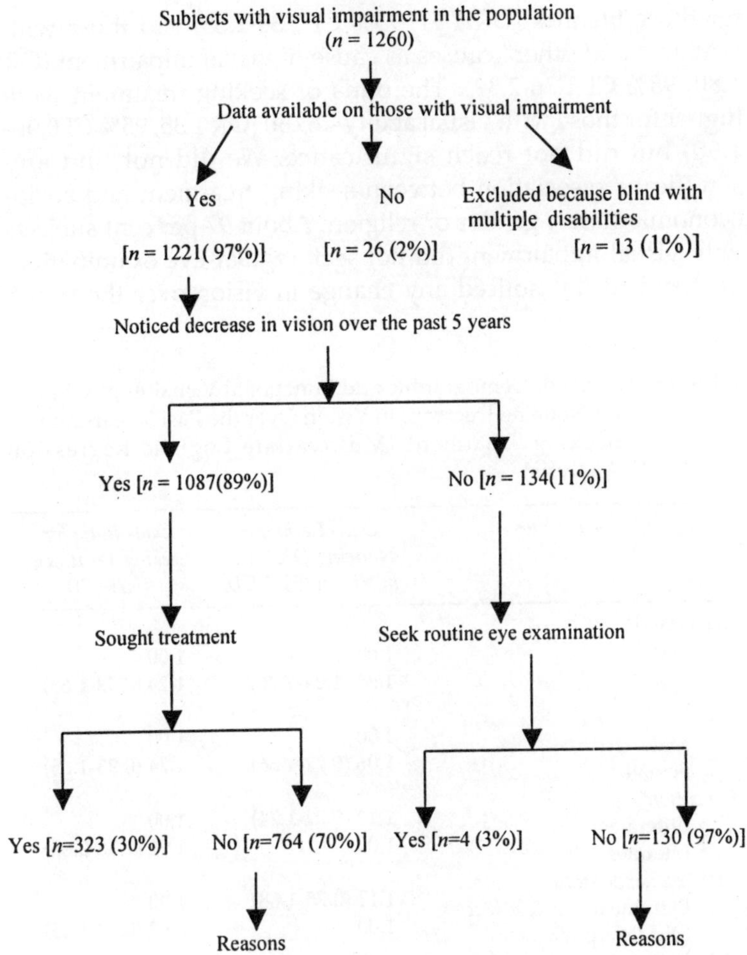

Fig. 15.1: Barriers to Eye Care in Rural Areas

The odds of noticing decrease in vision significantly increased with increasing age (OR 1.85, 95% CI 1.24-2.76) (Table 15.2). These with cataract plus other reasons as a cause of visual impairment had higher odds of noticing decrease in vision (OR 1.72, 95% CI, 1.15-2.55).

Only 323 (26.4%) visually impaired subjects had sought treatment after noticing decrease in vision in rural areas (Table 15.2), the odds of seeking treatment were significantly higher for those literates (OR 1.91, 95% CI 1.38-2.65) and those with "cataract and other" causes as cause of visual impairment (OR 1.80, 95% CI 1.36-2.39). The odds of seeking treatment were higher for those with visual acuity <6/60 (OR 1.35, 95% CI 0.96-1.90) but did not reach significance. We did not find any significant association between seeking treatment and socio-economic status, gender or religion. About 97 per cent subjects with visual impairment did not seek regular eye examination, as they had not noticed any change in vision over the past 5 years.

Table 15.2: Effect of Demographic and Functional Visual Acuity Levels on Noticing Decrease in Vision Over the Past 5 Years and on Seeking Treatment (Multivariate Logistic Regression Analysis)

Characteristics	*Odds Ratio for Noticing Decrease in Vision (95% CI)*	*Odds Ratio for Seeking Treatment (95% CI)*
*Age (years)**		
<60	1.00	1.00
≥60	1.85 (1.24-2.76)	1.24 (0.93-1.65)
Sex		
Male	1.00	1.00
Female	1.06 (0.72-1.56)	1.24 (0.93-1.65)
*Education**		
Illiterates	1.12 (0.72-1.74)	1.00
Literates	1.00	1.91 (1.38-2.65)
*Socio-economic status**		
Extreme lower & lower	1.12 (0.75-1.68)	1.00
Middle, upper	1.00	0.93 (0.68-1.25)
*Religion**		
Hindu	1.21 (0.48-2.95)	1.38 (0.66-2.88)
Muslim	1.00	1.00
*Level of visual impairment**		
<6/18-6/60	1.00	1.00
<6/60	1.00 (0.56-1.50)	1.35 (0.96-1.90)
*Cause of visual impairment**		
Cataract and others	1.72 (1.15-2.55)	1.50 (1.11-2.03)
Refractive error	1.00	1.00

* Categories for these variables combined to increase the power of analysis. Age groups <60 and ≥60 years combined to asses difference between the non-elderly and elderly groups. Cataract and others combined.

Barriers to routine eye examination in those with good vision were classified as personal in 87 per cent, economic in 8 per cent, and social in 5 per cent of the cases. Data were missing in 3 subjects as they did not want to provide information (Table 15.3).

Table 15.3: Reasons for not Utilizing Routine Eye Examination Services

Reason	*Category†*	*No (%)** *(n=130)*
1. Did not have serious problem	P	16 (12.3)
2. Able to see adequately	P	89 (68.5)
3. Eye diseases/decrease in vision are natural with growing old, hence do not need treatment	P	1 (0.8)
4. No one willing to escort for eye checkup	S	1 (0.8)
5. Family/harvest/business/other obligations	S	7 (5.4)
6. Do not have money to pay for eye checkup	E	10 (7.7)
7. Eye check up not a priority because of other serious medical problems	P	1 (0.8)
Other reasons		
1. Fear of surgery	P	1 (0.8)
2. Negligence	P	1 (0.8)

† P = personal, S = social and E = economic reason.

* Percentages do not add up to 100 because of rounding, as data is not applicable for 3 subjects.

Barriers to seeking treatment for those who had not sought treatment in spite of noticed decrease in vision over the past 5 years were personal in 52 per cent, economic in 37 per cent and social in 21 per cent respectively. Data were missing in 2 subjects, as they did not want to provide information (Table 15.4).

The associations between age, education, level of visual impairment, and cause of visual impairment and barriers to seeking treatment are shown in Figure 15.2.

Discussion

Despite noticing a decrease in vision a large proportion of the rural population does not seem to consider eye examination a priority. Personal and economic reasons were perceived as barriers to eye care. There was a significant association between age and noticing decrease in vision over the past 5 years in this

Table 15.4: Reasons for not Utilizing Eye Care Services Even after Noticing Change in Vision

	Reason	*Category†*	*No (%)* (n = 764)*
1.	Dominant person in family, if other than the subject didn't feel need for seeking treatment	S	23 (3.0)
2.	Did not have a serious problem	P	161 (21.1)
3.	Able to see adequately	P	22 (2.9)
4.	Eye diseases/decrease in vision are natural with growing old and so don't need treatment	P	40 (5.2)
5.	Afraid that seeing someone for eye checkup would reveal vision loss, and hence cause worry	P	12 (1.6)
6.	Don't know where to go for eye checkup	P	2 (0.3)
7.	Have to travel far for eye check up	P	5 (0.7)
8.	No one willing to escort for eye check up	S	22 (2.9)
9.	Family/Harvest/business/other obligations prevent eye checkup	S	114 (14.9)
10.	Do not have money to pay for eye checkup	E	283 (37.0)
11.	Don't feel comfortable with the indigenous practitioner that I have access to	P	4 (0.5)
12.	Don't feel comfortable with eye Doctor/General Medical Doctor	P	1 (0.1)
13.	Eye checkup not a priority because of other serious medical problems	P	37 (4.8)
14.	Would like eye checkup but other medical problems prevent me from going	P	12 (1.6)
15.	Other reasons	P	24 (3.1)

† P = personal, S = social and E = economic reason.

* Percentages do not add up to 100 because of rounding, as data is not applicable for 2 subjects.

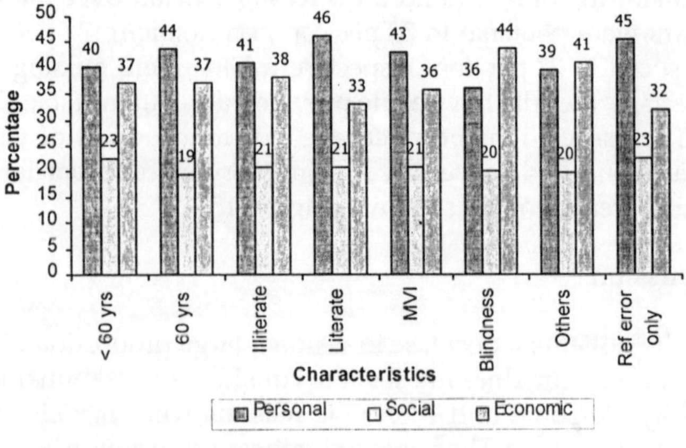

Fig. 15.2: Barriers for not Seeking Eye Care Services in Rural India

study. While this may be expected, even if there was perceived decrease in vision, no treatment was sought (Table 15.2). As reported earlier, this might be due to the health seeking priorities in relation to age in rural areas; age influences the decision that determines seeking health (Morgan, 1985). It could also be due to increased dependency visually, economically and socially on family as age advances. This is supported by our data that about 58 per cent of visually impaired subjects (< 6/60 +) of APEDS who had not sought treatment were economically deprived (Table 15.5). Also our data show that personal followed by economic reasons for not seeking treatment increased significantly with the increase of age (Figure 15.2).

Table 15.5: Working Status of Visually Impaired People in Relation to Seeking Treatment in Rural Andhra Pradesh

Level of VI	*Working Status of Those Who Sought Treatment (n=323)*		*Working Status of Those Who have not Sought Treatment (n=764)*	
	Yes	*No*	*Yes*	*No*
<6/18-<6/60	129 (50.99)	124 (49.01)	427 (66.20)	218 (33.80)
<6/60+	22 (32.35)	46 (67.65)	50 (42.02)	69 (57.98)

Strategies to address this group of barriers in those above 60 years include promoting community based free screening and free treatment, free transport to hospital for further treatment and low cost spectacles irrespective of economic status of subjects. This increases the chances of availing eye care services. The Aravind Hospital Model (Naichiar *et al.*, 1994: 987-993) shows that offering free screening, transport and surgery is effective and acts as catalyst in educating the other potential cataract patients to utilize eye care services. Newer approaches like setting up permanent eye care facilities closer to people like Satellite Eye Centres (Shamanna, 2000: 105-107) should probably be used as an alternative to periodic temporary methods like eye camps where possible.

It is interesting that although subjects noticed uecreased vision, it translated into seeking treatment only when vision fell to the blindness category level. These findings corroborate reports (Gupta and Murthy, 1995: 1337-1340) that the subjects with moderate visual impairment probably adjust to the symptoms first for a period of time and seek treatment, as the symptoms become more severe. With limited resources, it is only natural that treatment is delayed till it is deemed absolutely necessary. However, even people defined as blind and aware of the severity of the visual problem could not seek treatment primarily due to costs and other personal problems.

Decreased vision to the level of visual impairment alone does not seem to be sufficient to take the person to an eye care provider; this is related to personal, social and economic circumstance of the person and also the cause of visual impairment. For those defined as moderate visual impairment, treatment was not sought primarily due to personal reasons such as "do not have a serious problem", and "decrease in vision is natural with growing old and so do not need treatment". On multivariate logistic regression analysis, personal reasons were responsible for people with refractive error as cause of visual impairment for not seeking treatment (Figure 15.2). The chances of not seeking treatment for eye care were significantly lower in illiterates mainly due to personal and economic reasons (Table 15.2). We did not find any significant association of gender, socio-economic status with noticing decreased vision or seeking treatment as similar to a comparison with data reported on urban component of APEDS (Dandona *et al.*, 2000: 22-27).

Interestingly, about 60 per cent of visually impaired population who can be classified as moderate visually impairment among the APEDS subjects (Table 15.5) were still economically productive in spite of not seeking treatment for their decrease in vision due to personal reasons.

The majority of those blind were also illiterate. It would seem imperative to raise awareness of benefits of cataract surgery and its benefits in this group. This requires screening, patient counselling and more patient friendly systems for treatment for this category. Data from other studies suggest that the literate, the affluent and males have higher awareness about cataract and its treatment (Brilliant and Brilliant, 1985: 584-589). Treatment inequalities could also be due to imbalance of eye care human resources availability in the urban and rural areas (Kumar, 1993: 269-275). Elimination of illiteracy probably leads to higher utilization of eye care services. Only 50 per cent of those who had noticed decrease in vision because of cataract causing visual impairment sought treatment. Poor outcome of treatment itself could also attribute to this low uptake (Fletcher *et al.*, 1999: 1393-1399). The other most important reason for not utilization of cataract surgical services probably due to the poor outcome of cataract surgery. The percentage of blindness following cataract surgery in India ranged from 3.7-38.8 per cent (Anand *et al.*, 2000; Limburg *et al.*, 1999; Reidy *et al.*, 1991). It is important to recognize that despite the successful cataract surgery, many patients in rural India do not see well because of uncorrected refractive errors due to uncomfortable or lost spectacles (Limburg *et al.*, 1999; Kumar, 1993: 269-275).

It is clear that awareness of the eye diseases and the benefits of the intervention must be increased and treatment costs (Shamanna *et al.*, 1998; Jose, 1997: 10-16) increase if treatment is not sought. This could be possible by addressing three issues as follows:

1. Establishing good rapport with the catchments population;
2. Holding informal eye health awareness workshops for the target community; and
3. Patient friendly atmosphere at base hospital.

This would help foster community participation for eye care and in "marketing" sight restoration as a product (Morgan, 1985). Easy accessibility, free services (for those who cannot afford it), reputation of the operating team and advertisement were the major motivating factors that were cited by respondents for the utilization of the eye care camp facilities (Dandona *et al.*, 2001).

In conclusion, if these data from our study are roughly projected to the rural population >15 years of age in India, 564 million in 2001 (Census, 2001), there would be an estimated 91 million people (95% CI 69.26-97.12 million) with visual impairment, of which 68 million (95% CI 65.67-70.18 million) people would have perceived change in vision. A significant 47 million (95% CI 44.78-48.53 million) would not have sought eye care despite perceived change in vision. Our findings imply that elimination of illiteracy, awareness of eye care and removal of economic constraints might influence the subjects with visual impairment to go to an eye doctor. These findings underscore the importance of understanding the demographic variables like age, education, level of visual impairment and causes of visual impairment and their significant interaction with noticing decrease in vision and seeking treatment in addition to barriers to eye care in rural areas while implementing suitable eye care planning. If the "Vision 2020: The Right to Sight" is to succeed, it is imperative to determine the groups to be targeted and eliminate the barriers that prevent delivery of eye care. It would seem that currently we need to concentrate on those who are blind *versus* visually impaired, keeping in mind that visual impairment due to cataract will eventually progress to blindness.

REFERENCES

Anand, R.; Gupta, A.; Ram, J.; *et al.* (2000), Visual Outcome following Cataract Surgery in Rural Punjab, *Indian J Opthalmol*, 48, pp. 153-8.

Brilliant, G.E.; James M. Lepakowski; Betriz Zurita; *et al.* (1991), Social Determinants of Cataract Surgery, *Archives Ophthalmology*, 109: pp. 584-589.

Brilliant, G.E.; Brilliant, L.B. (1985), Using Social Epidemiology to Understand Who Stays Blind and Who Gets Operated for Cataract in a Rural Setting, *SocSci Med*, 21, pp. 553-558.

Census of India 2001 results, http://www.censusindia.net/results/summaryindia.html.

Dandona, L.; Dandona, R.; Naduvilath, T.J.; *et al.* (1998), Is Current Eye Care Policy Focus almost Exclusively on Cataract adequate to deal with Blindness in India? *Lancet, 10*, pp. 497-504.

Dandona, L.; Dandona, R.; Srinivas, M.; *et al.* (2001), Blindness in the Indian state of Andhra Pradesh, *Invest Ophthalmol Vis Sci*, 42, pp. 908-16.

Dandona, R.; Dandona, L.; Naduvilath T.J.; *et al.* (1997), Design of a Population based Study of Visual Impairment in India: the Andhra Pradesh Eye Disease Study, *Indian J Ophthalmol*, 45, pp. 251-7.

Dandona, R.; Dandona, L.; Naduvilath T.J.; *et al.* (2000), Utilization of Eye Care Services in an Urban Population in Southern India, *Br J Ophthalmol*, 84, pp. 22-27.

Dandona, R.; Dandona, L.; Vilas, K.; *et al.* (2002), Population-Based Study of Spectacles Use in Southern India, *Indian J Ophthalmol.*, 50, pp. 145-55.

Fletcher E. Astrid; Donogue Martine; Devavaram John; *et al.* (1999), Low Uptake of Eye Services in Rural India, *Arch Ophthalmol.*, 117, pp. 1393-99.

Naichiar, G.; Alan L. Robin; Ravilla D.; *et al.* (1994), Attacking the Backlog of India's Curable Blind; The Aravind Eye Hospital Model, *Arch Ophthalmol.*, 112: pp. 987-93.

Gupta, S.K.; Murthy, G.V.S. (1995), Where Do People with Blindness Caused by Cataracts in Rural Areas of India seek Treatment and Why? *Arch Ophthalmol.*, 113, pp. 1337-40.

Jose, R. (1997), National Programme for Control of Blindness. *Indian J. Comm. Health*, 3(2), pp. 10-16.

Kumar R. (1993), Ophthalmic Manpower in India—Need for Serious Review, *Int. Ophthalmol.*, 17, pp. 269-75.

Limburg, H.; Foster A.; Vaidyanathan K.; *et al.* (1999), Monitoring Visual Outcome of Cataract Surgery in India, *Bulletin of WHO*, 77, pp. 455-60.

Morgan, M.; Calnan, M.; and Manning, N. (1985), *Sociological Approaches to Health and Illness*, London: Routledge & Kegan Paul.

Rao, G.N. (2000), Vision 2020: The Right to Sight (editorial), *Indian J Ophthalmol.*, 48, p. 1.

Reidy, A.; Mehra, V.; Minassian, D.; *et al.* (1991), Outcome of Cataract Surgery in Central India. A Longitudinal follow up Study, *Br. J. Opthalmol.*, 75, pp. 102-5.

Shamanna, B.R.; Dandona, L.; Gullapalli N. Rao (1998), Economic Burden of Blindness in India, *Indian J Ophthalmol.*, 46, pp. 169-72.

Shamanna, B.R. (2000), Establishing Sustainable Eye Care Programmes in India—Some Issues and Thoughts, *JKSOS*, 12(3), pp. 105-7.

Vision 2020, The Right to Sight. (http/www.who.org/inf-pr-1999/en/pr99-12html).

16

Dalit Protest, Dalit Literature and Dalit Feminism

Towards a New Anthropological Approach

N.K. DAS

Dalits in India have faced centuries of oppression. For centuries they had lived at the mercy of their rich high caste masters. Under the impact of new thoughts, democratic political institutions and new economic order, the old structural and functional bases of the villages are crumbling. There is a new awakening among the Dalits today, their strivings to gain human dignity. The Scheduled Castes, Scheduled Tribes and Other Backward Classes in many parts of India have increasingly identified themselves as 'Dalit' (the oppressed). This emerging pan—Indian identity has been widely recognised in recent years. Anthropologists and Sociologists are however not in agreement unanimously about pragmatic relevance of this term. Historian Romila Thapar maintains that there is a political necessity for holding on to the Dalit category. She traces the roots of this category in Pali literature in which Dalit means "the oppressed". Some Scholars have argued that any attempt to accord a pan-Indian status to this category would rob other identities based on region and culture (Pandian and others, quoted in Guru and Geetha, 2000). Gajendran has noted that upper caste common sense saw Dalits as uncultured and primitive people doing menial jobs and lacking a written antiquity (Guru and Geetha, 2000). Pleading extension of the Dalit category, Illiah has advocated for inclusion of the category Bahujan within the Dalit category. Rege urges that the Dalit feminism should be treated differently from the standpoint of epistemology (Guru and Geetha, 2000).

The Scheduled Castes, Scheduled Tribes and the Other Backward Classes together constitute about 60 per cent of India's population. They together form the Dalit category. There are as many as 600 communities which are regarded as Scheduled Castes. The Scheduled Castes alone constitute a high per cent of the country's population (Khillare, 1997). According to 1991 Census the SC population was 13.82 crores. The genesis of Dalit category is associated with social movements among the Scheduled Castes in Maharashtra, where they identified themselves as Dalit. In this paper also we will concentrate on the Scheduled Castes in different parts of India. The People of India project of the Anthropological Survey of India has identified 450 Scheduled Castes, including 45 unlisted sub-groups. The total number of Scheduled Caste segments come to 751 (Singh, 1995). Numerically speaking, the Chamar outrank all other castes. Other numerically large Scheduled Castes, widely distributed in different parts of India, are Adi Dravida, Pasi, Madiga, Dusadh, Mala, Pariyan, Dhobi, Adi-Karnataka and Mahar. The Harijans, the 'Untouchables', were earlier identified as 'Depressed Classes'. From 1935 onwards they came to be known as Scheduled Castes. Besides agricultural labour, the Scheduled Castes traditionally worked as scavengers, gravediggers, dead-cattle removers, tanners and shoe makers.

Both the Scheduled Castes and Scheduled Tribes constitute the Dalit social category, but there are certain aspects in which the problems of the Scheduled Castes and Scheduled Tribes differ. The Scheduled Tribes mainly suffer from geographical isolation and being forest dwellers, their society is generally characterised by low level of techno-economic development. The Scheduled Castes, on the other hand suffer not only from economic backwardness, they also suffer from social disabilities and stigma. The lowness of the Scheduled Caste is ritually explained by their *permanent impurity* which derives from their association with death and organic pollution. They fulfil certain essential ritual functions within Indian society. "They remove impurity from the social world" (Deliege, 1992). Untouchability stands abolished by virtue of Article 17 of the Constitution and its practice in any form is punishable; but social discriminations against the Scheduled Castes still linger in many parts of the country. Thus, 76,748 cases of atrocities against persons belonging to Scheduled Castes and 17,101 cases of atrocities against Scheduled Tribes were reported between 1986 and 1990. Of these, 5339 cases were of rape.

Historically speaking, these so-called 'ritually low caste groups' had constituted the artisan and service class and provided services to high castes and rich landowners, under a rigid *jajmani* system in the past. Of the total Scheduled Caste population 88 per cent lives in villages. Broadly speaking, north India has greater concentration of Scheduled Caste communities than South India. In post–Independence era, allotment of agricultural land to landless Scheduled Caste families under land reforms or as a consequence of reclamation of agricultural land has strengthened their proportion in the primary sector as owner-cultivator. But these measures have hardly led to the diversification of occupational structure of the Scheduled Caste population to any great extent. Agricultural labour thus continues to be the main occupation of the Scheduled Castes. It is followed by cultivation, other services, manufacturing industries, livestock, plantations, fishing, storage, transport and communication, trade and commerce, construction, mining and quarrying in this order (Chandana, 1989:151).

In any discussion on national Dalit question, the Dalit women's issue deserves special consideration. There are linkages between gender, caste and class structure, the organisation of production, re-production and re-distribution. The two most important orientations which have been brought to centre of Dalit feminist standpoint are 'caste' and 'contemporary capitalism' (Rege, 2000; Datar, 1999). Caste in mediating the control over resources and the division of labour structures the divide between intellectual and manual labour.

The inter-linkages between caste-based division of labour and sexual division of labour control the production of life through the marriage circles and make way for patriarchal extraction of women's labour (Rege, 2000). The Dalit people including their womenfolk in some parts of India in recent years have mobilised themselves to fight for their rights on natural resources. In fact, the decade of the 1970s was marked by a series of forest movements, involving women folk in different parts of the country. Ecologists and environmentalists have been aggressively involved in campaigning in rural, coastal, forest and hill areas focusing on the rights of the rural Dalit people. According to Medha Patekar "The mass movements with the environmental vision have a great role to play" (Patekar, 2000).

Literary expression goes hand in hand with political agitation. The Dalits have variously expressed resentment and dissent in different parts of India in different historical phases. Dalit literature, which has been identified as a liberation literature is a part of Dalit culture. The Dalits indeed have their own unique vocabulary and speech. Dalit literature is people's literature. Shame, sexual exploitation, anger, sorrow and persistent hope are the main content of Dalit literature. According to Dangle (1992), Dalit literature is marked by revolt and negativism, since it is closely associated with the hopes for freedom of a group of people who, as untouchables, are victims of social, economic and cultural inequality. There are numerous theories about the origin of Dalit literature. Buddha (6th century B.C.), Chokhamela (14th century A.D.), Mahatma Phule (1828-90) and Prof. S.M. Mate (1886-1957) are regarded as among the originators. In modern context, however, it is Dr. Ambedkar who may be called the pioneer of Dalit literature. Dalit literature has a long tradition in South India (Karnataka, Tamil Nadu and Andhra Pradesh) and parts of northwest India such as Gujarat and Maharashtra. Dalit literature includes short stories, novels and drama, but has been most effective in poetry and autobiography[1]. The Dalit poems generally reflect the conflict between the past tradition and the contemporary movement. Zelliot (1992: 293-331) has compiled many Dalit poems, written by Daya Pawar and others. There are poems dealing with past village life of the Mahars. While much of this literature in bitter, a strain of humour and optimism runs through the works of the native poets. A few lines from a poem of Namdeo Dhasal are produced below. The poem "Poverty as my own independent piece of land" was first published in *Times Weekly*, 25, November, 1973 (Zelliot, 1992).

> *"...poverty itself is my own independent*
> *piece of land,*
> *And as I cultivate it my days rise*
> *And my days fal...*
> *Earlier men could have been the wretched*
> *slaves of the soil.*
> *I refused to make compromise..."*

Zelliot (1992: 300-301) and other scholars have translated *Vidrohi Kavita* (Poetry of protest) of Keshav Meshram. One such poem is partly produced here 'One day I crushed that mother-fucker, God...My neighbour...was shocked...would you cop a whole cart full of wood, for a single piece of bread!' Zelliot regards Babasaheb Ambedkar as key figure in the Dalit movement in India. Among his legacies are the Republican Party, a network of schools and colleges, a Buddhism conversion movement and a literary movement which is a new force in Marathi literature and growing now in Kannada and Gujarati linguistic areas (1992: 312).

The Dalits of Maharashtra have created a school of literature, Dalit Sahitya (Zelliot, 1976; 1978), which has changed the face of Marathi literature and inspired similar literary creativity among the Dalits of Gujarat and Karnataka. Dalit culture has now become something of a fashionable article of faith. *The Dalit Voice*, English Weekly from Bangalore, claims from time to time that *Devadasi* culture, which includes the classical dance form, Bharata Natyam, is a Dalit form of creativity. The June 1986 issue of *Religion and Society*, a scholarly journal published from Bangalore by the Christian Institute for the Study of Society and Religion, is entirely devoted to Dalit culture, Hindu as well as Christian. Even more striking, however, are the ways in which today's Dalits encourage cultural creativity. The poem by Daya Pawar on Valmiki both indicates a belief in the Dalit creative past and is itself an act of creation. Since the early 1970s, short stories, a few novels, many poetry and most recent autobiography have flowed from Dalit pens in great quantity (Zelliot, 1992:321).

The Delhi-based Ahwan Theatre, a Cinema and Mass Media group, has "definite plans to provide extensive exposure to the rich cultural heritage and traditional Dalit and folk arts of the country" (Ahwan Brochure, 1987, quoted in Zelliot, 1992:321). Several Dalit drama conferences have been held, and it is said that there are now more than forty Dalit theatre groups. Many write their own plays, a few adapt plays from the American Black theatre, some revive the arts of *tamasha*. B.S. Shinde of Pune, founding father of Dalit Rangabhumi, has written plays based on Buddhist themes and a drama built around the legendary Mahar hero, Amrutnak (Zelliot, 1992:322).

There seems to be no end to new Dalit cultural creativity. Dalit women in Mumbai organized the Dalit Stri Samwadini (Dalit Women's Dialogue) in 1986, probably the first women's literary conference in Maharashtra. A Dalit art exhibition was held in Nagpur in connection with the Asmitadarsh literary conference in 1979, and an all-India art conference was called in Hyderabad in 1987. Some Dalits believe that the sculptors of the classic period of Indian art were of an untouchable caste. (Zelliot, 1992:322). Among the earliest works on the untouchables, we may mention the pioneering work on the untouchable sweepers by Kolenda (1964). One of the recent and most thorough is Vincentnathan's study of a group that calls itself Harijan in the South (1988). The rejection of the idea of pollution may be much older than the modern period. A classic statement was made in the fourteenth century by the Mahar saint-poet Chokhamela who asked.

In the beginning, at the end,
There is nothing but pollution.
No one knows anyone who is born pure.
Cokha says, in wonder, who is pure?

(Abhanga 11)

There have been interesting developments in Dalit literature in the past few years. The movement has spread in south (Karnataka) and north (Gujarat) and there is now serious and important Dalit fiction and poetry in Kannada and Gujarati. In Maharashtra, beginning with Daya Pawar's autobiography Baluta, there has been a steady stream of pioneering autobiographies from Mahars, Buddhists, Chambhars, "De-notified tribes", and other Dalits (Zelliot, 1992:332). Women's poetry is also becoming important, and there are now many Dalit women poets. A Dalit Womens' Literary Conference, probably the first women's literary organization in Maharashtra, was organized in 1986 (Zelliot, 1992:332). The feminist Dalit literature has a unique historical tradition in many parts of India. Thus, in South India, a Dalit woman, Kalavve, challenged the upper castes in the twelfth century in the following words:

Those who eat goats, fowl and tiny fish,
Such, they call caste people.
Those, who eat the sacred cow,
that showers frothing milk for Shiva,
Such, they call 'out-castes'.

In the same poem, Kalavve points out how the Brahmans drink with glee water and ghee from bags made of cattle hide by untouchables (Shiva Prakash, 1999). Dharman (1999) argues that the problem of the Dalits has not sprung up in recent years. Dalit issues and the 'Voices' pleading the Dalit causes have been raised from the very beginning of Tamil literature. In one such old writing the Siddas had questioned: Is the pleasure of upper class women's flesh different from that of Pariah woman's? Do the flesh, bone and skin of women bear the stamp of their caste?

Now we have a sizeable body of Dalit literature not only in Tamil and Kannada, but also in Telugu, Marathi, Hindi, Gujarati, Punjabi and Bengali. In Andhra Pradesh we have not only a rich tradition of Dalit literature mainly contributed by Gaddar, but non-Dalit sections of exploited people, such as the Madiga, have come out with challenging voices.

Gaddar, the popular Telugu singer-poet, embodies many institutions in his struggle to re-shape the structure of caste/ class system. As a Dalit he wrote hundreds of songs that brought the Dalit Bahujan working class and women's life into literary texts. An early song (Ilaiah, 1997) that won the hearts of Telugu society was written around the life experience of a mother:

Oh, mother,
Lachumamma,
your blouse is torn,
your hair is soiled,
your sari is torn,
you have no money to buy new ones.
Even in that condition
what have you done ?
You planted saplings
walking backwards like a bull
in order to produce
food from the mud.

It was no accident that Gorky's most popular novel is about the mother's role in revolution. Gaddar's most popular song is also about a Dalit mother's role in the production of wealth (Ilaiah, 1997). Gaddar used a powerful song by another Dalit poet, Guda Anjaiah to educate the poor. When Gaddar sang *Ea Vuru Manadira* (this village is ours), thousands of people joined him in procession.

Gaddar constructs the producing castes and classes as *matti chetulu* (the hands that turn mud into food). He uses the basic Dalit-Bahujan language, idiom and symbolism by transforming the linguistic structure of literary Telugu. Gradually his influence spread to cinema. Gaddar's association with the Ambedkarite movement and thought raised new hopes.

In all his songs about women, the institution of the family comes under attack:

'Mogolla nollallo beedilai Kaletollam,
nindu amasanaadu 'o' Lachgummadi,
Aada pilla puttinaadi 'o' Lachagummadi'

'We women, burn as cigars in the mouths of men,
if a girl is born on a no-moon day, the
mother is forced to throw her away' (Ilaiah, 1997).

About Dalit life, Gaddar sings:

'matti batukulu –
yetti batukulu'.

'Dalit lives are not only the lives that live in soil, but they are bonded lives' as well (Ilaiah, 1997).

Shame, anger, sorrow and indomitable hope have always been main content of Dalit literature of the past and present. The relationship between such radical traditions of the past and present day Dalit literary movements, particularly those concerned with women's issues, need to be reviewed and analysed by the anthropologists in order not only to project the insider's perspective but also to 'deconstruct' preconceived notions and presumptions of the past.

The women remained invisible in anthropology till recently. Though they appeared in the literature in the context of 'kinship and marriage' but 'analysis of social reality were loaded with a distinct male bias which led to the distortion of facts (Moore, 1988). In most of Indian anthropological works of earlier period traditional familial roles of women were glorified (Mehrotra, 1990) which was only to justify the patriarchal domination of men-folk. Veena Majumdar (1986) has identified three ingredients in an Indian perspective on women's studies, 'Acceptance and recognition of Indian society as plural society', 'Recognition that women must fight for future and her involvement in political, economic and social processes in all levels' and 'That research and policy have to be pro-women'. Leela Dube (1980) stated that women's studies have been handicapped by a general lack of understanding of cross-cultural and inter-cultural variations in the organisational principles of societies and in the life contexts of women (1980).

A new emphasis on women as a person, as gender category is emerging as a recent trend in anthropology. Symbolic anthropologists are focusing on woman's body, her sexuality, notion of femininity and different metaphors used in language and culture to represent reality (Veena Das, 1988; Dube, 1986, 1988). Using cross-cultural data Sandy (1973) examined the theory of status of women on the basis of ecological and economic factors and concluded that female production is a necessary but not sufficient condition for the development of female power and that female status is likely to develop if women have control over valued products and strategic resources (Sandy, 1973). The Human Development Report, 1995, demonstrates that no country in the world treats women as well as it does its men. The term social status seems to be more of an artificial construct. It is generally agreed that, instead of use of term status we should be concerned with the placement of women in a system of access to power, property and legal and economic freedom. The term, status, is considered to be more limited in scope. Hence the term, women's autonomy, has gained currency in development of feminist literature. The women's autonomy denotes the independence the women have in their functioning.

Khare (1998) has argued that 'World anthropology today is multi-centred'. In India, the problems of the socially disadvantaged categories of people may not be ignored any longer. The anthropologist should not only be a seeker of truth but also of social justice. With specific reference to Dalit women and other powerless categories of people, Khare, says 'Anthropology is writing about culture or, more perceptively, "Writing culture", and unless this is done with (not about) the people, unless it incorporates and not merely appropriates their voices, 'doing' anthropology will be in vain'. Khare quotes a Dalit woman, "When others write about us, they misrepresent us; otherwise, we are mostly ignored or overlooked. This body is our book of life" (Khare 1998: 161f). After having been silenced for centuries by caste prejudice, there has emerged a keen self-awareness and a sense of having been exploited, wronged and abused, on part of the oppressed. There is a new consciousness and expression of aggressiveness, which is reflected in growing literature being created by the Dalit scholars themselves. There is need to accord greater recognition to their literature which shows the bitterness of their experiences.

NOTE

1. In their book *Viramma: life of a Dalit* J. Racine and J.L. Racine (2000) provide an 'Autobiography' of a Dalit woman. In her autobiography, Viramma, the Dalit woman, says "Her illiteracy, her ignorance of genuine connections between events, her lack of information, her lack of access to modern communication have stood in the way of her improving her social position". She further says, "The hierarchy of the castes was actually a graded access to land and a graduated share of the harvest". She also says ".... Political parties and political power are meant only to be manipulated in order to move up ...." (Racine and Racine, 2000).

REFERENCES

Agrawal, Bina (1992), The Gender and Environment Debate: Lessons from India, *Feminist Studies*. Vol.18, No. 1.

Bapat, Ram (1996), *Arthakarnachya Badalatya Disha*. Satara: Ambedkar Academy.

Chandana, R.C. (1989), *Spatial Dimensions of Scheduled Castes in India*. New Delhi: Intellectual Publishing House.

Dangle, Arjun (1992), Introduction, In *No Entry for the New Sun*, Arjun Dangle (ed), Bombay: Disha Books.

Das, Veena (1976), Indian Women: Work, Power and Status, In B.R. Nanda (ed) *Indian Women*, New Delhi: Vikas Publication.

Das, Veena (1988), Femininity and the Orientation to the Body, In Karuna Chanana (ed) *Education, Socialisation and Women*, New Delhi: Orient Longman.

Datar, Chhaya (1999), Non-Brahmin Renderings of Feminism in Maharasthra, *Economic and Political Weekly*. October 9, 1999.

Deliege, Robert (1992), Replication and Consensus, Untouchability, Caste and Ideology in India, *Man*, 27 (1): 155-73.

Dharman, Cho (1999), What is said and what ought to have been said, *Indian Literature*. 193, pp. 91-3.

Dube, Leela (1980), *Review of Studies on Women in South East Asia*. UNESCO.

Dube, Leela (1986), Seed and Earth: The Symbolism of Biological Reproduction and Sexual Relations of Production, In L. Dube, E. Leacock and S. Ardener (eds) *Visibility and Power*, pp. 22-53, Delhi: Oxford University Press.

Dube, Leela (1988), On the Construction of Gender: Hindu Girls in Patrilineal India, In K. Chanana (ed) *Education, Socialisation and Women*, New Delhi: Orient Longman

Guru, Gopal and V. Geetha (2000), New Phase of Dalit-Bahujan Intellectual Activity. *Economic and Political Weekly*, January 15, 2000.

Ilaiah, Kancha (1997), Gaddar: Embodying Many Institutions, *Seminar*, 456 August, 1997.

Khare, R.S. (1998), *Cultural Diversity and Social Discontent*. New Delhi: Sage.

Khillare, Y. (1997), *Present Status of Backward Classes in India*. Aurangabad: Centre for Studies on SC, ST.

Kolenda, Pauline (1964), Religious Anxiety and Hindu Fate, *Journal of Asian Studies*, XXIII, pp. 71-81.

Majumdar, V. (1986), Indian Perspectives to Women's Studies, In M. Krishnaraj (ed), *Women's Studies in India*, New Delhi (London): Sargam Books.

Mehrotra, Nilika (1990), Women's Issues in Indian Anthropology, *The Eastern Anthropologist*. Vol. 43, No. 2.

Moore, H.L. (1988), *Feminism and Anthropology*, London: Polity Press.

Patekar, Medha (2000), People's Movements, *Survey of the Environment. The Hindu*. Chennai.

Racine, J. and J.C. Racine (2000), *Life of a Dalit by Viramma*, Delhi: Social Science Press.

Rege, Sharmila (2000), Real Feminism and Dalit Women, *Economic and Political Weekly*, February 5, 2000.

Sandy, P.S. (1973), Towards a Theory of the Status of Women, *American Anthropologist*. 75, p. 5.

Shiva Prakash, H.S. (1999), The Out-Caste at the City Gate, *Indian Literature*. 193, pp. 5-11.

Singh, K.S. (1995), *The Scheduled Castes* (Second Edition), Calcutta: Anthropological Survey of India.

Zelliot, Eleanor (1976), Dalit Sahitya—The Historical Background, *Vagaratha*, 12.

Zelliot, Eleanor (1978), Dalit—New Cultural Context of an Old Marathi Word, *Contributions to Asian Studies*, XI, pp. 77-90.

Zelliot, Eleanor (1992), *From Untouchable to Dalit: Essays on the Ambedkar Movement*. Delhi: Manohar.

17

The Significance of Ethnographic Studies in Understanding Poor Response to School Education Among the Tribes in India

B.V. SHARMA

Introduction

Involvement of anthropologists in the study of formal education using qualitative methodology most often enhances the understanding of the processes involved in the acceptance of education through formal institutions, such as schools. However, anthropologists have, by and large, failed to pay much attention to such in-depth studies of formal education. The studies on education by anthropologists dealt more with the informal learning during the enculturation process. In view of the greater emphasis placed on the realm of informal learning, the studies on cultural transmission have become the focus of anthropological studies (Fredereck and Tindall, 1973). The Encyclopaedia of Educational Research pointed out the bias in the studies on education by anthropologists by saying that anthropology of education, means, informal learning, by and large, with family and kin group support (Mitzel, 1982). The studies that distinguished between education and socialization too did not refer to formal education. Socialization, for them, meant activities, "that are devoted to the inculcation and elicitation of basic motivational and cognitive patterns through on-going and spontaneous interaction with parents, siblings, kinsmen and other members of the community" (Cohen, 1971: 22). Education is the inculcation of standardised and stereotyped knowledge skills, values and etiquette by means of standardised and stereotyped procedures. The native mechanisms of 'education' such as repetitive recitation of lore, myth, and etiquette by grandparents to grandchildren around fires in crude shelters and working of the native institutional complexes like dormitories were studied, rather than the formal educational system.

Till recently, studies on formal education, if any, again focused more on the results of such education, but not the process (Spindler, 1963). Only on a few occasions the descriptive analytical approach, using case study method was adopted in the study of educational process to explain the poor response. The studies did not attempt specific theoretical paradigms, but explained the phenomena using the broad concept of culture. During that time scholars who reviewed the works in educational anthropology noted, "in this field of specialization, there is an abundance of uncrystallized thinking and unrefined terminology" (Theodore, 1963). In this context, Spindler (1963) also noted that anthropologists could make substantial contribution to education by building up a body of case materials using techniques of observation in different educational situations.

Among the qualitative approaches adopted by some to the study of formal education, the process of child rearing became a central concern. This importance may be seen in the statement by Mead: "Every intellectual capacity that is later tested by achievement, test, or observation is intimately linked with early childhood experience, with the level of education of parent and nurse, with the structure and furnishing of the home, with the contexts with which the members of the family and the neighbourhood are pre-occupied and with availability of the apparatus and technology on which abstract thought is dependent". The studies emphasizing on child rearing practices for understanding formal education in the West pointed out that the values, attitudes, etc. differ to a climate of experience that varies according to its family's social class. It is argued that the socialization experiences of working class children and middle class children are distinct and the experiences of middle class children are likely to be better preparation for school success. Musgrove (1966), for example, summarized his study as following: "The 'good home' is an aid to success in our school system. It is small; the parents are ambitious for their children; the father is at least a skilled manual worker; and if it is a working class home, the mother has preferably 'married down'. The father is somewhat ineffectual, perhaps, rather feckless, but one of the both parents are demanding, even ruthless in their expectations of achievement. Relationships in the home are emotionally bleak. The family is unstable and has moved often; the mother goes to work. The children grow up to be rather withdrawn and solitary, conscientious and given to self-blame. They are good grammar school material."

Margaret Mead observed the need to understand the culture of a community, particularly the socialization process, to explain the educational experiences of children of that community. Mead had suggested as to how the emphasis placed on either reward or punishment in a society in the socialization of children determined the education of the children. In the case of societies with repressive socialization, the children's school performance is badly affected for they would always act out of the fear of being wrong. On the other hand, societies with participatory socialization, the children actively seek rewards for being right. Mead explains that such consequences as the above are very important in the explanation of childrens' educational experiences.

Similarly, Mead suggests that the culture of a community would possess certain resources that make education of children easy and interesting. Referring to the acceptance of formal learning, she observed: "in primitive homes into which the idea of script will penetrate with conquest and community development programmes, are already a series of underlying expectancies that will partly shape the ways in which reading and writing will be learned. One of these expectancies will be the amount of curiosity that is cultivated within the particular socio-cultural setting. If there is a strong interest in the strange and the unknown, then the ground work is laid for looking at the pictures and later reading books about that which is not known".

The study of early childhood experiences of children in holistic perspective to understand the success or failure of them in modern education system was emphasized by Mead while commenting on the abstract and concrete thinking being so heavily emphasized today. She stated: "the child who is cared for in infancy and early childhood by individuals of a lower level of education then the child will later be expected to reach, faces a different educational situation than one who is reared from infancy by parents who represent the same level of education to which the child is expected to aspire."

Mead has further hinted: "on the cultural level it is possible to work out in some detail the consequences for later learning of living in houses constructed without benefit of any precise measurement, without clocks or calendars, or even toys that embody some of the principles on which the education is postulated......(*sic*) the child who comes from housing built on the basis of explicit geometrical knowledge makes a different order of discovery of geometry than the child who comes from a circular thatched dwelling, or from a crazy, sagging hut made of broken pieces of tin."

Henry made a study (1971) based on life histories of two Negro children. He observed the learning experiences of these two at school and at home. He showed how a particular boy, named Mr. David's experiences in the school are bad. For that, Mr. David's home environment is first characterized as: "He comes from a lower social class family; father and mother are separated and neither of them lives in the apartment; his household is held together by his illiterate 59 years old great grandmother. The only adult male member, his uncle, is 'violent'. The communication among the members of the household is limited. The adults' communication with the children is limited to commands and admonitions. The organizations of the activities are as disorganized as the furniture in the house."

After having characterized the home experiences, Henry explained as to why the boy is unsuccessful in the school. He is unsuccessful because he is an outfit in the school culture: "He acts up in a school which insists on strict order and discipline; teacher devalues David since she (the teacher) comes from a middle class; the principal and teachers believe that the only thing that makes an impression on kids is a strong arm; the school district is under pressure to 'make showing' and its kids like David who give them a 'black eye'; teacher promotion is related to achievement records of her children." The author felt that since the student has his own emotional problems that do not allow him to do well in the class, he is often inattentive, etc. Then he observed, "... under the conditions given above (school culture) the teacher is prone to express her irritation with children by violence. This makes the student's life as harsh as his environment at home. The result is an accumulation of anxieties beyond a point where school learning is possible."

A study by Clark (1983), similarly, emphasized the socialization process. On the basis of life histories of 10 children, it was pointed out that a black child succeeds because his or her family acquaints him or her with social survival skills or knowledge needed to adjust to school and to academic work in the classroom; and he or she fails if the family does not transmit the appropriate cognitive competences. Social survival skills, which were studied by Clark, include ability to accept and follow rules, to maintain self-control, to involve in construction of self-directed activities, to enjoy orderly social interaction, and to carry through and complete tasks.

Newson, Newson and Barnes (1977) similarly conducted a longitudinal study interviewing 700 mothers at regular intervals. Their study showed social class differences with regard to patterns of general cultural interests and also to what they called, 'home-school concordance' (whether child takes things to school to show to the teacher, whether parents help with the school work, and whether the child follows up school work with parents, etc. Their study shows that the children of the unskilled manual groups in contrast to the children of professional groups share less restricted and narrower cultural interests. Further their parents show little involvement in the discussion of school inspired topics and often submit their ignorance to the children's doubts.

Some of the ethnographic studies have taken a 'cultural differences' approach to explain the ethnic school failure and sought explanations focusing attention to specific areas such as language. Bernestein (1971) had studied, for instance, the failure of working class child from a different perspective. One of the main ingredients of culture, the language model, was systematically studied by him. According to him, 'the linguistic performance' and the 'forms of talk' or 'speech codes' as he calls them, within the family vary according to some socio-cultural features which different groups share. These speech codes determine the attitude to learning, the aspiration, motivation and the forms of social control. He observes that the 'restricted code' orients the speaker to relatively context-bound speech and 'particularistic orders of meaning'. This type of speech he associates with working class children and also attributes that in this case, the structure of communication is closed and social control is through imperative mode. The child according to him, in this case may lack autonomy but attain a strong sense of social identity. The middle class children, on the other hand, use an 'elaborated code', which suits to the school environment and hence brings success to those children.

The interest in language patterns and speech styles adopted in schools to explain the ethnic failures grew after the work of Bernestein (Philips, 1983). During the same time, ethno methodology of Harold Garfinkle too influenced the studies of educational anthropologists to make ethnographies regarding how educational failure was being 'socially construed' in the everyday interactions between the teachers and students. These scholars focused on the institutionalised communicative practices of school authorities. Such studies on Negroes pointed out that the 'black youth were given less counselling, attention in classrooms and the way to answer standardized tests (Foley, 1991). The ethnomethodologists too, in a sense emphasized cultural difference approach to explain the academic failure of ethnic minorities in West.

The recent interest in the detailed study of communication styles adopted by different actors in a particular settling revealed how the variability in academic performance may result when the teachers and students come from different cultural backgrounds. Erickson (1987) describes a situation in which teachers and students misunderstand the verbal and non-verbal communication styles of one another. Studies by Heath (1983) and Hymes (1974) similarly pointed out that the conceptions of appropriate classroom behaviour would differ depending upon the cultural background and socio-economic characteristics of individuals. What a student considers proper classroom conduct may be interpreted as being any thing from withdrawal to disruption by the teachers.

To sum up, the smaller samples in the qualitative studies helped the scholars to explain in detail the particular traits in the culture, which hinder or help a child to attain education. These studies though focused on different aspects of culture arrived at more or less similar conclusions. Bernstein's study as well as the studies by Jules Henry and Newson and Newson emphasized on the communication patterns in the households of those who fail to attain education. The 'restricted code' in the forms of talk essentially means limited communication. Newson and Newson pointed out the same phenomena when they observed that parents show little inclination to learn and explain children's questions'. Similarly, Bernestein stresses on 'imperative mode' in talks of form. The 'violent' behaviour of adults in the case presented by Henry can be understood as an extreme case of such 'imperative mode of communication'. The demanding nature of the parents and the ruthless expectations of the parents which Musgrove points out in his study result in the imperative mode of communication. Similarly, both Henry and Musgrove found a common feature that the relationships in the home are emotionally bleak.

Cultural Resources, Learning Experiences and Schooling

The qualitative studies can be discussed under the conceptual framework provided by Bourdieu (1971). He employs two crucial concepts in his account of the role of schools in transforming social and cultural inequalities from one generation to the next. They are 'habitus' and 'cultural capital'. The habitus is essentially, "the culture of particular social group or class that provides the basis for the 'durable disposition'—the ways of seeing and making sense of world—of the child". The habitus is constituted "afresh in each generation through the children's experience of socialization within their social group and in relation to the objective material conditions of their social world". He further observes that certain habituses constitute cultural capital in relation to the process of schooling while others do not. Bourdieu's attempt was to show that this cultural capital differs according to social class and is cause of the initial inequalities of children when faced with examination and tests and hence marginal achievement.

The linguistic models by Bernestein, the social survival skills by Clark, the inferences of Henry from the case study of home, and school environment of Mr. David, the observations of Mead with regard to cultural resources that would be made available to children in a country/family can all be put under the broad category of 'cultural capital'. The availability or non-availability of such cultural capital would determine the educability of the children. However, Henry's study suggests that the failure of the student is not just because of the absence of cultural capital, but because that problem is compounded at the school. Thus, he suggests the following model.

$$O = f(E + S + P)\,T$$

The O here stands for the student's total educational experience, E for his experience at home, P for his peer group experience, and S for the influence of the school culture and T for time. This model suggests that school success is a function of different elements. Negative role by any of these factors leads to school failure. But, possibility to overcome the negative influence by maximization of other factors is always there. Henry entered time factor (T) to suggest that the longer any process continues the greater the effect it will have. This model by Henry takes a holistic view of the study of educational attainment, than others.

Study of Formal Education among the Tribes in Indian Context

Following the traditions of sociology of education abroad, in India too many studies were conducted to know the social factors behind educability. The scholars associated with such studies, to mention a few, are: Chitnis (1972, 1975), Desai (1978), Goswami (1969), Madan *et. al* (1972), Sabarwal (1975), Shah and Patel (1977), Sharma (1975), Aphole (1962), Gorwaney (1974), and Shah (1975). Some of the variables, which have been identified as influencing the educational attainments elsewhere, were picked up and their influence in the Indian context were tested. These studies among different caste groups, thus, pointed out certain statistical correlations between educational attainment, choice of subjects etc. with factors like sex, caste membership, income level of the family, occupation of the father, educational aspirations of the parents, family size, etc. Such studies ignored the value of such factors as sibling similarities, self-fulfilling prophecy, frog-pond effect, etc. in dealing with educational failures. The conceptual models generated abroad while dealing with similar variables were also not taken into account. The attention to debate on how far the schools make a difference in the educational performance of children is also relatively low.

There are only few major works on response to formal education among different tribal groups in India. Studies undertaken by Sen Gupta (1964) among Santhals, Srivastava (1967) among Saoras inhabiting the Ganjam district of Orissa, Naik (1969) among Bhills, studies by Shah and Patel (1981) among different tribal groups in Gujarat, and by Shyamlal (1987) among the tribals of Rajasthan are the results of projects sponsored by bodies like University Grants Commission, ICSSR, and NCERT. The studies by Ratnaiah (1977) among the Gonds of Adilabad District of Andhra Pradesh and by Sita Toppo (1979) on tribals of Bihar were conducted for their doctoral degrees. In addition to the works mentioned above, different commissions and committees appointed by the Government of India pointed out a variety of factors that are hindering the spread of formal education among tribals. Most of the major studies on formal education among tribals followed the sociological studies among the caste communities. These studies too dealt with quantitative techniques and did not go beyond drawing inferences based on comparison of statistical data relating to enrolment, absenteeism, stagnation and drop-out among children of different communities. The anthropological studies generally lacked the qualitative rigour and failed to understand in depth the culture-school incongruence phenomena. The need is a special emphasis on cultural differences in value orientations and learning styles in schools and community and identify the schools with specific school cultures that would help optimize use of cultural resources a specific tribal community possessed. This calls for in depth ethnographic accounts of the tribal communities studied on the one hand and the cultures of the schools that the children attend.

REFERENCES

Aphole, C.A. (1962), Child in Home and School: A Study of Upbringing of Children in Maharashtra Hindu Families in Poona, Unpublished Ph.D. dissertation, University of Poona.

Bernestein, B. (1971), A Socio-Linguistic Approach to Socialization with Some Reference to Educability, In Bernstein (ed) *Class, Codes and Control*, London, Routledge and Kegan Paul.

Bourdieu, P. (1971), Intellectual Field and Creative Project, In MFD Young *et al.* (eds), *Knowledge and Control*, London, Collier-Macmillan.

Chitnis, S. (1972), Education for Equality: Case of Scheduled Castes, *Economic and Political Weekly*, 1675-81.

Clark, M.R. (1983), *Family Life and School Achievement: Why Poor Black Children Succeed or Fail?* Chicago: University of Chicago Press.

Cohen, A.Y. (1971), The Shaping of Men's Minds: Adaptations to the Imperatives of Culture, In L.M. Wax *et al.* (eds) *Anthropological Perspectives on Education*, New York, Basic Books Inc. Publishers, pp. 19-57.

Desai, R.H. (1978), Education of the Scheduled Castes and Scheduled Tribes in Gujarat, In A.B. Shah (ed), *The Social Context of Education, Essays in Honour of J.P. Naik*, New Delhi Allied Publishers.

Erickson, F. (1987), Transformation and School Success: The Politics and Culture of Educational Achievement, *Anthropology and Education Quarterly*, 18(4), pp. 335-56.

Foley, E.D. (1991), Reconsidering Anthropological Explanations of Ethnic School Failure, *Anthropology and Education Quarterly*, 22(7).

Fredereck, O.G. and Tindall, B.A. (1973), Anthropological Studies of the Educational Process, *Annual Review of Anthropology*, Vol. 2.

Gorwaney, N. (1974), Role Structure and Social Change: A Sociological Study of Female Students, Unpublished Ph.D. dissertation, Rajasthan University, Jaipur.

Goswami, R. (1969), School Teacher as a Determinant of Educability in India: A Sociological Study, In S.P. Ruhela (ed) *Social Determinants of Educability in India*, New Delhi: Jain Pub.

Heath, S. (1983), *Ways With Words: Language, Life and Work in Communities and Class Rooms*, Cambridge: Cambridge University Press.

Hymes, D. (1974), Ways of Speaking, In P. Barman and J. Sherzer (eds) *Explorations in the Ethnography of Speaking*, New York, Cambridge University Press.

Madan, T.N. *et al.* (1972), Caste and Community in the Private and Public Education of Mysore State, In S.H. Rudolph and L.I. Rudolphs (eds), *Education and Politics in India*, New Delhi, Oxford University Press.

Mead, M. (1955), Personal and Situational Factors associated with Perfect Attendance, *Personal Guild Journal*, 33, pp. 438-43.

Mead, M. (1971), Early Childhood Experience and Later Education in Complex Cultures, In M. Wax *et al.* (ed) *Anthropological Perspectives on Education*, New York, Basic Books.

Mitzel, E.H. (1982), Anthropology of Education, In *Encyclopedia of Educational Research* (V Edition), London, Free Press.

Musgrove, F. (1966), *Family, Education and Society*, London, Routledge and Kegan Paul.

Naik, T.B. (1969), *Impact of Education on the Bhils: Culture Change in the Tribal Life of Madhya Pradesh*, New Delhi, Research Programme Committee, Planning Commission.

Newson, J., and Newson, E., with Barnes, P. (1977), *Perspectives on School at Seven Years Old*, London: Allen and Unwin.

Philips, S. (1983), *The Invisible Culture*, New York, Longman Pub.

Rathnaiah, E.V. (1977), *Structural Constraints in Tribal Education: A Regional Study*, New Delhi: Sterling Publishers Pvt. Ltd.

Sabarwal, S. (1975), Education, Inequality and Industrialization, *Journal of Higher Education*,1(2).

Sengupta (1964), Tribal Education: Present Position and Future Progress, Indian *Education*, pp. 1-20.

Shah, V.P. and Patel, T. (1977), *Who goes to College? Scheduled Caste/Tribe Scholars in Gujarat*, Ahmedabad: Rachna Prakashan.

Shah, V.P. and Patel, T. (1981), *Social Contexts of Tribal Education in Gujarat*, Ahmedabad: Gujarat University.

Shah, V.P. (1975), *The Educational Problems of Scheduled Caste and Scheduled Tribe School and College Students in India (A Statistical Profile)*, Surat: Centre for Regional Development Studies.

Sharma, K.N. (1975), *Educational Arithmetic of Social Inequality (A study of admission and adjustment of IIT Kanpur Studies)* IIT, Kanpur (Mimeo).

Shyamlal (1987), *Education among Tribals*, Jaipur: Printwell Publishers.

Spindler, D.G. (1963), Anthropology and Education: An overview, In D.G. Spindler (ed) *Education and Culture: Anthropological Approaches*, New York: Holt, Rinehart and Winston.

Srivastava, L.R.N. (1967), Some Basic Problems of Tribal Education, In *Report of the National Seminar on Tribal Education in India*, New Delhi: NCERT.

Toppo, S. (1979), *Dynamics of Educational Development in Tribal India*, New Delhi, Classical Pub.

18

Anthropology in the Era of Entrepreneurship and Change

P.H. MAHAMMAD

The Background

Sol Tax had once aptly remarked that anthropology is "something between that of an Einstein dealing with the mysterious and that of an entertainer". These remarks have been reflected all through the journey of the discipline during the successive stages of its development till the present time. At one point of time anthropology was, in fact, considered to be a study of mere queer customs, potsherds, skulls, bones, etc. But later the discipline has rendered immense practical help to the society, as the anthropologists have proved sometimes that they can forecast the social weather with some accuracy. Because, as Kluckhohn has rightly pointed out, "The anthropologist will insist upon the stupidity of any policy that emphasises political or economic factors at the expense of cultural and psychological factors" (1985, 275). Hence, it is this deep understanding of cultural factors in studying any societal phenomenon that has ensured anthropology a status of a unique and special discipline among the rest other social sciences and humanities.

The present paper is another addition to the existing body of literature on how the phenomenon, entrepreneurship, which is mostly studied by the practitioners of management sciences, attains importance when studied from a cultural perspective. The paper presents, with the help of case materials how certain cultural factors, such as kinship, caste and other primordial ties help the communities to continuously strive for sustaining in any profession notwithstanding severe hardships and crises they have to face. On the contrary, how the communities without such cultural factors literally fall prey to many external market and other forces, eventually facing a situation of complete bankruptcy. As a case study, the paper examines such a situation among the weaving communities in the state of Andhra Pradesh.

The Problem

When one looks back to the beginning of anthropology as a human science, one can easily notice that it aimed at providing the basis for understanding the actual social situations, where the researchers from 'other cultures' could translate their ideas about indigenous societies and cultures into theories on their behaviour, particularly in small-scale societies (Kluckhohn, 1985). However, in the process of its journey towards 'modern' anthropology, there has been a paradigm shift in the anthropological research strategies and methods. One of the changes in interest could be viewed as a shift from the reconstruction of past societies to the investigation of the contemporary ones. In fact, this shift has led to the emergence of a domain in anthropological research, called development/ applied anthropology, which continues to play a very crucial role in the contemporary anthropological research.

As a mark of changing dimensions of anthropological interest, the situations of conflict and social stress, and the contexts of culture contact have been increasingly noticed in anthropological studies. Accordingly, the resultant processes of conflicts between different social institutions as well as the consequences of changes introduced into the indigenous economic systems have been highlighted. In these studies, the emphasis is laid on the socio-cultural parameters that have undergone changes due to the economic changes (Epstein,

1962). Hence, the priority items for the studies by social anthropologists could no longer be restricted to the collection of isolated pieces of information about particular customs or institutions, but extended to the new frontiers. This shift in anthropological research gained prominence in the wake of the liberalisation process, where the local or village affairs have been located in a wide spectrum of changes occurring in the global scenario.

In the present paper an attempt has been made to study the indigenous occupational groups/communities in the context of changing economic scenario, resulted by technological changes through the process of globalization and liberalisation. It focuses on how different occupational groups respond to new entrepreneurial opportunities that penetrate into the local economic and market environments. The paper argues that the innovativeness and adaptability by sections of particular occupational groups to these changes show the prevalence of more enterprising qualities among that particular endogamous group, unlike earlier characterisation of these groups as a verse to transformations. In fact, it is in the backdrop of the introduction of globalization process into the Indian economy (which made the economy more market oriented) that the paper dwells upon the dimensions of entrepreneurship and development among the traditional weaving castes/communities.

It has been observed by many noted theorists that the traditional institutional and normative patterns of the Indian society are not conducive to promote modern technology (Weber, 1930). It is often argued that the primordial attachments, such as the caste, caste-based occupations, and kinship affiliations act as stumbling blocks in the development of entrepreneurship and to pursue technological innovations. In this paper it is hypothesized, on the contrary, that the socio-cultural bases rather serve as launching pads for the communities, with enterprising zeal, to survive even in their caste-based occupational ventures.

Another objective of this paper is much more than adding the research findings to the existing body of literature on this particular subject. In fact, it also aims at advocating that the studies of this nature would put into perspective the situation of the local occupations and seek for appropriate policy formulations. This is because of the fact that the Indian government moves in the direction of modernising Indian industries, particularly the small and medium-scale ones, still living as traditional occupations, to cope with the international competitions. The indigenous industrial sector is expected to change accordingly to suit the needs of structural adjustment programme. Thus it is expected that the Indian industries would expand, modernise or diversify their operations in the wake of the easier terms and conditions for the international industries to enter the Indian industrial sector. When such a change is formulated, there is a need to explore the entrepreneurship bases among the indigenous small-scale industrial communities, which are the backbones of the Indian economy.

Globalization and Entrepreneurship

Entrepreneurship is viewed as an important factor in the whole process of liberalisation. In simpler terms, entrepreneurship is viewed as an attribute, which is responsible for the development/growth-oriented change. In fact, given the multi-faceted nature of the concept, defining entrepreneurship is paralleled with the phrase of "Hunting the Heffalump". To sum up what "Hunting the Heffalump", in the words of Peter Kilby (1971), is that "The Heffalump is a rather large and important animal. It has been hunted by many individuals using various ingenious trapping devices, but no one so far has succeeded in capturing it. All who have caught sight of it report that it is enormous, but they disagree on his particularities. Not having explored his current habitat with sufficient care, some hunters have used as bait their own favourite dishes and have then tried to persuade people that what they caught was Heffalump. However, few are convinced, and the search goes on". In this background, in the present paper, entrepreneurship is considered as an attribute to adapt to the changing market situations against many diverse definitions.

Study Area and Methodology

The paper is substantiated with the empirical data collected through usual anthropological techniques; participant observation being one of them, where the relevant case materials were collected. The case materials presented in this paper were collected as a part of the fieldwork undertaken among the weavers in the region of Yemmiganur in Kurnool District of Andhra Pradesh. Data for this paper is further supplemented from the secondary sources on the situation of the weavers in general, and that of the weavers of Siricilla town in Karimnagar District in the state, in particular, where suicide deaths by the powerloom weavers have been reported recently.

Weaving Communities and Their Organizations

Yemmiganur has been a centre for a variety of cotton products, for which it has carved a niche for itself in the Indian handloom industry. A well-established and popular cooperative society, the Yemmiganur Weavers' Cooperative Society (YWCS) has brought the handloom industry in Kurnool District into the limelight (YWCS Working Paper, 1983). The members of the YWCS are among the best organised in the handloom industry and also enjoy the benefits as members of an ideal cooperative society. Weaving castes engaged in the enterprise can be categorised into two:

(*a*) *Traditional*: The Kurini, Padmasale, Togatasale, Sakulasale and Devangam, given their traditional attachment with the industry as caste occupation, are considered as the traditional weaver castes.

(*b*) *Non-Traditional Weavers*: Members from the communities like the Muslim, Katika, Telaga and Boya, who are engaged in weaving in the study area, are categorised into non-traditional weavers.

Formation of YWCS

The formation of YWCS in 1938 has its own history due to the imperative economic conditions of acute drought prevailing during the colonial regime in this locality. It was the kinship and caste alliances of the 'Kurini' caste and their preponderance in the industry, which helped mobilising them to approach the colonial administrators to convince them to open a separate relief centre for weavers in 1936 due to their different work culture. Also, the importance of the same primordial factor was felt when the weavers were mobilised to demand the government officials to convert the then weavers' relief centre into a weavers' cooperative society in 1938, after the economic conditions were improved.

The enterprise traversed successfully through different stages and it continues to be a predominant source of employment to many weavers till today. However, decline in its membership has started due to the crisis emerged on various grounds. The membership has come down to a great extent posing a threat to the weaving industry in this area. However, the introduction of silk weaving is found as an alternative to the dwindling traditional cotton weaving enterprise.

Thus the formation of YWCS is viewed from the perspective that the entrepreneurial culture and atmosphere flowers in situations where there exists an organisation to reassure reduction in perceived risks to the entrepreneurs. The organisation prepares the entrepreneurs to manage the enterprise through the medium of social relations and trains them in different aspects of entrepreneurship. It becomes a springboard for entrepreneurial development. This holds well in case of YWCS that turned many weavers into entrepreneurs. In this process, the role of kin, caste and other primordial factors is quite significant. The concentration of entrepreneurs in certain traditional weaving castes can be attributed to the advantage of kin, caste and other primordial links that they enjoy over others. Thus, Kurini entrepreneurs enjoyed a definitive edge over the others in weaving enterprise, be it traditional cotton or now emerging modern silk.

Kinship as a Basis of Enterprising

The entrepreneurs among the traditional weavers with their meagre resources used their kinship and caste nexus and flourished in the profession over others who lacked them. The master weavers (who basically operate the enterprise with the capital investment) own the looms and lease them out to the fellow weavers along with the raw materials, such as the yarn. They procure the final products from the clients and pay them the piece rate prices. It was the master weavers belonging to Kurini caste, who were dominating the industry before any formal organisation for weavers was set up. After formation of the YWCS, these master weavers were roped into the YWCS as its directors. This particular step, which was initiated to tap the available human resources, had helped the young YWCS particularly in procuring qualitative yarn and extending credit facility. Because, the long standing association of these master weavers (turned directors of YWCS) with the profession has gained it by diverting their potentialities, expertise and professional connections towards the new venture, YWCS.

Kurini, in this context, is understood as a large extended social group with strong bonds of kinship. They live in close proximity and maintain close interpersonal relations with one another. All Kurinis are closely related either by marriage or through consanguinity. In this social setup, exchange of gifts, periodic visits, reciprocal support in personal emergencies, etc. further strengthen their relationship with one another. In fact, these widespread kinship connections had helped the master weavers, before formation of YWCS, to introduce the new weaving techniques and technology into their venture, which was operated in some places in the erstwhile Mysore state. The Kurini weavers living in Andhra Pradesh, during their visits to their kinsmen in adjoining Mysore, had noted these changes in their occupation and had introduced them in their enterprise in their own places in Yemmiganur area. Particularly, the introduction of twenty and thirty count saris, which they had observed had much of demand in the market, were weaved in Yemmiganur, particularly for the coffee plantation workers in Mysore state, proved to be an appropriate strong entrepreneurial move. Because, the particular saris were affordable for the buyers of this particular area, given the large number of the working class people here, who preferred wearing these thick coarse saris. The introduction of kerchiefs used by the Lingayat community members to cover the image of Lord Shiva (*Shiva Lingam*), wearing it around the neck and hanging at the abdomen was also a mark of successful entrepreneurship by the weaving communities of this area.

The area could see the presence of the master weavers who re-emerged in this profession after 1985, taking note of the crisis situation in the YWCS. This particular step helped the weaving enterprise in this area a promising future. In fact, the same cultural factors which dominated the formation and sustenance of the enterprise under the YWCS and outside have come to the rescue of the weaver groups this time also. It was the marital alliances of some weaver members in this area with those of the well-established weaver families in other parts of the region, which reinforced the faith in the profession.

Weaving as Exclusive Economic Enterprise

In contrast to the situation of weavers in Yemmiganur area, the recent reports on the plight of weavers in some other places show that certain small-scale industrial occupational groups have perceived threats of the technological changes and have preferred to end their lives by committing suicide. Particularly, the issue of suicide deaths by the weavers in recent times has been in constant media focus with the spate of suicide deaths committed by the powerloom weavers in Siricilla town of Karimnagar district in the state. Powerloom is considered to be a step forward than the pit and the weavers rather consider it as an advanced technology in the process of adaptation to the changing market conditions. In fact, given the technological advantage of powerlooms, a phenomenal growth of powerlooms and the mutual competitions among the weavers have been the most important development in the textile industry in recent times.

Haynes (1996) states that during 1920s and 1930s, the power loom industry was taken up by small weavers in their workshops or *karkhanas*. It was in the places like Bhiwandi, Sholapur, Malegaon, Surat, etc., in the then Bombay Presidency, where the powerloom developed initially. He states that these small weavers were able to combine the advantage of handloom weaving in that their product mix remained flexible, with the advent of mechanised production. Besides, he further states that, ".... their small size enabled them to adjust their production levels to the market conditions" (1996, 201-202). Mukund and Shyama Sundari (2001) have demonstrated that handlooms have continuously been concentrated on a product mix in which they have had a comparative advantage of high value-added fine cottons and silks. She reports that the weavers have produced different varieties of cloth, such as high priced cloth catering to the high-income people and coarse cloth for very low-income groups. Similarly, the powerlooms in more recent times have catered to the middle-income group demands. She further observes that modern technology has been adapted by the handloom sector whenever it has been economically viable. Example is that the shift even in the 19th century to machine spun yarn and chemical dyes.

Weavers of Siricilla town had the influence of the powerloom weaving activity undertaken by their fellow weavers in the neighbouring Maharashtra state. Hence, one could see the enormous growth of powerlooms in the town in the past decades, till its debacle in the recent past. They enjoyed the advantages of the occupation as long as there was demand for the powerloom products. But with the growth of mills in the neighbouring places the situation deteriorated in the area. The small and marginal weavers who were rather running their own looms than working under any master weaver could not withstand the competition from the mill sector and started looking for joining under the master weavers. But the master weavers could not generate employment to large proportions to satisfy the needs of the weaving community members in the locality, and in fact, they abandoned their *karkhanas*/workshops and let the industry in dire straits. The work culture that all the weavers were part all through, did not permit them to shift to agricultural or construction works. Because a weaver would prefer to sit on a loom in shade under the roof and does not work under hot Sun. In case of any such dislocation in his duties would cause him acute health disorders. The alternatives chosen by them did not really give them the long-term satisfaction. The occupation like *beedi* (country cigarettes) making, which is mostly taken up by women, demanded them to migrate seasonally to such places without their male members accompanying them. Because, the labour intensive works suitable for employing male labour was not available, in the places where the *beedi* leaves reserves are located. Hence, such migrations by the weavers proved to be quite uneconomical and posed them with new problems.

Srikanth (2003) in his case study on a traditional weaving community of Siricilla area has highlighted that "powerloom industry in Siricilla is affected by mistrust in the trade, unhealthy competition among master weavers, and decline in the quality of cloth that is produced" (2003, 51). The triangular non-formal financial arrangements between the master weaver, local financier and the common weaver have added owes to the existing problems of weavers. According to this arrangement, called *hundi* system, the master weaver would supply yarn to the client weaver along with a chit. The client weaver produces the chit to the financier for getting required amount from him. This amount to the weaver which is supposed to be his wages, would be given by financier as a part of his agreement with the master weaver who is supposed to sell his final products, procured from his clients, to the financier. But, the financier would deduct a part of it amounting to three months' interest from the money that was being lent to the client weaver. Hence, the client (labour) weaver has to bear the interest amount. The financier would finally collect all such amount, indicated through chits, from the particular master weaver at the time when the master weaver sells the clothes procured from the clients. Sometimes notwithstanding the pressure from the financier the master weaver has to sell the procured cloth for very cheaper rates which reflected very badly on the common weaver again. Ultimately, the financier became the contractor/middleman in the system, which resulted in the entrance of the non-weaver categories into the profession. Hence, the weaving industry could see lot of fluctuations with up and downs in prices and as a consequence the wages for the weavers came down very drastically. Srikanth has rightly pointed out that such developments in Siricilla have contributed to developing mistrust among the fellow weavers. Hence, all such dimensions have added panic to the weavers in the Siricilla area to take them to death trap.

The situation reveals that there has been lack of any social mechanism to control the situation from becoming worse. Instead of strong kinship bonds and caste like other primordial factors which helped the weavers in Yemmiganur area to establish certain norms, rules, procedures, ethics, etc., in the profession, the weavers in Siricilla area stricken in the hands of selfish and sheer commercially motivated master weavers. As noted already, the principles of kinship and caste had helped reinforcing the industry in Yemmiganur area during the time when they demanded a separate relief centre exclusively for weavers keeping their work culture in view, in 1936, and also while converting it into a cooperative society. In contrast, the weavers in Siricilla have failed to enter into any such social shield that could have balanced the crisis situations in the profession.

Conclusion

The main conclusion that emerges from the above discussions is that the weaving enterprise in Siricilla area with the influence of its neighbouring places in Maharashtra also has the history of adaptation to market situations as in the case of weaving enterprise in Yemmiganur area. This particular attribute of adaptation is considered to be an important aspect of entrepreneurship. But such an attribute has not helped the industry to regain its predominance for the weavers in Siricilla area. However, this could be made possible in case of the weavers in Yemmiganur area, from time to time. It is, therefore, concluded that what is lacking with the Siricilla weaving groups is the solidarity spirit and the primordial factors such as kinship, caste, etc., which, in fact, became the part of the entrepreneurial spirit of the Yemmiganur weavers. The entrepreneurship spirit built on strong social bases could turn the crises into promising developments. The sustenance of the weaving industry in Yemmiganur as highlighted in this paper is a case in point.

REFERENCES

Epstein, T.S. (1962), *Economic Development and Social Change in South India*, Manchester: Manchester University Press.

Haynes (1996), The Logic of the Artisan Firm in a Capitalist Economy: Handloom Weavers and Technological Change in Western India, 1880-1947, In Stein, Burton and Sanjay Subramanyam (eds) *Institutions and Economic Change in South Asia*, New Delhi: Oxford University Press.

Kilby, Peter (1971), "Hunting the Heffalump", In Kilby, Peter (ed) *Entrepreneurship and Economic Development*, New York: The Free Press.

Kluckhohn Clyde (1985), *Mirror for Man—The Relation of Anthropology to Modern Life*, Arizona: University of Arizona Press.

Mukund, Kanakalatha and B. Shyama Sundari (2001), *Traditional Industry in the New Market Economy: The Cotton Handlooms of Andhra Pradesh*, New Delhi: Sage Publications.

Srikanth, M. (2003), Traditional Occupation and Contemporary Problems: A Case Study of Padmasali Community in Karimnagar District, Unpublished M.Phil. dissertation submitted to the Department of Anthropology, University of Hyderabad, Hyderabad.

Weber, Max (1930), *The Protestant Ethic and the Spirit of Capitalism* (translated by Talcott Parsons), New York: Charles Scribner's Sons.

Yemmiganur Weavers' Cooperative Society (YWCS) (1983), *Working Paper. No. Y298—YGR.*

Index